THE
ESSENTIAL
GHALIB

Praise for *The Essential Ghalib*

'*The Essential Ghalib* will certainly be useful to the general reader, and those who are taking a first look at the ghazals of Ghalib will find it especially helpful. Like Professor Rahman's other books of Urdu literary translation, it will surely find an appreciative audience both in India and beyond.'

—**Frances W. Pritchett,**
professor emerita of Modern Indic languages
Middle Eastern, South Asian and African Studies,
Columbia University

'Anisur Rahman's *The Essential Ghalib* is an expertly assembled treasure trove of translations, analyses and vocabulary that enriches our understanding of the great poet. It is a rare work that is generous enough to cater to everyone from the novice reader to the connoisseur ... Let the *mushaira* begin!'

—**Daisy Rockwell,**
translator and winner of the International Booker Award

'A priceless introduction to Ghalib in English, marked by easy erudition and close reading and, equally, great familiarity and deep affection.'

—**Anjum Hasan,**
novelist, columnist and poet

'Dr Anisur Rahman's *The Essential Ghalib* is a remarkable new book in English that distils the poetry and poetics of Mirza Ghalib's oeuvre in Urdu by offering us a selection of 200 *shers*, or couplets, drawn from the full range of the poet's ghazals ... *The Essential Ghalib* is indispensable—especially for its fresh commentary on each verse—because Ghalib continues to be essential reading today.'

—**Vinay Dharwadker,**
professor of English, World Literature and South Asian Studies,
University of Wisconsin-Madison

'*The Essential Ghalib* and Anisur Rahman Ṣāḥib's magisterial selection, translation and commentary on two hundred verses from Ġhālib's Urdu ghazal-poetry blaze a clear path for contemporary readers through the densely daunting, sylvan thickets and brambles of Ġhālib's poetry.'

—**Satyanarayana Hegde,**
advocate, literary critic; Persian, Urdu and Sanskrit scholar of poetry and poetics

'The strengths of this delightful book lie not only in the impeccable selection of two hundred verses but also in the thoughtful commentaries that accompany each verse. This book should grace every poetry lover's bookshelf.'

—**Mehr Afshan Farooqi,**
professor, department of Middle Eastern and South Asian Languages and Literatures, University of Virginia

'*The Essential Ghalib* will be of interest to readers new to Ghalib as well as to established fans, as it opens new vistas for understanding and appreciating one of Urdu's most alluring poets.'

—**A. Sean Pue,**
professor, Indian and South Asian Studies, Michigan State University

'By placing selections from Ghalib's poetry in historical and linguistic context, this book also enables new, fruitful ways of reading it. And it reminds us why great literature is forever topical and necessary.'

—**Tabish Khair,**
writer and critic

The Transliteration Key pertaining to this book is available on the HarperCollins *Publishers* India website. Scan this QR code to access the same.

THE ESSENTIAL GHALIB

ANISUR RAHMAN

HarperCollins *Publishers* India

First published in India by HarperCollins *Publishers* 2024
4th Floor, Tower A, Building No. 10, DLF Cyber City,
DLF Phase II, Gurugram, Haryana – 122002
www.harpercollins.co.in

2 4 6 8 10 9 7 5 3 1

Copyright © Anisur Rahman 2024

P-ISBN: 978-93-6569-280-8
E-ISBN: 978-93-6569-964-7

The views and opinions expressed in this book are the author's own and the facts are as reported by him, and the publishers are not in any way liable for the same.

Anisur Rahman asserts the moral right
to be identified as the author of this work.

All rights reserved. No part of this publication may be reproduced, stored in a retrieval system, or transmitted, in any form or by any means, electronic, mechanical, photocopying, recording or otherwise, without the prior permission of the publishers.

Typeset in 9.5/13.5 HC Arc at
HarperCollins *Publishers* India

Printed and bound at
Thomson Press (India) Ltd

This book is produced from independently certified FSC® paper
to ensure responsible forest management.

To
Professor Frances W. Pritchett,
the distinguished Ghalibean

hai.n aur bhii duniyaa mei.n suKHanvar bahut achhe
kahte hai.n ke Ghalib ka hai andaaz-e bayaa.n aur

Many other poets in the world, there are many, who sway
But Ghalib, they say, has a different way to say a say

aate hai.n Ghaib se ye mazaamii.n KHayaal mei.n
Ghalib sariir-e KHaama navaa-i sarosh hai

These ideas come to me from the worlds unknown, indeed
Ghalib! The sound of a pen's movement is of angelic breed

ganjiin-i m'anii kaa tilism us ko samajhiye
jo lafz ke Ghalib mire ash'aar mei.n aave

That's magic from meaning's treasury, consider that for sure
The word that enters my verse, Ghalib, that's a magic pure

adaa-i KHaas se Ghalib huaa hai nukta-saraa
salaa-i 'aam hai yaaraan-e nukta-daa.n ke liye

Ghalib has opened his lips, as a connoisseur, with a unique elan
Here is an open call for discerning friends to join, if they can

—Mirza Asadullah Khan Ghalib

CONTENTS

FOREWORD BY VINAY DHARWADKER   xi

PREFACE   xvi

PUUCHHTE HAI.N VO KE GHALIB KAUN HAI:
AN INTRODUCTION   xix

MIRZA ASADULLAH KHAN GHALIB: A BRIEF TIMELINE   xxviii

VERSES AND COMMENTARIES   1

TRANSLITERATION KEY   403

ACKNOWLEDGEMENTS   405

FOREWORD

Dr Anisur Rahman's *The Essential Ghalib* is a remarkable new book in English that distils the poetry and poetics of Mirza Ghalib's oeuvre in Urdu by offering us a selection of two hundred *shers*, or couplets, drawn from the full range of the poet's ghazals. What makes it notable is the fact that, for each selected *sher*, the volume provides the standard text in Nastaliq script, in Devanagari and in Roman transliteration; a short list of key terms in the verse, with their denotations and connotations glossed concisely in English; a verse translation, with flexible rhythm, metre and end-rhymes, in the form of a couplet in modern English; and, finally, a compact yet detailed commentary that interprets the verse, explains its ambiguities and complexities of meaning, and places it in multifarious contexts, whether linguistic, textual, philosophical or cultural. Each *sher* and its accompanying material are designed to be displayed neatly on two facing pages in print, so that the reader can view the whole capsule at a glance—a perfect material aid to the process of focusing attention on one verse at a time, contemplating its many layers of signification and absorbing its imaginative impact. The physical interaction between such a text (on paper) and a projected individual reader is part of the configuration in which this book seeks to pinpoint an essential Ghalib. In conception, these two hundred couplets are primary building blocks in the structure we identify as the poet's oeuvre of Urdu verse, and if we grasp them one-by-one along a cumulative trajectory, then we are likely to arrive at a new discursive understanding of the poet and his life's work on a significant scale.

For me, the format that Dr Rahman has chosen for this project is particularly important because it pays nuanced attention to the very

xi

forms of attention that readers need and ought to practice. As deeper studies of textual technologies now show, digital scrolling—even when two pages are displayed side-by-side on a desktop, laptop, tablet or smartphone screen—actually has the perceptual effect of homogenizing verse and prose. The physicality of reading in so-called hard copy, especially in the seven-hundred-year-old form of print on paper, activates neurons in the human brain in a different way, and puts distinct forms of attention in motion that are central to our interaction with poetic texts. In the case of Urdu poetry, a copy of a text in Nastaliq (for example, in lithograph), or a transcription in Devanagari or roman script (conventionally in cast metal type), has the subtle feature of capturing the form of attention that a *sher* in a ghazal invites during a *musha'irah* (or a less formal recitation) or even a musical rendering. Print on paper allows the recursive contemplation of a verse and its meanings that repetition delivers in an oral performance—and that is undercut, somehow, by the ease and linearity of scrolling along a vertical axis, as distinct from the act of turning pages laterally, on a horizontal axis. If Ghalib's poetry has to be read (rather than heard), then this book furnishes the best kind of format to engage with it, whether for readers who are already familiar with the poetry or for readers who are new to it or have to access it only through translation and commentary in English. Ghalib is especially amenable to the form of attention that his much younger contemporary Friedrich Nietzsche, in a philosophical perspective, called 'slow reading'.

The task of leading us through Ghalib's Urdu *diivaan* that Dr Rahman undertakes is obviously a difficult one, but he follows a trajectory of distinguished Indian precursors. The centenary of Ghalib's death, in 1969, led to a commemoration of the poet's work in several forms, including new books in English. As part of this celebration, Choudhary Mohammad Naim—my teacher, mentor and friend at the University of Chicago since 1983, and also the teacher, a little earlier, of Frances Pritchett, to whom *The Essential Ghalib* is dedicated—published a small volume titled *Twenty-five Verses by Ghalib: English Versions from the Urdu* (Calcutta: Writers Workshop, 1970). In a prefatory Note, he observed:

FOREWORD   xiii

In the following pages I have attempted to present for the pleasure of non-Urdu-knowing readers some selected couplets of Mirza Ghalib (1797-1869) in a format derived from Stanley Burnshaw's *The Poem Itself*. My purpose is not to translate these verses [poetically] but to present them in such a way and with such commentary that a reader who does not know Urdu can go back to the original verse in Urdu (given in transcription) and see how that verse works—i.e., he can get not only some idea of the poet's thoughts but also of his craft.

These couplets have been selected from various *ghazals*. As is well known, each couplet in a *ghazal* is a discrete unit in itself. Thus it is possible to enjoy these couplets of Ghalib without making any reference to other couplets in the same *ghazal*.

Naim crystallized a paradigm that underwent a more elaborate variation the following year, when Aijaz Ahmed, as editor, published *Ghazals of Ghalib* (New York: Columbia University Press, 1971). This larger book remains a classic in the field— besides a substantive scholarly Introduction, it offered its international audience thirty-seven ghazals, some in their entirety but many represented by select *sher*s. For each ghazal, Ahmed furnished the original text (but only in the Nastaliq script), his own line-by-line 'literal translation', and, for each couplet, an explication of its 'essential vocabulary' and, when necessary, a 'general explanation'; this collage was then followed by one or more poetic translations in English, each crafted by a prominent American poet of that period. Ahmed had invited seven poets to collaborate with him on the project; since none of the American collaborators knew Urdu, and none of them was familiar with the ghazal genre at the time, Ahmed worked closely with each poet and on each ghazal to help prepare the final, polished renderings. In this process, '*Har qadam doori-e-manzil hai numayan mujhse*' (represented by five of its *sher*s), for example, was accompanied by three translations—by W.S. Merwin, Adrienne Rich and Mark Strand, respectively—each of which was marked by its American craftsman's distinctive style. Despite the extraordinary collaboration, however, none of the book's renditions captured either the tone or the texture of Ghalib's verse; as Robert Lowell noted in the context of his own work with European poems, from Homer to Montale, in *Imitations* (1961): 'Boris Pasternak has said that the usual reliable translator gets the literal meaning but misses the tone, and that in poetry *tone* is of course everything' (emphasis added). Neither Ahmed nor the American poets were individually responsible for the volume's shortcoming; in my perspective, the method of bringing together a 'native informant' (for the source language) and a poet (in the second language) who is unacquainted with the original does not produce a satisfactory translation in practice, especially in the long shadows of Orientalism.

The Essential Ghalib does not refer to these earlier books, but it converges with both and also diverges from them in fascinating combinations. Dr Rahman's volume differs from Ahmed's in that it focuses on one *sher* from one ghazal at a time; more importantly, it provides verbal glosses, textual explication and poetic translation by one and the same hand, imparting his enterprise with what may be termed an 'organic' authorial integrity. Correspondingly, this book also diverges from Naim's project in two main respects: it offers us a much larger and more varied selection—of two hundred *shers*, many of them from different ghazals in the Urdu *divan*—and it seeks to represent them in verse, not explicatory prose. At the same time, however, *The Essential Ghalib* has two features in common with both earlier books—in its renditions across languages, it treats each couplet as a discrete poetic unit, and, in its well-rounded interpretations, it seeks to showcase 'the poem itself'. Ghalib fashioned each *sher* as a miniature poem in itself, even as he used it as a building block to simultaneously construct his individual ghazals and his oeuvre as a whole.

The Essential Ghalib is indispensable—especially for its fresh commentary on each verse—because Ghalib continues to be essential reading today. He is essential because, in a panoramic view of history, he is the last major poet in a modern Indian language who is trained as a craftsman fully and exclusively in an indigenous system of literary education and transmission. He is essential because he completes his first Urdu *divan* in Delhi, at the age of nineteen under the poetic signature 'Asad', at the same time as the earliest Indian-English poets and poems begin to appear in print in the territories controlled by the East India Company. He is essential because, throughout his career, he is contemporaneous with colonial moderns in a different sphere—not only with Rammohun Roy from the 1810s to the early 1830s, but also, say, with Madhusudan Dutt in the 1840s and Sir Syed Ahmad Khan in the 1850s and 1860s. (These 'connections' are not abstract or remote; Dutt launched Indian drama in English with his play *Rizia*, written in Madras in 1848–49; Raziyah Sultana's *mazar* stood just a kilometre from Ghalib's *haveli* in Gali Qasim Jan, and Sir Syed's home lay half a kilometre beyond the gravesite memorial, closer to Daryaganj.) Ghalib remains essential because, in the final decade of his life, under the stimulus of the English literature and English translations of world literature around him, and after reflecting on the *dastan* of Amir Hamza and the genre of the Persian 'romance' (in a preface written in 1866), he begins to imagine the possibility of writing modern short stories in Urdu. Trained in Arabi and Farsi by a Parsi polymath in Delhi, he chose to be a writer in Farsi as well as Urdu (or Rekhta or 'Hindi', as he called it at different times), and elected to practise a full-fledged *literary bilingualism* fifty to seventy-five years before it became notable with early and late modernists like Constantine Cavafy, Fernando Pessoa and Samuel Beckett. Under these cross-currents, Ghalib continues to serve as the most distinguished 'classical' lens through which we can observe the appearance of modernity on the Indian aesthetic landscape—before that modernity permeates the world and transforms it utterly.

Vinay Dharwadker
Professor of English, World Literature and South Asian Studies,
University of Wisconsin–Madison, USA

8 December 2023

PREFACE

*T*he *Essential Ghalib* brings you two hundred select verses from the Urdu *diivaan* of Mirza Asadullah Khan Ghalib in English translation along with close critical commentaries on them. It addresses the perennial readership of this canonical poet that has known him as naturally as one has known the markers of one's life and culture. It brings together an immense variety of verses drawn from his ghazals; some only too well known, and others waiting to be known better and read better still. With these classic verses, selected carefully, translated judiciously and commented upon comprehensively, you would come across a poet who wrote a kind of poetry that has ever remained both emblematic and enigmatic. Indeed, his poetry has created literary archetypes that compare well with the finest ones in any language. The book promises to bring you the experience of ecstatic fulfilment that Ghalib's verses are typically known for—much better than those of the many established poets, who wrote before or after him.

    Translators and annotators from different literary cultures and languages have been endlessly allured by canonical poets and authors. Like others in this tribe, I too have had an enduring engagement with translating many of the Urdu poets into English. This time, I chose to exclusively engage with Ghalib, who had allured me all along. How would his verses sound auditorily and appear visually in English if I tried my hand on them, I kept asking myself over and over again. I wondered how best I could try, translate and critically comment on these verses which formed parts of his individual ghazals, yet survived as aggressively independent units. Since his verses have had a way of acquiring their spaces in readers' collective memory, I decided to bring them to

Ghalib's readership in English in my own way with rhymed translations and multilayered commentaries for a broader understanding of his worldview and poetics. Howsoever much I desired, I found it much too trying, almost well-nigh impossible, to translate and comment upon the entire Ghalib oeuvre of two hundred and thirty-five ghazals with any distinction. So, I thought of making a selection—a personal one for that reason—to represent him in all his thematic and stylistic varieties. Making a critical assortment of his verses that could lend themselves to me as the translatable ones proved to be a long process into itself. Further, locating Ghalib's possible intent to be able to comment upon his verses that I had selected for my purposes was no less than a trial of romance I faced both with pain and pleasure. Although this inimitable poet has lent himself in different ways to a host of his translators, annotators and commentators across ages and places; I chose to critically define my dual job of translating and commenting upon his verses to see how best I could approach him with any measure of merit.

Apart from unravelling the Ghalibean ambiguities for myself, I also needed to develop a translation methodology for my individual purposes. I realized rather naturally that I needed to develop a linguistic register and a pattern of rhyme and rhythm in the English language that could represent both Ghalib's intent and his tone of voice. So, I evolved a methodology of my own making which involved finding my own diction with a certain echo, deciding on my number of syllables with certain weight and volume, determining the line breaks and their length to ensure their readability in translation, and finally approximating Ghalib's tone of voice which differed from verse to verse. To me, this was a way of evolving a rhythmic design in English which tended to correspond with the rhythmic design of the two lines of a verse in Urdu. In order to make Ghalib easily accessible, I chose further to provide the generic and contextual meaning of difficult words and expressions in English that could help the readers appreciate my critically tempered and multilayered commentaries on the verses. It is in these respects that this work strikes a difference in relation to numerous other works that have been available to us so far.

I hope that these select two hundred verses of this incomparable poet will introduce him with all his resilience and splendour to the eternally curious readers. As you proceed with these verses and their critical readings, you will discover a poet who is philosophical now, now plebeian; pungently pleasant now, now pleasantly pungent. He comes across with intricate ideas and expressions at one time, and humble and modest at another. He expresses himself in a manner that is easily accessible at one time, while quite unreachable at another. So is the case with his wit and humour that is sparkling at one place while artfully muted for a gain at another. These qualities prominently mark his verses and singularly qualify his ghazal. I hope that the readers will get a broader idea of this poet who played with concrete and abstract ideas together, and in styles entirely personal. This work of translating and critically commenting upon Ghalib's select verses, completed over a long period of time, is aimed primarily at bringing the essentiality of Ghalib to our lives and living, as also at sharing the pleasures of my engagement with him.

Puuchhte Hai.n Vo Ke Ghalib Kaun Hai:
AN INTRODUCTION

> *puuchhte hai.n vo ke Ghalib kaun hai*
> *koii batlaao ke ham batlaaei.n kyaa*
> They ask, Ghalib—Ghalib who?
> Let someone say, I have no clue

Prologue

Poetry might descend upon the poets spontaneously, although it dawns upon the readers with all its magic only gradually and steadily. Such a hiatus between poetry and its readers also becomes a reason for readers and poetry to get curiously closer to each other with time. Mirza Asadullah Khan (1797–1869), who chose the *nom de plume* of Ghalib for himself, found his kindred kind in poetry, where he could express himself the best and intrigue his readers the most, with his fascinating complexities of ideas and language. He lived during times of turmoil and expressed himself variously in prose and poetry that now plainly reveal, now artfully conceal, his existential angst. His geniality with life at a broader level is also his way of negotiating with it in literary terms. As he brought life and art to bear upon one another, he secured a place for himself in the common imaginary of his readers ever since he started writing from the early years of the nineteenth century.

Word as a nucleus of possible meaning has been much debated upon in the domains of ancient and modern poetics. Ghalib drew upon this in his own manner and eulogized himself for his creative engagement with words in several of his verses in explicit terms. He addressed his readers in many of his verses and led them to believe that the words which found their place in his poetry were purely magical and they created an inimitable treasury of meaning. He, thus, assigned the position of the high priest of poetics to himself, who struck a delicate balance between word and thought, and discovered what lay behind and beyond them. Unlike a jeweller who inserts his gemstones in his jewellery using his hard-earned craft with labour, Ghalib etched his words in his verses with natural ease. The words he brought together in his verses thus carried their semantic, phonetic and morphological overbearing with them for the readers and enriched their experience of engagement with him.

Ghalib created a music of words and ideas together which distinguished his poetry from those of his predecessors and successors. His ideational structures and artistic representations create a synchronous world of beauty. The beauty of his poetry is multi-layered, as are the ways of reading poetry itself. These can be explored authentically in reading it patiently, pondering over it seriously and wondering genuinely if there was a better way of poetic expression than what Ghalib had evolved for himself and his readers. The curiosity to explore the worth of his work, which began with his contemporaries and has continued growing ever since, only confirms the legitimacy of his *nom de plume* which, interestingly enough, signifies a person who can overcome and prevail.

A Life Not Easy

A Turkish descendent of the Aibak dynasty connected in origin to King Afrasiyab, Ghalib was born on 27 December 1797, in Agra, where he also got his early education. He was later nurtured by a Zoroastrian tourist, or a wandering scholar from Iran called Hormuzd, who, on embracing Islam, came to be known as Mulla Abdussamad, and helped him hone his skills in Persian, Arabic and logic. Although Ghalib had the pride of a grand lineage, he was sadly destined to grapple both with the onslaughts of a difficult life and a terribly consequential era of history. Coming from a family of warriors, his grandfather, Mirza Ququan Baig, had emigrated to Lahore from Samarqand and later joined the services of the Mughal emperor Shah Alam II in Delhi. As the tradition of serving the crown and the nobility continued, his father, Abdullah Baig Khan, too, followed the same profession and served Nawab Asifuddaula (or Asaf-ud-Daula) of Lucknow, the Nizam of Hyderabad and, later, the Maharaja of Alwar, but he did not live long enough to see Ghalib beyond his fifth year. His uncle, Nasrullah Baig Khan, a *risaalaadaar*, or a troop commander in the British Army, looked after him subsequently, but he too passed away even before Ghalib could reach his tenth year.

Miseries kept multiplying with time in Ghalib's life. He was destined to enter a long struggle against his outrageous fortune. With the confiscation of his uncle's large estate, an annuity of ten thousand rupees was fixed, but Nawab Ahmad Bakhsh Khan, from whose estate the amount had to be paid, gave Ghalib's family only one-third of the amount. With several recipients from his extended family, Ghalib's personal share came to rupees seven hundred and fifty per year. Married at an early age of thirteen to Umrao Begum, aged seven, he shifted to Delhi as a young boy of about fifteen in 1812-13, where he lived all along. Shifting his residence from place to place in the walled city, he got exposed to a world of greater tribulations which had a direct bearing on his intellectual make up and writing. His persistent persuasion for improvement in his pension, first with Ahmad Bakhsh Khan and then with the authorities of the British East India Company, that his uncle had served as a military officer, came to stay as a prolonged and a tedious plot in the larger saga of his life that continued growing difficult, year after year. However, grants in appreciation from the last Mughal emperor and also the nawab of Rampur kept him going somehow.

Ghalib knew no ways of yielding even in impoverishment as he was critically conscious of being an aristocrat by descent and temper. He refused favours and shunned free mixing. He had no house of his own, no books he could claim his own and no siblings, out of the seven, to live long and stay with him beyond their childhood. He was indeed an exceptional individual who drew loans, drank incessantly, played dice, violated norms and was imprisoned, but chose to continue with his manners rather defiantly. Even with all these, he pursued his intellectual pursuits and wrote the finest kind of poetry and prose in Urdu and Persian.

A Time Too Terrible

Ghalib had seen and suffered the onslaughts of his times and climes—the decline and fall of the Mughal Empire and the British rule exercising its controlling hand. He was a sore witness to the upheavals of his age; a sad and helpless observer of one culture replacing another in the wake of cataclysmic events. He grieved the way history was charting its course, rather swiftly but recklessly. As Delhi was ravaged in 1857, his heart bled. He recorded his anguish in his letters to his close friends in no uncertain terms. He wrote about Delhi that was once known for its unique spots and lamented its tragic decay. He grieved that there existed a city once in the land of Ind and wondered if that city was still alive. In this Delhi of his dear dreams and rude realities, however, he remained indebted to both the empires—the Mughals and the British—for his sustenance. The ambivalence of his attitude towards the British, which has concerned many critics, is understandable on account of his personal limitations. It may not, in any case, be considered a betrayal of his essential pride that characterizes his poetry quite prominently. He recorded in *Dastanbuy* (1858), his Persian diary of 1857, that he received his bread and salt from the table of the British masters, the conquerors of the world, right from his early childhood. It would, therefore, be unfair to ignore this frank and honest admission and consider it as a sign of his servility to the British Empire.

Ghalib's Urdu letters collected in *'Ud-e Hindi* (1868) and *Urdu-e Mu'alla* (1869) unequivocally represent his helplessness at his dichotomous existence that he found too terrible to withstand and absorb internally. They reflect his deep human concern, as much as they represent his anguish and anxiety. They are characteristically intimate in design and are written to close friends, who loved and respected him as a gentleman and a poet. Uniquely conversational in their tone, and suave in their narration, they may be read like tracts of history from a poet-narrator. Ghalib historicized his times both with pain and sympathy, and he found his metaphors of suffering and survival in those tracts of history that he creatively configured in his poetry. His poetry, in any case, may appropriately be read as a philosophical representation of human predicament at large.

Both his diary and his letters are intimate conversations and take us into confidence instantly. They reflect his literary personality and his human catholicity, and may be read as personal interpretations of an age in sheer crisis. These works not only impress us with their dramatic design, for which they are so well known, but also with the deep sympathy they evoke with the readers. With his keen interest in sharing his personal predicament and that of his time, he emerges as a storyteller of tragic times, where objects appear as characters and characters as speaking icons. The dramatic qualities of his narratives hold the attention of his readers who stand astonished at his infinite capacity to bear pain. Like his verses, his prose works combine the best elements of the Perso-Arabic tradition with the linguistic patterns of the Urdu language. Read with his verses, his prose works emerge as complementary writings on contemporary history, politics and culture.

Literary Identities

Ghalib was a poet and a prose writer, an epistolarian and a diarist, a lexicographer and a polemist, a critic and a historian, and above all, an arbiter of taste. Even though he was a great reader, loved the literature of classical temper, and was naturally given to preserving the vanishing glory of the past, the acquisition of knowledge in his case was more a matter of personal reflections and observations than of merely culling from textual sources. He started writing at the age of nine and had already written most of his remarkable Urdu ghazals by his nineteenth year. He compiled his first Urdu *diivaan* known as *NushKHa-i Amroha* or *NusKHa-i Bhopal* in 1816, the second version of his *diivaan* known as *NusKHa-i Hamidiya* in 1821, and the third version of his *diivaan* called *NusKHa-i Shirani* in 1825. In 1833, he compiled his ghazals yet again in a final version which is now referred to as his most popular *diivaan*. Ghalib was extremely meticulous in making the selection of his verses for his *diivaans* and rejected many of the verses he considered inferior by his own exacting standards. As a sensitive choice maker of his verses and a keen editor of his ghazals, he has handed us a slim *diivaan* of two hundred and thirty-five ghazals only on which his reputation as a poet of exceptional merit rests firmly and finally.

In pursuing his literary vocation, Ghalib did not strictly follow the established tradition of a given genre as he treated each of these in his individual style, imparting each one the freshness expected of a literary iconoclast or the genius of a language. Unlike the poets and writers of our age, those in the past had a constant and wholetime engagement with writing. So, Ghalib too, apart from writing his poetry in Urdu and Persian in different genres, wrote in various genres of prose with equal passion. Apart from his Persian diary of 1857 and his inimitable Urdu letters discussed above, some of his other works that deserve special mention include a *mathnavii* he wrote in rebuttal of linguistic blemishes in his works (*Baade MuKHaalif*, 1828), a Persian *diivaan (MaiKHaana-i Aarzuu-e Saranjaam*, 1834–35), a scholarly work on letter writing, Persian infinitives, technical terms, reviews and miscellaneous writings under five heads (*Panj Aahang*, 1849), a historical narrative up to Humayun of the Mughal empire (*Mehr-e Niim Roz*, 1854), a Persian and Urdu vocabulary verse (*Qaat'i-e Naama*, 1856), a polemical writing against *Burhaan-e Qaat'i (Qaat'i-e Burhaan*, 1862), a collection of Persian poetry (*Kulliyaat-e Nazm Farsi*, 1863), a Persian *mathnavii (Abr-e Guharbaar*, 1864), and a collection of prose works in Persian (*Kulliyaat-e Nasr-e Farsi*, 1868).

Ghalib is a classic example of a comprehensive scholar, a critical reader and an inclusive writer. Different disciplines that we broadly place under the larger umbrella of the humanities caught his attention. He was an untutored genius but an intellectual in the true sense of the phrase who evolved his own knowledge and knowledge systems. Even though 'originality' as a concept is much contested, Ghalib has a claim to originality as a genius of language, poetry and poetics in all fairness. Drawing upon a large hinterland of intellectual resources, he created his own plots and *dramatis personae* to produce his individual mythos in his life and works. There are types and protypes of men and women, lovers and beloveds, heretics and believers, as well as a series of situations and moments that are plebian and sublime in various manifestations. He knew his exact word and how that word could be turned into an image, an image into a simile, a simile into a metaphor, a metaphor into a symbol and, finally, a symbol into a myth. Ghalib excelled in all these ways to emerge and remain a canonical figure.

Ghalib: Our Contemporary

Ghalib did not know of modernism as a movement and modernity as a quality, as the more critically informed and theory-oriented scholars know today. He was indeed a progenitor of both in his own way. As a ghazal poet, he is our contemporary in many ways. He foreshadowed modernism and modern thought, and developed his own metaphysics of ghazal that certainly was his real forte. He was the most modern mind around who wrote the most urbane ghazals of his time that continues to be so even today. He spoke in three distinct voices—his own, his imagined addressees and his *dramatis personae*. Ghalib, thus, turned his ghazal into a theatre of situations, sounds and echoes that immensely enriched this romantic-cum-mystical genre of Urdu poetry. His extraordinary insight into prosodic subtleties, resourcefulness with figures of speech and sensitivity to the rules of grammar helped him establish his individual identity. Like the English metaphysical poets of the early seventeenth century who gained currency in modern times, he mixed his metaphors, sharpened his conceits and challenged his reader's imagination. A poet of unusual imaginative vitality, he balanced his exaggeration against ratiocination, and artfully negotiated between thought-binding and meaning-making with special reference to life, love, death and God.

Ghalib created a discourse around language and diction, evolved conceptual contiguities and antinomies with words of a certain feather to write an intriguingly individual kind of verse. He recognized the merits of classical literature, as also of history, philosophy and ethics, which he nurtured on his own, and made his poetry metaphysically rich and stylistically accomplished. Logicality, which is alien to poetry, imparted certain credence to his verses. Reading Ghalib is, therefore, an experience in exploring a new horizon of meaning and discovering a new kind of aesthetic pleasure. Like a playful being, he treated the world lightly but marked the existential layers of meanings seriously. To put it precisely, his complexity lay in his simplicity and his simplicity in his complexity. In many of his verses, the meaning cannot be determined unitarily; there is at best only a possibility of richly ambiguous meaning(s) that the readers might comprehend in a variety of ways. Even though many of his compositions turned too cerebral, his readers did not get impatient with him. Indeed, they prepared themselves to engage with him, as he chose to prepare a class of critical readers that he expected would increase in times to come.

Ghalib balanced his racial memory against his contemporary backdrop and the Perso-Arabic poetics against the evolving Urdu poetics. He did not represent a unitary tradition but chose to blend the major marks of Persian literary culture into Urdu and transformed it into a more homogenous language than it had ever been before. His richness is a matter of his context where cultures, languages and historical periods intersected and gave birth to his comprehensive sensibility, amalgamating multiple traditions and influences. The states of ecstasy and sorrow, the conditions of being and nothingness, the moments of leisure and pleasure, all find their configuration in his ghazals. Since poetry imparts infinite imaginative space to poets, Ghalib made use of the same in full measure and achieved ecstasy in imaginative fulfilment as a poet who strikes us as our contemporary.

Epilogue

Ghalib remains an unfinished project. In fact, every work on Ghalib can at best be a work in progress. This is how we recognize the significance of this poet whose works open up afresh with every reading, and keep on opening incessantly. He was duly acknowledged during his lifetime and remains so even after more than a century and a half of his passing away in 1869. He received his place and his honours at the Governor General's *darbaar* in 1829 and access to the Mughal court after the ascendency of Bahadur Shah Zafar to the throne in 1837. His worth was further acknowledged with his employment as the emperor's literary mentor after the demise of his *ustaad*, Sheikh Ibrahim Zauq, and by the offer made to him to write the history of the Mughal dynasty. The high titles of *Dabir-ul mulk* (honour of the country), *Najm-ud daula* (star of the realm), *Nizam Jung* (head of war) and *Mirza Naushaah* (the young monarch/groom), which he earned from the royalty further confirm the recognition of his genius.

AN INTRODUCTION

With all the disappointments he lived with and all the appreciations he received, he remained a persistently philosophical plaintiff in the court of life where he seemingly lost his case. The questions he raised and the complaints he articulated in his works engrossed the attention of his readers as he made them with clinical detachment and dignity, but at times with defiance and irreverence. He wrote as if to find a way through his existential crisis and possibly to seek his resolution, as artists often do, at a metaphysical rather than a mundane level.

Sick with many a desire, Ghalib passed away on 15 February 1869, at the age of seventy-two. To date, he remains the most contemporaneous of the literary masters in Urdu. A major maker of the classical tradition, he simultaneously falls in line with the newest of the new. A modern mind by all means—philosophically and scientifically—he has been subjected to a variety of interpretations in the past. This continues even today, because he remains a literary phenomenon to readers in Urdu and many other languages in translation.

Mirza Asadullah Khan Ghalib:
A BRIEF TIMELINE

1750s: Asadullah Khan's grandfather, Mirza Quqan Beg Khan, arrived in Lahore from Samarqand. Shifted to Delhi later, and first served Prince Shah Alam II and later Zulfiqar-ud Daulah (1771) and Maharaja of Jaipur (1782).

1763–1765: Mirza Quqan Beg Khan got married; Abdullah Khan, Asadullah Khan's father, was born in Delhi.

1793: Abdullah Beg Khan, Asadullah Khan's father, got married to Izzat un-Nisa Begam.

1797: Asadullah Khan was born in Agra on 27 December.

1810: Asadullah Khan is said to have attended the *maktab* of Maulvi Muhammad Mu'azzam in Agra.

1810: Asadullah Khan, aged eleven, got married to Umrao Begum, aged seven.

1811: Hormuzd, later called Abdus Samad after his conversion to Islam, gave lessons in Persian, Arabic and logic to Asadullah Khan for a couple of years while staying at his home in Agra.

1812–3: Asadullah Khan took permanent residence in Delhi and lived in a street called Qasim Jan.

1816: Asadullah Khan put together his first Urdu *diivaan*—later known as the *NusKHa-i Amroha*, or *NusKHa-i Bhopal*.

1816: Asadullah Khan adopted 'Ghalib' as his *nom de plume*, apart from another one 'Asad'.

A BRIEF TIMELINE

- 1821: Ghalib put together the second version of his Urdu *diivaan*, later known as *NusKHa-i Hamidiya*. It contained most of his ghazals from the 1816 *diivaan*, apart from several new ghazals.
- 1825: Put together the third version of his Urdu *diivaan*, now known as *NusKHa-i Shirani*. It contained most of the ghazals from the 1821 compilation, apart from some new ghazals.
- 1828: Reached Calcutta, and petitioned the Company officials for his long due and neglected pension issues.
- 1828: Participated in Persian language mushairas where he was lambasted by his rivals for his linguistic blemishes, which he duly addressed in his *mathnavii Baad-e MuKHaalif*.
- 1828: Company officials directed him to approach the Delhi officials for his pension matters.
- 1829: Received a position and honours in the Governor General's *darbaar*.
- 1829: Returned to Delhi from Calcutta.
- 1831: Claim for pension was finally denied.
- 1833: Put together his Urdu *diivaan*, now read as the final version, published in 1841.
- 1834-35: Compiled his Persian *diivaan*, *MaiKHaana-i Aarzuu-e Saranjaam*.
- 1837: An English wine merchant sued him for not paying off his debt; he stayed indoors to avoid creditors, was arrested briefly and released when Aminuddin Khan, son of the ruler of Loharu, paid the amount due.
- 1841: Arrested for running a gaming-house in his own home, paid rupees one hundred to seek release.
- 1841: Published his Urdu *diivaan* already compiled earlier in 1833.
- 1845: Published his Persian *diivaan* already compiled in 1834.
- 1847: Second edition of his Urdu *diivaan* published.
- 1847: Arrested for gambling, sentenced to six months of imprisonment along with a fine, which was paid by friends, and was released after three months.

1849: Published his Persian work, *Panj Aahang*, a collection of miscellaneous writing under five heads.

1850: Appointed by Bahadur Shah Zafar to write the history of the Timur dynasty. Received titles of *Najm-ud daula, Dabir-ul mulk, Nizam Jung* from the emperor, and was granted an annual pension of rupees six hundred.

1853: Published the second edition of *Panj Aahang*.

1854: Succeeded Sheikh Ibrahim Zauq, after his demise, as the poet-mentor of Emperor Bahadur Shah Zafar.

1854: The first part of Timurid history, *Mehr-e Niim Roz*, was published. Reprinted twice within a year.

1855: Awarded cash and pension by Wajid Ali Shah, the nawab of Avadh.

1856: Published *Qaadir Naama*, mnemonic Persian/Urdu vocabulary verses for children.

1856: Composed a *qasiida*, a poem of praise, for Queen Victoria.

1857: Protected by the maharaja of Patiala during the rebellion, lost all valuables, secretly transported by his wife to Mian Kale Sahib's house for a safe stay.

1858: Poems of praise written for the queen; British officials rejected it considering it an act of flattery.

1858: Published *Dastanbuy*, his Persian diary, describing the events of 1857.

1859: Started receiving a pension of rupees one hundred per month from the nawab of Rampur

1860: British pension reinstated with help from Sir Sayyid Ahmad Khan and the nawab of Rampur. Received rupees two thousand two hundred fifty as arrears.

1861: Rejected the third edition of Urdu *Diivaan-e Ghalib* on account of misprints and wrong entries published without his permission.

1862: Published *Qaat'i-e Burhaan*, a polemical writing, attacking *Burhan-e Qaat'i*.

1862: Revised edition of Urdu *diivaan* published.

1863: Restoration of official darbaar honours.

1863: Publication of *Kulliyaat-e Nazm Farsi*.

1863: Publication of the fifth edition of Urdu *diivaan*.

1864: Separate publication of Persian *mathnavii Abr-e Guhar Baar* which had already appeared in his Persian *Kulliyaat*.

1864: Publication of the second edition of *Qaadir Naama*.

1865: Publication of the second edition of *Dastanbuy*.

1868: Publication of *Kulliyaat-e Nasr-e Farsi*.

1868: Publication of *'Ud-e Hindi*, a collection of his Urdu letters, which contained errors and displeased him.

1869: Died following a coma on 15 February; buried in Nizamuddin, now in New Delhi, where his present tomb was built in 1955, eighty-six years after his death.

VERSES AND COMMENTARIES

1

نقش فریادی ہے کس کی شوخیٔ تحریر کا
کاغذی ہے پیرہن ہر پیکر تصویر کا

नक़्श फ़रयादी है किस की शोख़ी-ए तहरीर का
काग़ज़ी है पैरहन हर पैकर-ए तस्वीर का

naqsh faryaadii hai kis kii shoKHii-i tahriir kaa
kaaGhazii hai pairahan har paikar-e tasviir kaa

(*naqsh*—image, facsimile, portrait;
faryaadii—appellant, seeker, implorer;
shoKHii—playfulness, flippancy, coquetry, caprice;
tahriir—writing, composition;
pairahan—robe, mantle;
paikar—figure, form, body)

Whose crafty creation am I; the image implores—
Every image stands enrobed—but in paper robes

Ghalib opens his *diivaan* with a unique stroke of his genius. The imploring in the first line, followed by an answer in the second line, opens up various avenues of interpretation. The implication here is that the implorer is seeking justice as he has been subjected to oppression. Apart from being an individual, he is also a stock figure —an everyman— in a state of eternal entreaty, insofar as he represents the perpetual human condition marked by suffering. This imploring is being made to God, or to the one in the seat of power on this earth. The implorer thus underlines what we know today as a discourse on the dialectics of power and powerlessness, or the oppressor and the oppressed. Interestingly, the image of the implorer is also like the one that a painter paints on a paper canvas, puts in a frame and hangs on a wall, as a reminder of the eternal human condition. In this much-debated but iconic verse, Ghalib creates a cosmos of meaning relating to the metaphysical meaning of human existence and survival which constitutes the kernel of his poetry at large.

It should now be easy to mark the significance of the deeply implicated questions Ghalib puts frontally: (a) whose caprice, or craft, does the image stand as witness to? (b) why has the creator cast the image in a paper robe, which is essentially ephemeral? (c) is the creator a flippant being to have done so? (d) why is the created one so still and silent in his protest and appeal? and (e) is it the individual or the entire phenomenon, which is subjected to eternal suffering? Answers to all these questions are clearly self-suggestive.

Ghalib was once told to his face that this was a meaningless verse. He then asked a friend in a letter to listen to the 'meaning of this meaningless verse' and related it to a custom in Iran where the appellant used to put on a paper robe and appear before the ruler to protest and seek justice. This was similar to carrying a lighted torch in India, or hanging the blood-soaked clothes of the murdered one on a stick in Arabia. This allusion takes us to the heart of the verse and adds to its foundational strength. Far from being meaningless, this verse represents a metaphysical meaning. This is one of the most precise verses of Ghalib where words act like metaphors: *naqsh* for the picture of suffering, *faryaadii* for the oppressed ones, *shoKHii-i tahriir* for the craftiness of scripting, *kaaGhazii* for ephemerality, *pairahan* for perishability, and *paikar-e tasviir* for the suffering human being inside a robe, which together bear the structural and thematic burden of the verse.

2

جذبۂ بے اختیار شوق دیکھا چاہئے
سینۂ شمشیر سے باہر ہے دم شمشیر کا

जज़्बा-ए बे-इख़्तियार-ए शौक़ देखा चाहिये
सीना-ए शमशीर से बाहर है दम शमशीर का

*jazba-i be-iKHtiyaar-e shauq dekhaa chaahiye
siina-i shamshiir se baahar hai dam shamshiir kaa*

(*jazba*—passion, desire;
be-iKHtiyaar—overwhelming, uncontrolled;
shauq—ardour, zeal;
siina-i shamshiir—cutting edge of scimitar;
dam—sparkle, sharpness, breath)

This uncontrollable passion, this ardour,
is worth a watch indeed
The sparkle of a scimitar shows
beyond its breath, beyond its breed

The passion of genuine lovers for their love is always uncontrollable. An idea as simple as this gets an exceptionally rich poetical configuration with the terribly beautiful image of a *shamshiir* (scimitar). Ghalib invites us to watch the lover's ardour and zeal in terms of the sparkling scimitar, which compares well with the sparkling desire of lovers for each other. As the scimitar's sparkle shows beyond its sheath and sharpness, the verse is enriched with multiple imports with reference to the desire of the lovers. It is in this aspect that the unique beauty of the verse lies.

A master of creating connotations, Ghalib projects several possible meanings for us. He seems to suggest: (a) the scimitar lies breathing as if in the sheath of its own breast, just as the passion of lovers breathes in their breasts (b) just as the scimitar cannot hold its sparkle within its own breast, the lovers too cannot hold their desire within their breasts (c) the lovers' overwhelming passion is as sparkling as the scimitar itself, and (d) the sparkling edge of the scimitar and the lovers' heart, brimming with desire, are two images of the same beauty and they reflect upon each other.

Two expressions, in particular, hold the key to this verse. While *siina-i shamshiir* (cutting edge of scimitar) implies the shining breast of the scimitar, *dam* (sparkle/breath) suggests the breath of life. Both these expressions are metaphorically charged and are richly suggestive in the larger context of the verse. Importantly enough, the second line far outweighs the first line in its impact, as the first one is only an inviting statement, while the second one flows out of it with its own resilience to complete the web of meaning. The verse clearly works through the device of establishing a reason to express a reason which adds a magical quality to it. We may refer to another verse of Ghalib here to mark how differently he plays upon the sparkling beauty of a scimitar here: *'ishrat-e qatl-gahe ahl-e tamannaa mat puuchh / 'iid-e nazzara hai shamshiir kaa 'uryaa.n honaa*. If we consider the two verses together, we may mark how a poet's imagination soars to seek poetic strength in different verses with different images.

3

تھا خواب میں خیال کو تجھ سے معاملہ
جب آنکھ کھل گئی نہ زیاں تھا نہ سود تھا

था ख़्वाब में ख़याल को तुझ से मुआमिला
जब आंख खुल गई न ज़ियाँ था न सूद था

*thaa KHvaab mei.n KHayaal ko tujh se mu'aamila
jab aa.nkh khul gaii na ziyaa.n thaa na suud thaa*

(*ziyaa.n*—loss, damage;
suud—gain, profit, advantage)

In dream, my thoughts had a deal with you to obtain
But when the eyes opened, there was no loss, no gain

The two states of dream and awakening have long constituted the major themes in the poetry of love and longing. Ghalib mythicizes this common experience in this verse. In plain terms, the lover suggests that in his dream his thoughts had a deal with his beloved but when he woke up, he realized that the deal got him neither a profit nor a loss. This brings a sense of futility to the lover and makes him reflect upon his miserable predicament.

Playing upon these two states, Ghalib imagines such prospects for the lover that portray him in a truly romantic disposition. Several possible interpretations come to the fore: (a) in psychological terms, dreams are the manifestations of desires lying in the subconscious, which, in this case, relates with the lover's desire for union with the beloved (b) it was the thought, not the lover, that had a deal with the beloved in his dream (c) the thought could be the lover's persona itself (d) this thought could also be of a sexual or material nature, as the word *mu'aamila* suggests in semantic terms (e) dreams are deceptions and are soon forgotten, and finally, (f) the dream could be meaningful if metaphorical, but meaningless if literal.

The kernel of meaning in the first line lies in three inter-contextual words—*KHvaab* (dream), *KHayaal* (thought) and *mu'aamala* (deal)—that collectively create a context for the lover to engage with himself. They make way for the concluding thought in the second line that highlights the essence of reality which, upon awakening, brings to the lover in terms of *ziyaa.n* (loss) and *suud* (gain). The second line completes the circle of meaning, and leaves the lover forlorn and wondering. This verse acquires its strength in the way Ghalib defines the two states of being for the lover and how he places him in those states. Interestingly enough, he also defines how the lover can find himself in two different states when his eyes are closed and when his eyes are open. The hiatus between the two states is where lies the crucial meaning of the verse which may be appreciated further with reference to the disinhibition model of hallucination theory.

4

ڈھانپا کفن نے داغ عیوب برہنگی
میں ورنہ ہر لباس میں ننگ وجود تھا

ढांपा कफ़न ने दाग़-ए उयूब-ए बरहनगी
मैं वरना हर लिबास में नंग-ए वुजूद था

*Dhaa.npaa kafan ne daaGh-e 'uyuub-e barahnagii
mai.n varna har libaas mei.n na.ng-e vujuud thaa*

('*uyuub*—defects, faults, blemishes;
barahnagii—nakedness, nudity;
na.ng—disgrace, shame, ignominy/honour;
esteem, reputation;
vujuud—living, existence, being)

My shroud veiled the blemishes of my nakedness
from everyone's seeing
In each of my dress although, I ever remained
a disgrace to my being

Man has long pondered over the illusion and reality of veiling, and unveiling in physical and spiritual terms. Ghalib's speaker makes a larger statement that he was a sheer disgrace to his being in whatever robe he wore, but it was the shroud at the end that veiled the blemishes of his nakedness. He projects a philosophical point on man's inability to keep away from blemishes. He also develops a design of meaning regarding man's states of dress and undress in life and death. It resembles a swan song, sung with humility while passing from one state of existence to another.

The voice that comes through this verse seems to be that of the poet's alter ego and makes a number of suggestions: (a) death draws a veil on the face of life and it outlives life (b) living is only a shame and dying a sacred shroud on shame (c) dress is, at best, a deception and nakedness is the ultimate reality (d) all dresses are blotted and the shroud is the ultimate dress, which is without a blot in spite of being white (e) every human being is defiled in life and purified in death, and finally (f) it also leaves us wondering if he is speaking as one alive or dead.

With three interwoven expressions—*kafan* (shroud), *barahnagii* (nakedness) and *na.ng-e vujuud* (disgrace to, or honour to existence)—Ghalib develops a pattern of thought in a natural succession. Two more points must be added here. First, Ghalib plays upon the word *na.ng* which means both disgrace and honour. Out of the two diametrically opposed meanings, he seems to appropriate 'disgrace' but 'honour' too would be equally meaningful, although that would entirely overturn the above interpretation of the verse. Second, this verse also reminds of a Qur'anic verse (7:26) where Adam's progeny is told that it has been bestowed with raiment to cover and adore itself, and the best of the raiment is righteousness. In this context, it should be rewarding to consider another verse by Ghalib here: *puuchhe hai kyaa vujuud-o 'adam ahl-e shauq kaa / aap apnii aag ke KHas-o KHaashaak ho gae.* This helps us ascertain how certain seminal ideas seek their expression in contiguous ways in different texts.

5

عشق سے طبीعت نے زیست کا مزا پایا
درد کی دوا پائی درد بے دوا پایا

इश्क़ से तबीअत ने ज़ीस्त का मज़ा पाया
दर्द की दवा पाई दर्द-ए बे-दवा पाया

'ishq se tabii'at ne ziist kaa maza paayaa
dard kii davaa paaii dard-e be-davaa paayaa

(*ziist*—life, living, existence)

Love brought me the joys of life, for sure
A cure for pain, a pain of no cure

Paeans to love are common in ghazals. Love brings all the relish of life and provides a cure from pain, but ironically enough, it also brings pain that has no cure. Ghalib makes a simple statement initially, but then complicates it, which is his characteristic style. He re-defines love both as pain and pleasure, and suggests that it helps enjoy life in totality. Importantly, he chooses to underline the essential quality of human nature, which is easily pleased with love, more than anything else.

This verse reflects differently on the phenomenon of love and makes the following suggestions: (a) the very first word—*'ishq* (love)—brings love to the centre stage and underlines its attributes (b) it defines pleasure and enjoyment that human beings yearn for (c) this love keeps one eternally engaged, irrespective of what pains and pleasures it brings, or might bring (d) there is a certain romance in lingering in a state of pain without reaching out for a cure, as pain can also be a cure unto itself (e) the love capitalized upon in this verse could be both *majaazii* (romantic) and *haqiiqii* (divine) because both bring pleasure and fulfilment to the seekers, although they are seekers of two different kinds and they pursue two different kinds of desires.

The basic appeal of the verse lies in the antithesis that Ghalib draws upon as a literary device to his great advantage. The first line speaks cheerfully and directly to us, suggesting that life was a pain and love brought a cure. It is the second line, however, that works principally through two punchy paradoxes—*dard kii davaa* (cure for pain) and *dard-e be-davaa* (pain of no cure). Together, they hold the pulse of the verse and make it worthy of literary value. Interestingly, they may also be read as *dard-e be-davaa* and *dard be-davaa* with equal justification and relevance. The two lines of the verse leave us pondering over both the ideas, on the one hand, and the experience of love, on the other. The spontaneity of utterance and simplicity of diction add to the immediacy of appeal which is one of the hallmarks of this verse. It should be worthwhile to listen to Ghalib's major predecessor, Mir Taqi Mir, in this respect who offers a definitional verse on love: *'ishq 'aashiq hai 'ishq hai m'aashuuq / yaanii apnaa hii mubtalaa hai 'ishq*. The two poets and their verses on love quite often echo each other with respect to experiential richness and variety.

6

سادگی و پرکاری بے خودی و ہشیاری
حسن کو تغافل میں جرأت آزما پایا

सादगी-ओ-पुरकारी बे-ख़ुदी-ओ-हुश्यारी
हुस्न को तग़ाफ़ुल में जुरअत-आज़मा पाया

saadgii-o pur-kaarii be-KHudii-o hushyaarii
husn ko taGhaaful mei.n jur'at-aazmaa paayaa

(*pur-kaarii*—cleverness, skilfulness, artfulness;
be-KHudii—selflessness, rapture, ecstasy;
taGhaaful—negligence, indifference, inertia;
jura't-aazmaa—testing courage)

Simple but cunning, lost but alert—
Beauty was brave—even if inert

Lovers know their beloveds for their peculiar qualities. Sometimes, these qualities stand in contrast with each other, but this is what precisely distinguishes them as well. Ghalib presents a uniquely endowed beloved in this verse. As she is a peculiar kind, she can make advances even in her state of feigned indifference. She is indeed a crafty beloved and has all the makings of one who can artfully entice.

Several layers of implication can be explored here: (a) the beloved is naïve yet ingenious enough to test the lover's commitment (b) she is selfless yet self-possessed to charm her lover (c) she has the nerve to feign ignorance, yet makes advances to her lover (d) the speaker here may be the lover himself who enjoys saying what she says (e) this lover who is aware of all her qualities is also attracted by her mysterious charms, and (f) all these images of the beloved personify her in rich, but complex, terms.

Ghalib artfully puts together six adjectives in three pairs to portray the beloved as a curious figure of romance. It should be noted that like the English metaphysical poets, he yokes with creative violence *saadgii* (simplicity) with *pur-kaarii* (cleverness), *be-KHudii* (selflessness) with *hushyaarii* (alertness) and *taGhaaful* (negligence) with *jur'at* (courage). Each pair of adjectives combines the contraries which Ghalib does on design to portray a beloved who is stranger indeed than a strange one. The two lines of this verse seem disconnected on the surface, and the second line of the verse doesn't apparently seem to flow out of the first line, but it is Ghalib's touch of genius that by reconciling the discordant images of the beloved in both the lines, he strikes a unique continuity between the lines. This is how he succeeds in portraying an atypical beloved who is also a type of her own. Hasrat Mohani, known for his romantic verses in particular, engages with this kind of experience and comes close to Ghalib with this verse: *hairat Ghuruur-e husn se shoKHii se iztiraab / dil ne bhii tere siikh liye hai.n chalan tamaam.*

7

غنچہ پھر لگا کھلنے آج ہم نے اپنا دل
خوں کیا ہوا دیکھا گم کیا ہوا پایا

गुंचा फिर लगा खिलने आज हम ने अपना दिल
ख़ूँ किया हुआ देखा गुम किया हुआ पाया

Ghuncha phir lagaa khilne aaj ham ne apnaa dil
KHuu.n kiyaa huaa dekhaa gum kiyaa huaa paayaa

(*Ghuncha*—bud)

Buds bloom yet again;
yet again, they are around
I saw my heart in cold blood;
lost for good, I found

Images drawn from the garden often find their symbolic configurations in Urdu ghazals. In this verse, Ghalib draws upon the stock symbolism of *Ghuncha* (bud), but with a difference. He suggests that spring has arrived, and this is the time for the bud to show up again and become a *gul (*blossom), but he also implies rather indirectly that just as the bud would bloom, it would attract the *bulbul*, which in turn would attract a hunter (*sayyaad*). It should be plausible, thus, to suggest that it is the bird here that appears to be the lover of the blossom that would lose its life at the hands of the hunter, and finally lie dead by the feet of the blossom. Ironically, while the hunter would live on, the bird would die and the blossom would wither.

The bud, the blossom and the hunter appear as archetypes that project together a pattern of multiple meanings: (a) the world is a garden where all objects have their life spans like birds and blossoms, and they are subject to decay and death (b) the bud is going to be a blossom this spring season yet again, and yet again the bird, its lover, would be killed by the hunter and the blossom would wither (c) buds unfurl into blossoms in the spring and it is both ironic and tragic that it is in this time of rejuvenation that the blossom should see its lover—the bird— killed by the hunter in cold blood and lose it forever (d) the speaker, that is the bird itself, is an eternal watcher, eternal sufferer and eternal lover, and finally, (e) the verse can be appreciated as the bird's soliloquy on the perennial philosophy of existence and perishing, and it reaches us in a natural act of pain-sharing.

Let this be added further that the two sets of four rhyming expressions in particular— *Khuu.n kiyaa huaa dekhaa* (saw as killed) and *gum kiyaa huaa paayaa* (found as lost)—add an auditory aura and stylistic finesse to the verse. The six synchronous sounds that emanate from the basic sound of *aa* add immensely to the auditory and semantic grandeur of the verse. Keeping this verse by Ghalib in mind, one may refer to a verse by Mir Taqi Mir to compare how the magnanimity of pain may find its voice in a different diction and imagery: *dil KHuu.n huaa zabt hii karte karte / ham ho hii chuke dukho.n ko bharte bharte.*

8

شوق بر رنگ رقیب سر و ساماں نکلا
قیس تصویر کے پردے میں بھی عریاں نکلا

शौक़ हर रंग रक़ीब-ए सर-ओ-सामाँ निकला
क़ैस तस्वीर के पर्दें में भी उर्याँ निकला

shauq har ra.ng raqiib-e sar-o saamaa.n niklaa
Qais tasviir ke parde mei.n bhii 'uryaa.n niklaa

(*shauq*—affection, passion, love;
raqiib—rival, opponent;
sar-o saamaa.n—wherewithal, assets;
belongings, possessions;
Qais—Laila's lover, known as Majnuu.n;
'uryaa.n—bare, naked, nude)

A zeal in every hue found a rival
in all assets ever
As Qais came out in a picture's veil,
as naked as ever

True love does not accept any barriers and it makes its own mark. Ghalib mythicizes this idea by drawing upon an allusion concerning the eleventh-century star-crossed lover of Arabia called Qais Ibn al-Malavva, also known as Majnuu.n, the possessed one. He defied all constraints and came to be fabled as a primeval lover in art and literature. Although he abandoned home, composed poems, wandered naked, lived with animals in the wilderness and endlessly pined for Laila, he could never be united with her. Finally, he breathed his last at her grave, and came to be painted naked and allegorized as an embodiment of unfulfilled desire.

This verse opens up multiple layers of meaning: (a) Qais was an archetypal lover like none else (b) he was an inspired rebel of his own make (c) he was possessed by lunacy with which alone he could ever reach his desired goal (d) he was sick with desire and stood naked in a painting in symbolic terms, and (e) he moved beyond the constraints of colour and painting, veil and nakedness, and acquired his own mythic life.

Ghalib brings together a rich complex of key words—*shauq* (passion), *raqiib* (rival), *sar-o saamaa.n* (possessions), *parda* (veil) and *'uryaa.n* (naked)—to cumulatively construct the image of Qais and his world. He underlines his defiance with the expression—*raqiib-e sar-o saamaa.n niklaa* (appeared as a rival of worldly possessions) in the first line and then he completes the paradigm of meaning with *'uryaa.n niklaa* (appeared naked) in the second line. Yet another turn of phrase—*tasviir ke parde mei.n* (in the veil of a painting)—is a great example of Ghalib's imaginative vitality by which he philosophically suggests that a creation is worthy of itself only in its nakedness, as all veils on them are only illusory. It is here that the verse acquires its extraordinary vitality of implicational meaning. A verse from Imdad Imam Asar adds yet another perspective to Ghalib's idea and enriches the institution of Qais as a primal lover: *purshish-e haal ko jaatii hai kahaa.n ai Laila / Qais kii shakl hai kyaa Qais kii tasviir se puuchh.*

9

زخم نے داد نہ دی تنگئ دل کی یا رب
تیر بھی سینۂ بسمل سے پرافشاں نکلا

ज़ख़्म ने दाद न दी तंगी-ए दिल की या रब
तीर भी सीना-ए बिस्मिल से पर-अफ़शाँ निकला

zaKHm ne daad na dii ta.ngi-i dil kii yaa Rab
tiir bhi siina-i bismil se par-afshaa.n niklaa

(*daad*—praise, appeal, justice;
ta.ngi-i dil—narrow space in heart;
bismil—injured, wounded;
par-afshaa.n—flapping/fluttering of wings)

The wound couldn't appeal, O God!
against the narrow space in heart's nest
Flapping its wings, the arrow too
shot out of the injured one's breast

In this self-proclaimed 'meaningless verse', Ghalib seems to suggest that the lover is complaining to God that his wound did not find the comfort of a home in the heart which was its abode because it was too constricted. To emphasize upon this state of the wound's deprivation, Ghalib executes the images of *tiir* (arrow) and *siina* (breast) to stress that the arrow, too, did not find a space in the heart and it fluttered its wings like a bird, as it shot through the injured lover's narrow breast. He thus suggests that the lover's heart remained wounded, and stayed in a state of perpetual pain and suffering.

Several implied layers of meaning appear before us: (a) the lover is typified as *bismil*, the injured one, that also happens to be a stock symbol of the Urdu ghazal (b) his wound remains uncared for forever and he remains in pain endlessly (c) even the arrow crosses through the injured lover's breast and deprives it of love (d) the heart is likened to a nest that is ruined, and (e) the arrow is personified as a bird that pierces through the heart to find its way out.

Ghalib uses the literary device of irony to enliven this verse. Laden with five telling images of *zaKHm* (wound) and *dil* (heart) in the first line and *tiir* (arrow), *siina* (breast) and *bismil* (injured) in the second line, the verse represents a conglomeration of concrete visual images. One may also notice the ingenious use of the word *daad* in two meanings of 'praise' and 'justice', which implies that the heart did not receive either of them and was left impoverished. This is further supplemented and strengthened by *par-afshaa.n* (flutter) which suggests the image of a helpless bird, and creates a condition of misery for the injured and devastated lover. A variation on this theme may be seen in yet another verse of Ghalib, which has its own individual appeal: *koii mere dil se puuchhe tire tiir-e niim kash ko / ye KHalish kahaa.n se hotii jo jigar ke paar hotaa.*

10

بوئے گل نالۂ دل دود چراغ محفل
جو تری بزم سے نکلا سو پریشاں نکلا

बू-ए गुल नाला-ए दिल दूद-ए चिराग़-ए महफ़िल
जो तिरी बज़्म से निकला सो परेशाँ निकला

buu-e gul naala-i dil duud-e charaaGh-e mahfil
jo tiri bazm se niklaa so pareshaa.n niklaa

(*buu-e gul*—flower's fragrance/smell;
naala-i dil—heart's lament, wailing;
(*duud-e charaaGh-e mahfil*—smoke from assembly's lamp;
bazm—assembly)

Flower's fragrance, heart's wailing,
assembly's lamp smoke—all for nought
Whosoever came out of your assembly
came out all distraught

The beloved's assembly is the place to be for the lover. Ghalib typically reverses this ideal notion in this verse. By evolving an analogy with the blossom's fragrance, heart's lamentations and lamp's smoke floating away helplessly, he indeed suggests that the lover too wandered out of the beloved's assembly in a ruffled state. It implies further that whosoever left the beloved's assembly remained in a state of disarray ever after. The larger implication is that the beloved's assembly, far from being enjoyable, is a place that the lover has to leave helplessly and in a miserable state.

A closer reading of the verse brings forth several notable layers of meaning: (a) the beloved invariably causes suffering to the lover, as it seems to happen in the case of this lover (b) leaving the beloved's assembly is in itself a cause of distress for this lover torn between desire and disappointment (c) it appears as if there were other admirers in her assembly, but there was no space for him there, which made him unhappy, and (d) he postulates in retrospect that he remained distressed as much in her company as in separation from her.

The artistic merit of the verse may be marked in the way Ghalib establishes likeness among three unrelated senses—olfactory (*buu-e gul*), auditory (*naala-i dil*) and visual (*duud-e charaaGh-e mahfil*)—to discover a pattern of unity among them. He underlines their essential helplessness and ephemerality, and connects them with the figure of the lover who remains distressed, both in and outside the assembly. *Bazm* (assembly) and *pareshaa.n* (ruffled) are the two key words of opposite nature that hold the essential import of the verse; one representing gaiety and the other suggesting distress. It must also be noted that by making the first line in Persian embrace the second line in Urdu, Ghalib strikes a natural dialogic relationship between both the lines to create a cause-effect relationship. In the given perspective, consider how like Ghalib, Momin Khan Momin also portrays his lover in a similar kind of misery: *maashuuq aur bhii hai.n bataa de jahaan mei.n / kartaa hai kaun zulm kisii per tirii tarah.*

11

تھا زندگی میں مرگ کا کھٹکا لگا ہوا
اڑنے سے پیشتر بھی مرا رنگ زرد تھا

था ज़िंदगी में मर्ग का खटका लगा हुआ
उड़ने से पेशतर भी मिरा रंग ज़र्द था

thaa zindagii mei.n marg kaa khaTkaa lagaa huaa
uDne se peshtar bhii miraa ra.ng zard thaa

(*marg*—death;
peshtar—before, prior, earlier, formerly;
zard—yellow, pale, wane, dull)

In life, I feared the impending death that jaded
I had turned pale even before my colour faded

The apprehension of death in life is one of the most common for human beings; something they suffer all their lives. Ghalib's speaker makes a universal statement in the first line of this verse. He impregnates this idea with greater implications in the second line, when he says that it was not the fear of death that turned him pale because he had already faded and lost his sheen even before he met his death. With death as the central concern of this verse, he makes an existential statement in terms of the symbolic pale colour which is suggestive of decay leading to death. In broader terms, he makes a philosophical point that the fading of colour implies fading out from life's canvas and leaving it blank.

There are several levels of connotational intents in this verse: (a) there is a constant apprehension of death in life which makes life wearisome (b) this apprehension does not allow man to enjoy the pleasures of life (c) living a life in constant apprehension is akin to living death in life (d) life and death are brought face-to-face against each other where life is represented by colour and death by colourlessness, and finally, (e) colourlessness is the real and the unchangeable colour which has a clearly metaphysical import behind it.

Ghalib plays artfully with three keywords — *khaTkaa* (apprehension), representing a psychological condition, *uDnaa* (flying), dramatizing the act of flying in the sky as also the fading of colour, and *zard* (pale), portraying an existential condition. In addition to these, the word *peshtar* (prior) indicates the stage before flying, or fading out, and implicates the two states of *zindagii* (life) and *marg* (death) upon which the semantic structure of the verse rests. It is interesting to note that Mir Taqi Mir also uses the colour *zard* to portray the condition of painful survival, although he uses this in the context of the lover's suffering which is akin to suffering death in life: *Mir jii zard hote jaate ho / kyaa kahii.n tum ne bhii kiyaa hai 'ishq.*

12

دہر میں نقش وفا وجہ تسلی نہ ہوا
ہے یہ وہ لفظ کہ شرمندۂ معنی نہ ہوا

दहर में नक़्श-ए वफ़ा वज्ह-ए तसल्ली न हुआ
है ये वो लफ़्ज़ कि शर्मिंदा-ए मानी न हुआ

dahr mei.n naqsh-e vafaa vajh-e tasallii na huaa
hai ye vo lafz ke sharminda-i m'anii na huaa

(*dahr*—age, time, world;
naqsh-e vafaa—mark of love;
tasallii—consolation, reassurance, satisfaction;
sharminda-i m'anii—bearing of meaning)

Love's mark was no cause for solace
in any time and age
This word didn't bear a meaning,
nor came out of the word's cage

Love and faithfulness are two stock concepts that ghazal poets have often developed. In most of the cases, they eulogize love, but sometimes they also make complaints regarding the beloved's indifference and their loveless relationships. In this particular verse, the lover laments that his love did not either show any signs of reciprocation or offer solace to him. The absence of any possible reassurance makes him despondent and compels him to say rather sadly that the word 'love' does not bear any meaning for him. As such, the idea and experience of love prove futile and inconsequential to him.

Drawing closely to the spirit of the verse, one notices certain finer shades of meaning here: (a) beloveds are characteristically careless and unacknowledging, without realizing how they torment their lovers (b) they provide no solace to the lovers and don't assuage them even in their misery (c) it is thus unfair to expect any reciprocal act of love from them (d) indifference towards love and loyalty is not limited to romantic relationships alone, but extends to all human relationships (e) as such, beloveds may realize the value of love only when they are left unloved or abandoned, which the lovers do not indulge in any case.

Ghalib's disapproval of the beloved's ways and manners is best expressed in the phrase *sharminda-i m'anii* (bearing of meaning) which implies that the emotion of love is not beholden to the meaning that the word 'love' holds. In this context, the word *tasallii* (consolation) acquires a deeper shade of pathos which reflects the sad state of the lover. This takes us to another verse by Ghalib himself that may be read as a variation on this very experience: *ham ko un se vafaa kii hai ummiid / jo nahii.n jaante vafaa kyaa hai.*

13

میں نے چاہا تھا کہ اندوہ وفا سے چھوٹوں
وہ ستم گر مرے مرنے پہ بھی راضی نہ ہوا

मैं ने चाहा था कि अंदोह-ए वफ़ा से छूटूँ
वो सितमगर मिरे मरने पे भी राज़ी न हुआ

mai.n ne chaahaa thaa ke andoh-e vaafa se chhuuTuu.n
vo sitamgar mire marne pe bhii raazii na huaa

(*andoh*—grief, pain, sorrow, agony;
vafaa—loyalty, fidelity, faithfulness;
sitamgar—tyrant, oppressor)

I had wished to get rid of love's grief and pain
But that tyrant didn't even let me die in bane

Seeking release from the pain of love is sometimes unimaginable for the lover. Speaking in the first person, however, the lover in this verse helplessly confesses that he wished to get rid of love's travails, but the beloved did not agree, and she did not allow him to even die and seek his release from her. As such, love is a prison for him which he is made to accept—albeit with insufferable pain. One also wonders if he enjoys some kind of secret pride or pleasure in suffering the onslaughts of his beloved, which he tries to conceal. However, he continues being with her, also portraying her as an oppressor.

This verse seems to unveil the stock image of a dejected lover. Here are certain implied layers of meaning for us to explore: (a) instead of pleasure, love brings agony to the lover which is ironical at the core (b) being in love is being held captive by the beloved's manoeuvres which, too, is a suffocating experience (c) there is no respite from love's travails, either in life or in death, which turns the lover into a prisoner (d) it was the lover's desire to get rid of love's pain but all desires are unfortunately subjected to the beloved's approval, and finally, (e) the beloved would not agree to let him die, even if the lover wished to die, because she wants to keep him in attendance.

The verse acquires its appeal in the way Ghalib imparts a situational context to a plain statement from the lover. Direct exposition of a state, lucid diction and a conversational tone clearly mark the merits of this verse. It gains impact through a play of three interlaced key expressions—*andoh* (agony), *sitamgar* (tormentor) and *marnaa* (death)—that Ghalib brings together to construct a condition of pain and suffering. This condition of a dejected lover acutely reminds us of a verse by Momin Khan Momin, who also constructs the figure of such a lover in a similar manner: *huu.n jaa.n ba-lab butaan-e sitamgar ke haath se / kyaa sab jahaa.n mei.n jiite hai.n Momin isii tarah.*

14

مری تعمیر میں مضمر ہے اک صورت خرابی کی
ہیولیٰ برق خرمن کا ہے خون گرم دہقاں کا

मिरी तामीर में मुज़मर है इक सूरत ख़राबी की
हयूला बरक़-ए ख़िर्मन का है ख़ून-ए गर्म दिहक़ाँ का

miri t'aamiir mei.n muzmar hai ik suurat KHaraabii kii
hayulaa barq-e KHirman kaa hai KHuun-e garm dahqaa.n kaa

(*t'aamiir*—construction, creation, making;
muzmar—concealed;
KHaraabii—destruction, desolation, affliction;
hayulaa—appearance, matter;
barq—lightening;
KHirman—harvest, heap, stack;
dahqaa.n—peasant, farmer, labourer)

In my creation is a way
of my destruction, concealed
The farmer's hot blood is indeed
a lightning on his yield

Issues in creation and destruction form the core of existential philosophy as well as of art and literature. Ghalib engages with those ideas in a symbolic framework here. The plain meaning is that when lightning strikes, it ruins the harvest which the farmer had, metaphorically, nurtured with his own blood. This also implies that his blood had become so hot with his hard work in the field that it turned into lightening and burnt the harvest.

Several possible implications may be marked further in this verse: (a) philosophically, every construction leads to destruction (b) politically, wherever there is yield, there is exploitation (c) symbolically, while working in the field, the peasant's blood becomes so hot that it burns his own harvest (d) ironically, the creator himself turns into the destructor (e) logically, thus, human efforts made, howsoever painstakingly, do not necessarily meet with rewards (f) one wonders whether the speaker here is a human figure, or is it a natural phenomenon which speaks its own inscrutable language.

While engaging with the opposite ideas of *t'aamiir* (construction) and *KHaraabii* (destruction), as also *barq* (lightening) and *KHirman* (harvest), Ghalib comes close to Marxist ideology concerning social class, peasantry and their predicament. The figure of the *dahqaa.n* (peasant) remains at the focal point, who connects the two lines of the verse together that work in a corroborative manner to develop a commentary on suffering and survival. Ghalib's preoccupation with these seminal issues is expressed in yet another verse by him: *kaargaah-e hastii mei.n laala daaGh saamaa.n hai / barq-e KHirman-e raahat KHuun-e garm-e dahqaa.n hai.* In one of his well-known verses, Mohammad Iqbal comes around Ghalib's idea, but with his own vision and in his characteristic style: *jis khet se dahqaa.n ko mayassar nahii.n rozii / us khet ke har KHosha-i gandum ko jalaa do.*

15

محرم نہیں ہے تو ہی نوا ہائے راز کا
یاں ورنہ جو حجاب ہے پردہ ہے ساز کا

महरम नहीं है तू ही नवाहा-ए राज़ का
याँ वरना जो हिजाब है पर्दा है साज़ का

mahram nahii.n hai tuu hii navahaae raaz kaa
yaa.n varna jo hijaab hai parda hai saaz kaa

(*mahram*—confidant;
navahaae raaz—secret voices;
hijaab—veil, curtain;
saaz—harmony, synchrony, music instrument)

You alone are not the confidant
of the voices of secrecy
Whatever lies in between
is only a veil of synchrony

Appearance and reality both contradict and supplement each other. This verse unveils the vital difference between what appears and what remains hidden. The moot question, however, is as to who has the potential to decipher the secrets of creation. Ghalib asserts that creation is essentially a veil which reverberates with the music of its own kind, but man is unaware of this reality and is unable to listen to this music. By defining the creation as a veil, he drives home a philosophical point on the enormity of creation and the inconsequentiality of man.

The verse opens several layers of implied meaning. It takes us to conclude that: (a) the creation, or what we know as the world, is a mystery (b) there is an inherent musical harmony in the physical world which is a divine phenomenon unto itself (c) man's potential is too limited to delve deeper into reality, and (d) man can be subjected to a stark, but subtle, commentary on his limitations, in spite of all the potentiality gifted to him by the divine power.

The structure of meaning in this verse rests on four key words— *mahram* (confidant) and *raaz* (secret) in the first line, and *hijaab* (veil) and *parda* (veil) in the second line. Together, they replicate the idea of secrecy with fine distinction. In the complex of these two pairs of semantically corresponding words, the central word is *saaz* (harmony) which unwraps a philosophical understanding of the phenomenon. In addition, the verse gains its strength through the directness of expression which contributes towards the immediacy of its appeal. Seemab Akbarabadi broadly draws upon this idea with his own metaphors of *zarra* (speck), *hijaab* (veil) and *aaiina* (mirror) in his verse and offers a comparative perspective to read Ghalib's verse: *sargashta-i jamaal kii hairaaniyaa.n na puuchh / har zarre ke hijaab mei.n ik aaiina milaa.*

16

بے خیال حسن میں حسن عمل کا سا خیال
خلد کا اک در ہے میری گور کے اندر کھلا

है ख़याल-ए हुस्न में हुस्न-ए अमल का सा ख़याल
ख़ुल्द का इक दर है मेरी गोर के अंदर खुला

hai KHayaal-e husn mei.n husn-e 'amal kaa saa KHayaal
KHuld ka ik dar hai merii gor ke andar khulaa

('amal—action;
KHuld—paradise;
gor—grave, tomb)

In thoughts of beauty is a thought
akin to a beauteous wave
There is but a door to heaven
that opens here in my grave

Beauty has multiple manifestations and calls for multiple responses. This verse is a paean to beauty and is conceived in imaginary terms. Ghalib asserts that imagining beauty is experiencing the beauty of imagination. The idea of beauty is thus defined as an idea of enjoyment unto itself. From this perspective, it is a heavenly experience to think of the beloved's beauty. This thought brings blessings to the lover even after death and opens, as if, the door of the heaven into his grave. This corresponds with the popular belief that the doors and windows of the pious ones open into the heavens. As such, Ghalib seems to imagine the lover, too, in terms of the pious ones which adds an entirely new dimension to the station of lovers.

Thinking further of the implications involved in this verse, it may be noted that (a) remembering the beloved is enjoying the heavenly bliss (b) her face is blissful and is as beautiful as heaven itself (c) equating the lover with the spiritually accomplished ones is a bold stroke of imagination (d) love is a faith unto itself for the lovers (e) the stark difference between spiritualist as lover and lover as spiritualist is demolished as the two constitute one entity, and finally, (f) the two incompatible spaces of grave and paradise are defined afresh here.

Ghalib gleefully plays with the word *husn* (beauty) in two different ways. He blends *KHayaal-e husn* (imagining of beauty) with *husn-e 'amal* (beauty of imagining) and adds the element of rare elation to his thought. Further, he places *KHuld* (paradise) and *gor* (grave) against each other as two thoughts and two visual experiences, and makes them mirror one another. It is equally important to note that Ghalib individualizes the entire experience by adding the personal pronoun of *merii* (mine) in the second line, and turns it into a plausible experience which makes the verse immensely expressive and appealing. Here is how a play with words (*KHayaal-e husn* and *husn-e KHayaal*) also makes way for the play of meaning.

17

شب کہ برقِ سوزِ دل سے زہرۂ ابر آب تھا
شعلۂ جوالہ ہر یک حلقۂ گرداب تھا

शब कि बर्क़-ए सोज़-ए दिल से ज़हरा-ए अब्र आब था
शोला-ए जव्वाला हर यक हल्क़ा-ए गिर्दाब था

*shab ke barq-e soz-e dil se zahra-i abr aab thaa
sh'ola-i javvala har ik halqa-i girdaab thaa*

(*barq*—lightening, blaze;
soz-e dil—burning of heart;
zahra-i abr aab—gall to enter water,
take courage, face fright;
sh'ola-i javvala—spinning flame;
halqa—circumference, circle;
girdaab—whirlpool, vortex)

The night bore my heart's blaze
but it had the courage to face the fright,
Each circle of the whirlpool
was a dancing flame within my sight

The little human heart is a continent that calls for endless explorations. This verse venerates the magical quality of the heart and its immense potential. Ghalib dramatizes a situation in which the night was ablaze with the burning of the heart. This burning spun a flame in water and gave it an extraordinarily raging life with circles of whirlpool emerging around. It may be surmised that water was indeed the cloud's lifeforce and the whirlpool that it got was the rage of the burning heart. As such, the cloud feared the heart's burning because each circle of the devastating whirlpool was a dancing flame unto itself, endowed with great power of devastation.

With reference to the astonishing power of the heart, several other implications can be noticed: (a) both nature and the human heart are endowed with astonishing power (b) heart is the storehouse of far greater energy to devastate than nature (c) the heart holds supremacy over the elements which are the prized creations of the divine, and (d) such a heart could only be the lover's heart that frets, fumes and burns with anger to devastate.

This verse is characterized by its heavily Persianized diction. Ghalib makes an astute selection of words and brings together five words with similar semantic burden like *barq* (lightening), *soz-e dil* (heart's burning) and *sh'ola* (flame) on the one hand and then *halqa* (circle) and *girdaab* (whirlpool) on the other to compose a vibrant complex of meaning. *Sh'ola* is further strengthened with a booster adjective *javvala* (spinning) which helps establish the strength of fire, and finally adds to the remarkable vibrancy of the verse. Dagh Dehlavi, who is generally associated with typically romantic verses with the extraordinary repository of his characteristic diction, comes up with an idea which harks back to Ghalib:
muhiit-e 'ishq kii har mauj-e tuufaa.n KHez aisii hai / vo hai.n girdaab mei.n jo daaman-e saahil mei.n rahte hai.n.

18

یاد کر وہ دن کہ ہر یک حلقہ تیرے دام کا
انتظارِ صید میں اک دیدۂ بے خواب تھا

याद कर वो दिन कि हर यक हल्क़ा तेरे दाम का
इंतिज़ार-ए सैद में इक दीदा-ए बे-ख़्वाब था

yaad kar vo din ke har ik halqa tere daam kaa
intizaar-e said mei.n ik diida-i be-KHvaab thaa

(*halqa*—circle, loop;
daam—snare, trap, net;
said—victim;
diida—eye;
be-KHvaab—sleepless)

Recall the day when your snare's each loop
Looked like sleepless eyes, waiting for the dupe

The figure of the beloved who snares the lover can well be the subject of a verse. Ghalib creates such a situation in this verse and speaks in the voice of the lover to address the beloved. There are two possible meanings involved here. First, the lover asks the beloved to recall the day when she was always on the lookout to snare a lover in her net, but that is not the case any longer as she has already got one now. Second, she did not have a lover and waited helplessly to get one without pausing for even a wink, which kept her eyes sleepless. Ghalib executes appropriate metaphors of entrapment which makes the verse worthy of emotional appeal and critical attention.

This double-edged verse makes other suggestions as well: (a) the beloved is sly and crafty, and the lover her helpless prey (b) this beloved is the one who ensnares rather than the one who attracts (c) she has forgotten the past of which the lover reminds her in the present moment (d) although she has a lover now, he does not receive her favours, and finally, (e) there is a hidden sense of disapproval from the lover over how she conducts herself which leaves the lover rueful.

There are two sets of entwined images to take note of: first, *halqa* (circle) and *diida* (eyes), which are round and open in visual terms and go together, second, *daam* (net) and *said* (victim) that complement each other semantically. All these four images, together, construct the essential intent of this verse. The circle of meaning is completed by another corollary image of *diida-i be-KHvaab* (sleepless eyes). The word *intizaar* (wait) in the second line, in its association with *nazar* (eye), turns immensely relevant in the way the poet plays with the idea of seeing and waiting to underline the central import of the verse.

19

بسکہ دشوار ہے ہر کام کا آساں ہونا
آدمی کو بھی میسر نہیں انساں ہونا

बसकि दुश्वार है हर काम का आसाँ होना
आदमी को भी मयस्सर नहीं इंसाँ होना

bas-ke dushvaar hai har kaam kaa aasaa.n honaa
aadmii ko bhii mayassar nahii.n insaa.n honaa

(*bas-ke*—although;
dushvaar—difficult, arduous, troublesome;
mayassar—attainable, achievable, possible)

It's hard to make it easy; past man's acumen
Just as it is for a man to be a human

'What oft was thought but never so well expressed' is a familiar line we often repeat to underline the beauty and appropriateness of a felt thought, or a universal truth, expressed artfully. This statement applies well to this verse where Ghalib says in simple and plain terms that it is difficult to make every task easy, just as it is for a man to become a human being. This verse may best be read as Ghalib's keenest discourse on man—his lacking as well as his potential—but more importantly, and ideally, on his infinite capabilities which he fails to exercise and become an ideal figure.

This seemingly simple verse may, however, be read to mark several suggested meanings behind it: (a) the reference to man invokes two concepts of man, that is, the ordinary man and the superman (b) both are created in the image of God, but they do not necessarily have the same standards of humaneness (c) the crux of the matter lies in man becoming a human being, endowed with superior qualities, but (d) it is not easy for man to attain those qualities that may make him a superior human being, which is essentially ironical.

Ghalib begins his precise discourse with a very consequential expression—*bas-ke* (although)—which suggests that he has picked the thread of a discourse from somewhere in the middle and that much has already been said before. It also suggests that what he proposes now is the sum and substance of a larger discourse. He further capitalizes upon two sets of dichotomous expressions—*dushvaar* (difficult) and *aasaan* (easy), as well as *aadmii* (man) and *insaa.n* (human)—to develop a definite scheme of meaning. *Mayassar* (attainable) is another important counter of expression which suggests that man might achieve his goal with his labour and ardour, if he tried. In an equally unassuming manner, characteristic of a genuine verse, Mir Taqi Mir too expresses this idea in a more personalized manner: *Mir sahib tum farishta ho to ho / aadmii honaa to mushkil hai miyaa.n.*

20

کی مرے قتل کے بعد اس نے جفا سے توبہ
ہائے اس زود پشیماں کا پشیماں ہونا

की मिरे क़त्ल के बाद उस ने जफ़ा से तौबा
हाए उस ज़ूद-पशेमाँ का पशेमाँ होना

kii mire qatl ke b'aad us ne jafaa se tauba
haai us zuud-pashemaa.n kaa pashemaa.n honaa

(*jafaa*—oppression, cruelty, beloved's tyranny;
tauba—penitence, renunciation;
zuud-pashemaa.n—repentant, embarrassed,
remorseful too soon)

She vowed not to be oppressive,
after ravaging me
Ah! Her repentance too soon!
Ah! Her idiosyncrasy!

Beloveds are known to turn oppressive, act unfairly and be tyrannical to their lovers, but also turn kind, subsequently. Although they cannot make amends for the damage done, they can always be repentant and make good for the pain caused to the lover. Ghalib brings to us a beloved in this verse who is unique in the sense that she causes pain, but takes no time to bring the pleasure of reconciliation and companionship to the lover. This is what makes her a special and a fascinating figure in this verse.

There are certain other aspects of this beloved that attract our attention: (a) beloveds, being beloveds, blow both hot and cold (b) lovers, being lovers, bear the pain and bask in the pleasure of union, as both pain and pleasure are the gifts of the game (c) her act of oppression might be a weird act but freaky acts in love are only natural, and (d) lovers are yielding and keep loving because the repentance of the beloveds brings genuine pleasure to them.

We may also note that five key words in this verse—*qatl* (killing), *jafaa* (oppression), *tauba* (penitence), *haai* (alas), and *zuud-pashemaa.n* (remorseful too soon)—stand out as the blocks on which the structure of the verse rests. All these words construct the figure of the beloved exactly as she is characterized. Ghalib's merit lies in bringing constitutive words of a given category here to represent a playful thought with vividness. These words, as they appear in this order, represent the entire plot and constitute the kernel of meaning with great finesse. This verse may be appreciated as a fine example of poetic elegance. A verse from Shahryar may be quoted here that echoes Ghalib's verse: *ham ne to koii baat nikaalii nahii.n Gham kii / vo zuud pashemaan pashemaan sa kyu.n hai.*

21

دوست غم خواری میں میری سعی فرماویں گے کیا
زخم کے بھرتے تلک ناخن نہ بڑھ جاویں گے کیا

दोस्त ग़म-ख़्वारी में मेरी सई फ़रमावेंगे क्या
ज़ख़्म के भरते तलक नाख़ुन न बढ़ जावेंगे क्या

dost Gham-KHvaarii mei.n merii sa'ii farmaave.nge kyaa
zaKHm ke bharte talak naaKHun na baRh jaavenge kyaa

(Gham-KHvaarii—sympathy, commiseration, consolation;
sa'ii—attempt, effort, endeavour, effort)

What can my friends do to soothe me in pain
Till my wounds heal, wouldn't the nails grow again

Both pain and suffering together constitute human fate. This verse may be read and appreciated as Ghalib's commentary on man's eternal fate that has pain and suffering writ large in it. It makes sense even at the first reading, but it evokes sympathy when considered seriously as to what the speaker has to say in the verse. He complains ruefully that howsoever much his friends may try to console him and get him out of his misery, they would not be able to help him for good. This is because pain has a way of staying back as new pains keep replacing the old ones and subject men to incessant suffering.

On a closer reading of the verse, one may deduce further that the speaker (a) inflicts misery upon himself again, and yet again (b) he sadly accepts that he is destined to suffer perpetually (c) he suffers from self-pity but shuns it, and (d) he questions himself, but also wonders if he would ever recover permanently from his perpetual suffering.

Ghalib expresses a philosophy of life with the metaphor of a wound that knows no healing. It should also be noted that there is a sense of questioning blended with a sense of wondering imbued with anxiety in each line of the verse. In the first line, it is about how (if at all) the friends may help him, and in the second line about would or wouldn't the nails grow again to nibble at the wound. The two images of *zaKHm* (wound) and *naaKHun* (nail), put against each other in oppositional terms, also serve as central metaphors to construct the meaning of the verse. The basic idea of this verse has been appropriated variously in ghazals: *KHaalii ai chaara-garo honge bahut marham-daa.n / per mire zaKHm nahii.n aise ke bhar jaaenge* (Sheikh Ibrahim Zauq), *tumhaarii yaad ke jab zaKHm bharne lagte hai.n / kisii bahaane tumhei.n yaad karne lagte hai.n* (Faiz Ahmad Faiz), and *ham to samjhe the ke ik zaKHm hai bhar jaaegaa / kyaa KHabar thii ke rag-e jaa.n mei.n utar jaaegaa* (Perveen Shakir).

22

گر کیا ناصح نے ہم کو قید اچھا یوں سہی
یہ جنون عشق کے انداز چھٹ جاویں گے کیا

गर किया नासिह ने हम को क़ैद अच्छा यूँ सही
ये जुनून-ए इश्क़ के अंदाज़ छुट जावेंगे क्या

gar kiyaa naaseh ne ham ko qaid achhaa yuu.n sahii
ye junuun-e 'ishq ke andaaz chhuT jaavenge kyaa

(*naaseh*—preacher;
junuun-e 'ishq—craziness in love)

If the preacher chose to imprison me, let that be
But will my crazy way of loving, ever leave me

Genuine love remains uncontrollable. Ghalib proposes his speaker's aesthetics of love here as against the institutionalized concept of love represented by the preacher. The oppressive attitude of the preacher who has incarcerated him metaphorically, rather than literally, makes him react sharply. He thus throws a challenge to him and asserts firmly that the preacher's edicts would not keep him away from his way of loving.

A closer look at the verse would reveal several other aspects of its meaning: (a) there is a clash of values in the two views of love—one represented by the preacher as an institution, and another by the speaker as a lover (b) the speaker stands for human love, while the preacher stands for a narrower understanding of this love (c) the speaker believes in a liberal view of love while the preacher believes in a constrictive view of love (d) the speaker asserts that love is not a taboo but a genuine human emotion, while the preacher negates it, and finally, (e) human love is a matter of faith for the speaker; it is a taboo for the preacher.

With respect to Ghalib's diction, *junuun* (craziness), *'ishq* (love) and *andaaz* (manner) appear as the most striking ones. These three words go hand-in-hand to represent the speaker's way of loving and living. Most significantly, he qualifies love as *junuun* (craziness). With the rich complex of these words, the speaker represents a liberal view of love as against the preacher's restrictive view of love. The word *chhuT* (get rid) works as a linchpin in the verse which highlights the idea that love is a habit for the speaker that he cannot get rid of whatever be the condition which is most defiantly expressed in *achhaa yuu.n sahii* (come what may). Equally remarkable is the wordplay of the opposites—*qaid* (prison) and *chhuTna* (release)—which contains a challenge for the preacher and is posed as a daring question to him. Consider how love as *junuun* has been represented in an iconic verse by Siraj Aurangabadi: *KHabar-e tahayyur-e 'ishq sun na junnu.n rahaa na parii rahii / na to tuu rahaa na to mai.n rahaa jo rahii so be-KHabarii rahii.*

23

یہ نہ تھی ہماری قسمت کہ وصال یار ہوتا
اگر اور جیتے رہتے یہی انتظار ہوتا

ये न थी हमारी क़िस्मत कि विसाल-ए यार होता
अगर और जीते रहते यही इंतिज़ार होता

ye na thii hamaarii qismat ke visaal-e yaar hotaa
agar aur jiite rahte yehii intizaar hotaa

(*visaal*—union, conjunction, meeting)

To be united with my love—
that wasn't my destiny ever
Had I lived any longer—
I'd have kept pining forever

Pining for union with the beloved has ever been the destiny of lovers. The speaker in this verse plainly states that he was not lucky enough to achieve union with his beloved. Had he lived longer, he muses, he would have kept waiting for this union and thus pined for her all his life. As Ghalib portrays the colossal disappointment of the archetypal lover, he seems to impart a tongue to him to say that since there is no union, it is better to die. In other words, he suggests that waiting for love is as good as dying in love.

This verse raises several doubts and poses several self-explanatory questions: (a) is union only a dream for the lover, or can it be a reality as well? (b) is it not better for the lover to die than to keep longing? (c) is the lover already dead in life, or is he musing only after his death? (d) is this lover essentially a fatalist? (e) is it the physical union only that this lover pines for? and (f) is this what happens in love with every lover, and is every lover destined to remain in a state of waiting, and suffer endlessly thereby?

As for the artistic merit of this verse, it is the natural continuity of thought that strikes us clearly. The first line logically and seamlessly joins the second line. Although the two lines read like two prosaic statements, but three central words—*qismat* (destiny), *visaal-e yaar* (union with beloved) and *intizaar* (wait)—hold the meaning of the verse and make it magically poetical. These words spell out the entire plot and suggest the basic mark of despondency that is writ large on the face of the verse. Faiz Ahmad Faiz expresses this sentiment from a different angle and adds the elements of curiosity and yearning to the experience of fruitless waiting: *nahii.n nigaah mei.n manzil to justujuu hii sahii / nahii.n visaal mayassar to aarzuu hii sahii.*

24

کوئی میرے دل سے پوچھے ترے تیر نیم کش کو
یہ خلش کہاں سے ہوتی جو جگر کے پار ہوتا

कोई मेरे दिल से पूछे तिरे तीर-ए नीम-कश को
ये ख़लिश कहाँ से होती जो जिगर के पार होता

koii mere dil se puuchhe tire tiir-e-niim-kash ko
ye KHalish kahaa.n se hotii jo jigar ke paar hotaa

(niim-kash—half-drawn;
KHalish—unease, prick)

Let someone ask my heart—
what it is to bear an arrow half-shot
What pain would there be,
had it pierced through and been fully-shot

Only the lover can tell what it means to suffer the injuries in loving. Let someone ask me, says the lover, what it means to bear the pain caused by an arrow half-shot. He makes his plea rather simply but quite ironically. His wish, expressed in the first line, finds an answer in the second line that he would not have been in such anguish had this arrow been fully shot through his heart. The poet portrays here the stock figure of the lover who suffers in multiple ways, one of them being a suffering without an end.

A closer reading of the verse opens several implications of the lover's suffering that cannot be brought to an end. It may be read (a) as a soliloquy where the lover begs to be heard about his suffering (b) this desire to be heard shows the human desire to share pain which brings relief to the sufferer, but the sufferer does not get sympathetic ears (c) pain is felt intensely when it makes a home in the heart, just as the arrow finds its home in the heart and causes agony to the lover (d) pain proves temporal if it finds its way out, which does not happen here as the arrow is still stuck in the heart, and (e) this pain could be because of the ruthless beloved's coquetry, or her piercing looks that cause him ceaseless suffering.

The artistic merit of the verse may be noticed in how Ghalib uses a half-shot arrow as a visual image which pierces another visual image of the heart. Further, three central words bearing upon one another—*tiir* (arrow), *niim-kash* (half-shot) and *KHalish* (unease)—create together a symbiotic scheme of meaning. It may also be noted that *KHalish* is an expression of understatement, which is a lesser state of suffering than bearing the pain borne with the piercing of an arrow. Ghalib resorts to understatement only to portray the suffering of the lover in ironic terms. This state of suffering is presented with a certain difference in a verse by Munir Niyazi. A sense of greater helplessness comes out in a tone and tenor typical of him: *dil kii KHalish to saath rahegii tamaam 'umr / dariya-i Gham ke paar utar jaaei.n ham to kyaa.*

25

رگ سنگ سے ٹپکتا وہ لہو کہ پھر نہ تھمتا
جسے غم سمجھ رہے ہو یہ اگر شرار ہوتا

रग-ए संग से टपकता वो लहू कि फिर न थमता
जिसे ग़म समझ रहे हो ये अगर शरार होता

rag-e sa.ng se Tapaktaa vo luhuu ke phir na thamtaa
jise Gham samajh rahe ho ye agar sharaar hotaa

(*rag-e sa.ng*—stone's vein where fire resides;
sharaar—spark)

From the stone's vein would drip blood;
unceasing, without relief
What if that was a spark,
that you think is grief

A poet's flight of imagination can turn a real predicament into a mythic one. Ghalib's speaker addresses the beloved, and by implication everyone else in love, to underline the magnitude of pain inflicted on him which could annihilate him. He puts forth a piercing question: what if it was a spark which you consider grief, and how terrible it would be if it vanquished him? He further implies that his suffering is so intense that it could move even the stone to bleed ceaselessly from its veins. In sum, Ghalib underlines how immeasurable suffering in love can be.

This distinctively complex verse unfolds several layers of meaning: (a) ceaseless dripping of blood suggests ceaseless pain caused to the lover (b) grief is a spark that could cause blood to ooze even from veins of the rock, where actually fire resides (c) grief is more inflammatory than a spark that only humans, not even rocks, can endure (d) the spark is rock's energy, just as blood is vein's energy (e) unable to bear the lover's suffering, grief finds an equivalent in the spark, which could vanquish the lover (f) both grief and spark are the vanquishing agents.

This verse is one of the finest examples of Ghalib's creative imagination. It gains in poetic appeal through the placement of the two lines of this verse in a reverse order of both thought and logic. There is a moment of silence, or pause, between the two lines that makes the reader imagine the implications of being in love and suffering its pain. The three central images—*rag-e sa.ng* (stone's vein), *lahuu* (blood) and *sharaar* (spark)—work as three key expressions and create meaning in metaphoric terms. Ghalib has used the expressions of *sharar* and *sharaar* in different verses to underline the immensity of suffering in love and life which may be looked at to develop a comparative perspective: (1) *ik nazar besh nahii.n fursat-e hastii Ghalib / garmii-i bazm hai ik raqs-e sharar hote tak* (2) *phir garm naala-haae sharar-baar hai nafas / muddat huii hai sair-charaaGhaa.n kiye huve* (3) *ik sharar dil mei.n hai is se koii ghabraaegaa kyaa / aag matluub hai ham ko jo havaa kahte hai.n* (4) *aatish-parast kahte hai.n ahl-e jahaa.n mujhe / sargarm-e naala-haae sharar-baar dekh kar.*

26

ہوئے مر کے ہم جو رسوا ہوئے کیوں نہ غرق دریا
نہ کبھی جنازہ اٹھتا نہ کہیں مزار ہوتا

हुए मर के हम जो रुस्वा हुए क्यूँ न ग़रक़-ए दरया
न कभी जनाज़ा उठता न कहीं मज़ार होता

huve mar ke ham jo rusvaa huve kyu.n na Gharq-e dariyaa
na kabhii janaaza uTthta na kahii.n mazaar hotaa

(*rusvaa*—disgraced, dishonoured, defamed, exposed;
Gharq—drowning, sinking, immersion;
janaaza—bier;
mazaar—tomb, mausoleum, shrine)

I suffered shame in death, why not in a river
I was ever drowned
My bier wouldn't have moved ever,
nowhere my shrine around

Death is not just the passing away of an individual; it carries more meanings beyond this. This verse projects a desire and comes to us as a soliloquy from an intimate speaker. He ruminates that instead of being a reminder of his failings through his bier and shrine, he would have better drowned in a river and disappeared for good. He thinks of burial and entombment as the living epitomes of his failure and cause enough, thereby, of his exposure and humiliation before the world. So, he sadly ponders that drowning in water could have saved him from a ritualistic end that brought him disgrace.

The speaker makes some daring points in retrospect, that is, after he has been dead and buried: (a) dying by drowning in water would have washed him off and left no trace of his being anywhere upon this earth, whereas his burial would remind the world of his existence upon this terrain once upon a time (b) by his own estimate, he has been of no consequence in this world, and thereby a cause for his own disgrace, which is why he would like to be traceless (c) he makes an audacious move by making an unusual choice and by denying the religious injunction of burial (d) he also disavows the prayers for atonement he might have received from others, and finally, (e) he asserts an iconoclastic view on life and death, marked by dissent to prescribed norms and established order.

The verse has a distinct rhythmic design which brings out its thematic burden in an appealing manner. Four rhyming words—*rusvaa* (disgrace) and *dariyaa* (river), in the first line, and *uThtaa* (raised) and *hotaa* (happened), in the second line—create a design of sound and meaning together. This is a fine example of how assonance works as a poetic device to create the structure of meaning. This apart, the two key words—*janaaza* (bier) and *mazaar* (tomb)—put in a sequential order, mark an established practice of offering a respectful parting with the dead for good.

27

یہ مسائل تصوف یہ ترا بیان غالبؔ
تجھے ہم ولی سمجھتے جو نہ بادہ خوار ہوتا

ये मसाइल-ए तसव्वुफ़ ये तिरा बयान ग़ालिब
तुझे हम वली समझते जो न बादा-ख़्वार होता

ye masaail-e tasavvuf ye tiraa bayaan Ghalib
tujhe ham valii samajhte jo na baada-KHvaar hotaa

(*masaail-e tasavvuf*—issues in mysticism,
matters of spirituality;
valii—saint, patron;
baada-KHvaar—drinker, boozer)

These mystic matters, these sparkles
you bring me, Ghalib
If not a boozer, I would take you
for a saint, Saahib

Can a mystical saying be said only by a mystic? Ghalib appears to address this question but indirectly. As it appears in the first reading, Ghalib addresses himself in this verse to say that you reach out to the complexities of mystical thoughts and unfold them exceptionally well; had you not been a wine-drinker, you would have been taken for a saint. While taking pride in himself, he locates the saint and the wine drinker in two different contexts, but tries to thin out the distinction between the two and consider both as one.

The verse has multiple implications: (a) Ghalib praises himself for his understanding of the secrets of mysticism and his eloquence in explaining those (b) since he uses the pronoun *ham* (we), which is both a personal pronoun and a collective pronoun here, the speaker may be both Ghalib himself or others addressing him (c) a critical concern is foregrounded in relation to the hardcore subject matter and the possibility of developing a discourse around it (d) a mystic and a drinker are two different beings as one is drunk on the divine wine and the other on the worldly wine, but here they bear upon one another both in contrast and comparison, and finally (e) the verse challenges the worldly and puerile ways of understanding the reality.

Artistically, the central intent of the verse is built upon two sets of concerns. While the first line focusses on *masaail-e tasavvuf* (issues in mysticism) and its *bayaan* (elucidation), the second line draws upon two dissimilar beings—*valii* (saint) and *baada-KHvaar* (wine drinker). Together, both sets develop a logical structure of a philosophical discourse. The double entendre in *ham* (we) adds significantly to the richness of the verse and its larger implication. Dagh Dehlavi apparently draws upon Ghalib and comes up with a jovial verse in his characteristic manner in this verse here: *gae hosh tere zaahid jo vo chashm-e mast dekhii / mujhe kyaa ulat ne dete jo na baada-KHvaar hotaa.*

28

بوس کو ہے نشاط کار کیا کیا
نہ ہو مرنا تو جینے کا مزا کیا

हवस को है नशात-ए कार क्या क्या
न हो मरना तो जीने का मज़ा क्या

havas ko hai nishaat-e kaar kyaa kyaa
na ho marnaa to jiine kaa maza kyaa

(*havas*—greed, lustful desire, excessive appetite;
nishaat-e kaar—pleasure of action, passion for action,
zeal of performance)

This lust beckons a passionate act in vying
What fun living at all, if there's no dying

Death can also be welcome but with conditions attached to it. Man's lustful desire knows no end, but what surely comes to an end is life itself. This end, known as death in worldly parlance, also helps recount the pleasures of life and living. In other words, there is no pleasure in living if there is no dying. Ghalib suggests that since desire chases life and life chases death, one is impelled to achieve the most before dying. The elements of curiosity, aspiration and fulfilment mark the first line and those of wonder, denial and inquiry mark the second line.

This verse foregrounds layers of rich ambiguity at the level of meaning: (a) since the joy of living lies in dying, life without reaching an end is monotonous (b) while life is a cycle of following and fulfilling desires, death is the fruit of life (c) desire and fulfilment mark the flux of life (d) instead of being a vice, lustful desire is also a virtue as it keeps a man impelling, and (e) more than putting forth a question in the first line, there is a delightful amazement there which helps us enjoy the verse for its worth.

The artistic merit of this verse lies as much in bringing the antinomy of *jiinaa* (living) and *marnaa* (dying) together, as it lies in counterbalancing the sweetness of *havas* (lustful desire) against *nishaat-e kaar* (passion for action). While the double occurrence of *kyaa* represents gestural wonderment and exclamation in the first line, its single occurrence in the second line represents a question. With this simple word used differently in two lines, the verse acquires its magical appeal. Further, the beauty of the verse lies in its casual way of poeticizing a serious concern relating to human aspiration as well as life and death.

29

بندگی میں بھی وہ آزادہ و خودبیں ہیں کہ ہم
الٹے پھر آئے در کعبہ اگر وا نہ ہوا

बंदगी में भी वो आज़ादा-ओ-ख़ुद-बीं हैं कि हम
उलटे फिर आए दर-ए काबा अगर वा न हुआ

*bandagii mei.n bhii vo aazaada-o KHud-bii.n hai.n ke ham
ulte phir aae dar-e k'aba agar vaa na huaa*

(*bandagii*—worship, devotion, service;
aazaada—liberated, free;
KHud-bii.n—egotistical, conceited;
vaa—open)

In my worship, I am so liberated,
I am so much free
I'd return if the doors of k'aba
didn't stand open to me

Pride, especially a poet's pride, can take unimaginable turns. Speaking in his own voice, Ghalib's makes an audacious claim and an equally impudent statement in this verse. He declares that he enjoys his self-respect and exercises complete freedom in the matters of worship. He asserts this with unusual pride of a believer and pronounces blatantly that when he arrives at the *k'aba* and finds that its doors are still not open for him, he would return forthwith. Is this his stark audacity, or his intense faith in the spirit of his genuine worship, one wonders, and this is what makes this verse worthy of attention.

This oft-quoted verse portrays the speaker's quintessential personality, demonstrates his intriguingly individual nature and opens many possibilities of interpretation: (a) the very idea of visiting the *k'aba* is an indication of his desire to make a visit to the house of God (b) he is not ready to knock at the door, but expects that it remains open for an extraordinary visitor like him (c) it exudes his sense of both utter pride and self-respect, which is far from self-conceit (d) he seems to ask as to why God expects the believer to knock, or wait at the door, for entry to his house (e) why doesn't God receive his worshipper with the doors of his house thrown open, and finally, (f) with his proud positioning, he appears to be a much more ardent believer than those traditionally identified as staunch believers.

Two key words in the verse—*bandagii* (worship) and *KHud-bii.n* (egotistical)—that stand in opposition to each other, brilliantly constitute the kernel of meaning. The word *bhii* (also) used with *bandagii* adds a deep sense of irony and enriches the complex of meaning. The phrase *ulte phir aae* (return forthwith), which is one of common parlance, is used here to express a sense of pride. Similarly, the word, *aazaada*, a variation on the word, *aazaad* (liberated), speaks of Ghalib's way of richly manipulating language with creative freedom. It strikes a note of freshness and adds strength to the meaning of liberation itself.

30

درد منت کش دوا نہ ہوا
میں نہ اچھا ہوا برا نہ ہوا

दर्द मिन्नत-कश-ए दवा न हुआ
मैं न अच्छा हुआ बुरा न हुआ

dard minnat-kash-e-davaa na huaa
mai.n na achhaa huaa buraa na huaa

(*minnat kash-e davaa*—obliged/indebted to medicine)

My pain wasn't obliged to drug
to get a cure, for sure
That I didn't get well,
wasn't too bad to endure

Who wants to remain in pain but the poets and philosophers alone who conceive their experiences of pain and suffering differently. Ghalib's speaker seems to be musing here on the nature of pain and panacea. Triumphantly, he says then that it is better to remain in pain and live with pride than be cured and remain indebted and obliged to medicine. He plays with the dichotomy of pain and cure, and good and bad, in an inverse manner, bringing a philosophical aura to his experience.

This verse opens up a variety of questions that reflect upon three central concerns of illness, wellness and treatment. Although the verse seems to make an easy-going statement, it raises interesting questions that reflect upon the existential meaning of disease and cure (a) did medicine fail him? (b) did staying in pain serve him well? (c) does he have a sense of pride in not being indebted to medicine? (d) does cure really owe little to medicine? (e) does he declare his triumph over pain? and (f) does one remain obliged to medicine, if cured?

The appeal of this verse lies in the inverse placement of two sets of expressions—*mai.n na achhaa huaa* (I was not cured) in the first line and *buraa na huaa* (that wasn't really bad) in the second line. Far from being a play of, or upon words, Ghalib creates a remarkable design of logic to find his appeal with his addressees. If poetry is a matter of evolving a fresh way to make an assertion, here is an example of this kind. Further, there is an in-built irony in the expression—*minnat kash-e davaa* (under obligation to medicine)—which is also a paradoxical statement made sportingly, but quite artfully. In his own objective way, Mir Taqi Mir gives this idea a pathetic bent in his verse and vents his feeling in a simple and conversational manner: *shifaa apnii taqdiir hii mei.n na thii / ke maqduur tak to davaa kar chale.*

31

جان دی دی ہوئی اسی کی تھی
حق تو یوں ہے کہ حق ادا نہ ہوا

जान दी दी हुई उसी की थी
हक़ तो यूँ है कि हक़ अदा न हुआ

jaan dii dii huii usii kii thhii
haq to yuu.n hai ke haq adaa na huaa

(*haq*—truth, responsibility, due, privilege, claim)

I gave up life, this life was a gift, it's true
I couldn't pay indeed what all was its due

Giving could be more important than receiving. This idea holds Ghalib's attention who chooses to gloss on life and God's gifts to man in multiple ways in his verses. In this particular verse, his speaker firmly asserts that God bestowed life upon man as a trust, but man rendered it back to Him because he failed in meeting the obligations expected of him. He expresses his sense of gratitude, as also of regret, over his failure as a keeper of trust with regard to life.

The verse opens multiple windows to meaning: (a) life is God's great gift to man and it goes back to God only (b) life is greater than man and man stands as a supreme trustee of God's gift (c) life makes demands upon man who is God's supreme creation, but, ironically enough, he is too incapable to meet its obligation and value the trust reposed in him (d) this inability of man creates a sense of remorse in him, and he ultimately (e) realizes his failure even while alive and admits this with a certain tinge of repentance.

Artistically, this verse can be appreciated well for three distinct reasons. First, it is the pun on *jaan dii* (gave back life) and *dii huii* (that was given) that holds our attention for its emphasis on the same words with two different meanings in the first line. Second, the word *haq* is used twice with extraordinary skill in the second line with two different meanings once again. It means 'truth' and 'responsibility' one after another by which Ghalib literally means, 'the truth is that I could not meet my responsibility'. Third, there is a rhythmic flow created with five monosyllabic rhyming words of equal volume—*dii, huii, usii, kii, thii*—that imparts a tone and a mood to the first line, which instantly appeals to our auditory imagination and prepares us to reach the second line.

32

گلہ ہے شوق کو دل میں بھی تنگئ جا کا
گہر میں محو ہوا اضطراب دریا کا

गिला है शौक़ को दिल में भी तंगी-ए जा का
गुहर में महव हुआ इज़्तिराब दरिया का

gila hai shauq ko dil mei.n bhii tangii-i jaa kaa
guhar mei.n mahv huaa iztiraab dariyaa kaa

(*gila*—complaint;
tangii-i jaa—lack of space;
guhar—pearl, gem;
mahv—absorbed;
iztiraab—impatience, restlessness)

My desires complain of no space
even in my breast
So, in the pearl, the restive river
found a home to rest

The heart is a huge continent but a narrow space for desires to find their place in. Ghalib makes an exquisite comment on infinite human desire and the inability of the heart to hold them all in its narrow space. This idea reaches its climactic point when he equates the heart with a pearl which is smaller than the heart, but it can absorb the river's restlessness into itself. In sum, he wants to metaphorically suggest that human desires are uncontrollable and infinite, but even then, they may be contained in the heart's narrow space, which is much deeper and bigger than the restless river.

This richly ambiguous verse on the trilogy of desire, heart and river, opens multiple avenues to meaning: (a) desires were too many and the heart was too narrow to keep them all in it (b) they could not flutter their wings for lack of space (c) so, they got absorbed by the pearl and lost their lifeforce (d) as such, they stood as complainants against the narrowness of heart (e) heart is a world unto itself that can incorporate all that shows and all that remains hidden (f) heart is broad, but desire is broader (g) river is contained in a pearl, and (h) both river and desire ever remain restless.

The verse leaves the question open as to what is greater—desire or the heart. The first line makes a statement; the second evolves a metaphor. Their causal relationship lies in the comparison of desire with a river and the heart with a pearl. The key words—*guhar* (pearl), *iztiraab* (restlessness), *mahv* (absorption) and *bhii* (also)—are strengthened with the paradox of a pearl that has greater space than the river to absorb its restlessness. It should be pertinent to see in this context how Firaq Gorakhpuri discourses over the experience of restlessness as a perennial condition and imparts it a philosophical character: *furqat ho yaa visaal vahii iztiraab hai / teraa asar hai ai Gham-e furqat kahaa.n kahaa.n.*

33

نہ بندھے تشنگی ذوق کے مضموں غالبؔ
گرچہ دل کھول کے دریا کو بھی ساحل باندھا

न बंधे तिशनगी-ए शौक़ के मज़मूँ ग़ालिब
गरचे दिल खोल के दरिया को भी साहिल बांधा

na ba.ndhe tishnagii-i shauq ke mazmuu.n Ghalib
garche dil khol ke dariyaa ko bhii saahil baa.ndhaa

(*tishnagii-i shauq*—insatiability of longing;
saahil—bank of river/sea)

I couldn't bind my insatiate longings, Ghalib,
with my verse for sure
Graciously though, I could bind the river
with the bank evermore

How does a poet strive to express himself and how far does he succeed in doing so? This is the central issue this verse aims to address. Ghalib's speaker says that he tried his best to give expression to his experience, but he could not succeed in his effort. In poetic terms, he could not control the river to become a shore where one arrives ultimately, that is, he could not shed the burden of his experience in poetic terms and versify his emotions, as he desired to do.

Several layers of implied meaning may be identified here: (a) the bank remained unsatiated as the water receded every time it kissed the shore, that is, the intent could never be expressed or bound in words (b) the shore kept the river close to itself but the two could not establish communication (c) this happened even though the poet made all efforts with all the skill at his command to express himself, that is, to versify his thoughts; at another level, this verse is (d) a statement on the immensity of experience and the insufficiency of the tools of expression that a poet may have at his command, but without bringing any profit to him (e) by implication, this is an exposé of Ghalib's poetics itself that his genius proved lesser than his experience that he wished to represent, and finally, (f) this frank admission of his inability to versify underlines his humility as a poet.

Poets often use the expression *baa.ndhnaa* (binding) in Urdu for the act of binding an idea into verse, or the act of versification itself. Ghalib uses it in the first line to literally say that he could not versify his thoughts well enough. He admits his inability to do so in the second line by asserting that he experienced *tishnagii* (state of insatiateness) in expressing himself with any amount of success. This is justifiable because ideas or experiences, which form the staple material for poetry, remain elusive many a time and the poet cannot reach out to them in poetic terms. Although Ghalib's speaker seems to represent Ghalib's own voice here, it could be any poet's voice since no poet can claim complete success in expressing himself. This is because art is greater than the artists and it tests the artist's potential to carry the burden of experience and express it with success.

34

میں اور بزم مے سے یوں تشنہ کام آؤں
گر میں نے کی تھی توبہ ساقی کو کیا ہوا تھا

मैं और बज़्म-ए मै से यूँ तिशना-काम आऊँ
गर मैं ने की थी तौबा साक़ी को क्या हुआ था

mai.n aur bazm-e mai se yuu.n tishna-kaam aauu.n
gar mai.n ne kii thii tauba saaqii ko kyaa huaa thaa

(*bazm-e mai*—assembly of wine drinkers;
tishna-kaam—thirsty;
tauba—penitence, renunciation)

Me! To return thirsty from the assembly of
drinkers, undeserving!
If I had vowed abstinence, what had stopped
the saaqii from serving

Wine and drinking have been the stock images of ghazal poets. As in many other verses, Ghalib mythicizes the figure of the drinker once again here, but with a difference. He is light-hearted but interrogative, and wryly suggests that it was he who had taken a vow to abstain from drinking, not the cup-bearer from serving him. This attitude creates a jovial atmosphere in the verse and adds colour to the entire institution of drinking, drinkers and the tavern.

As the verse redefines the institution of the tavern and its visitors along with the cup-bearer, interesting aspects of meaning are revealed further: (a) the drinker appears to be present in the tavern which shows that he is still inclined towards drinking, even though he has taken a vow of abstinence (b) there was every possibility of his coming back to drinking, if he was offered a drink (c) the cup-bearer should have shown his courtesy, or even made him drink in the way he drank earlier (d) since the cup-bearer did not do so, the drinker questions his discourtesy with utter amazement, but, on the other hand, (e) the cup-bearer's insistence would have only reiterated his own image as a server of drinks to all the visitors and also as a spoiler of everyone's piety.

Four expressions—*mai.n* (me!), *bazm-e mai* (assembly of wine drinkers), *yuu.n* (this way!) and *tauba* (vowing)—create a dramatic condition in the verse. The first word (*mai.n*) underlines the irony that out of all the persons, how can the drinker be singled out for deprivation? The second word (*bazm-e mai*) highlights the status of the tavern as an institution and not merely as a place for the coming together of drinkers. The third word (*yuu.n*) registers clear resentment against the cup-bearer, and the fourth one (*tauba*) extends the implication of vowing even beyond the religious vowing. As an apt reminder of a drinker taking a vow of abstinence like Ghalib's drinker, we may refer to Khumar Barabankvi's verse and compare the two verses for their rendition of this situation. Khumar says: *guzre hai.n maikade se jo tauba ke b'aad ham / kuchh duur 'aadatan bhii qadam dagmagaae hai.n.*

35

گھر ہمارا جو نہ روتے بھی تو ویراں ہوتا
بحر گر بحر نہ ہوتا تو بیاباں ہوتا

घर हमारा जो न रोते भी तो वीराँ होता
बह गर बह न होता तो बयाबाँ होता

ghar hamaaraa jo na rote bhii to viiraa.n hotaa
bahr gar bahr na hotaa to bayaabaa.n hotaa

(*viiraa.n*—desolate, deserted;
bahr—sea, ocean;
bayaabaa.n—wilderness, wasteland)

Even if I didn't cry, desolate my house
would surely be
It would be wild all around,
if the sea would not be a sea

What is the idea of a home and what makes or unmakes it? Hovering around this question, there is a remarkable poetic discourse here. In literal terms, Ghalib's speaker posits that even without his weeping over his lot, his home would have been a desolate place because pain was the essential condition of his life in whatever way he suffered it. This is just as there would have been desolate plains all around had there been no ocean. He broods over the nature of the human existence philosophically and connects himself with it in a metaphoric manner.

In metaphoric terms, this verse may be appreciated (a) as a stark commentary on suffering as a constituent of the inescapable human predicament (b) developing his argument from the other end of logic, the speaker suggests that his house has turned into a sea because he has wept there ceaselessly and tears have overflown all over and turned it into a desolate place (c) had there been no sea, it would have been a huge and arid plain all over because that is how Earth manifests itself, and it appears that (d) the speaker is a fatalist because he accepts whatever his destiny has brought to him.

The implied affinity established between river and tears add up to the metaphoric meaning of the verse. The ideational structure, however, rests on four essential referents—*ghar* (home), *viiraanii* (desolation), *bahr* (sea) and *bayaabaa.n* (wilderness)—that constitute the entire earthly phenomenon. In the context of this verse, home, desolation and wilderness bear upon one another, as they represent one condition only which the speaker wants to highlight essentially. The word *bhii* (used in the sense of even though) adds an ironic punch which distinguishes the verse for its artistic merit. This reminds of how Miraji engages with this experience of desolation but adds a different perspective at the end of his verse: *rashk-e sehra hai ghar kii viiraanii / yehii rang-e bahaar hai apnaa.*

36

نہ تھا کچھ تو خدا تھا کچھ نہ ہوتا تو خدا ہوتا
ڈبویا مجھ کو ہونے نے نہ ہوتا میں تو کیا ہوتا

न था कुछ तो ख़ुदा था कुछ न होता तो ख़ुदा होता
डुबोया मुझ को होने ने न होता मैं तो क्या होता

na thaa kuchh to KHudaa thaa kuchh na hotaa to KHudaa hotaa
Duboyaa mujh ko hone ne na hotaa mai.n to kyaa hotaa

When there was nothing, there was God;
had there been nothing, there'd be God
My being there drowned me for good;
what if I wasn't there, O God

W hat does the existence of God mean and how does man's existence in the larger frame of the cosmos matter? Such complex questions are best expressed in philosophical and poetical terms. Here is a characteristically argumentative Ghalib who makes a profound statement on the problematic of man's being itself. He puts his case in as simple terms as this: when there was nothing, there was God; had there been nothing, God alone would have been there. Then comes another set of arguments: I was vanquished because I existed; had I not existed, what difference would it have made? Ghalib's speaker philosophizes upon the issue of existence and non-existence by keeping God at the centre and man alongside.

This verse is thickly populated with multiple intents and implications about the centrality of God and the insignificance of man's existence as follows: (a) God has been the only real entity to have existed since the very beginning (b) God was there even when nothing else existed (c) that was God who created man and this is man who turned his back on Him with his questions about his own existence (d) the speaker's existence itself is the cause of his own destruction, not God (e) there would be no difference if He did not exist at all, and finally, (f) God alone is the source and manifestation of the entire phenomenon, including man.

Ghalib lets us enjoy the play of words in this verse. The word—*hotaa* (being)— occurring twice in each of the two lines creates a complex net of meaning here. There is a rich sense of questioning and amazement in the fourth and the ultimate use of this key expression. Another remarkable expression—*Duboyaa* (drowned)—used literally as a proverb, points towards metaphorical drowning in nothingness from where none can ever emerge. We may also keep another verse of Ghalib in view to mark how a multilayered idea may find its expressions in ways more than one: *juz naam nahii.n suurate-e 'aalam mujhe manzuur / juz vahm nahii.n hasti-e ashyaa mire aage.*

37

بلبل کے کاروبار پہ ہیں خندہ ہائے گل
کہتے ہیں جس کو عشق خلل ہے دماغ کا

बुलबुल के कार-ओ-बार पे हैं ख़ंदहहा-ए गुल
कहते हैं जिस को इश्क़ ख़लल है दिमाग़ का

bulbul ke kaar-o baar pe hai.n KHanda-haae gul
kahte hai.n jis ko 'ishq KHalal hai dimaaGh kaa

(*KHanda-haae gul*—smile/laugh of the blossom;
KHalal—folly)

The bulbul's sing-song makes the flowers all jolly
What's called love is nothing but human mind's folly

Bulbul and blossom have been configured often as archetypal symbols in Urdu ghazal. Ghalib draws upon these symbols to mark their relationship as lover and beloved. If the bulbul, known for its melodious notes, sings its song of love for the blossom, the blossom smiles. But here in this verse, it does not smile with love but with certain derision for the bulbul. This is because the bulbul is so much obsessed with its love for the blossom that the blossom thinks that the bulbul has gone crazy. It suggests that love also fails at times, and that too because of the beloved's disapproval of the lover's craziness.

In the special context of this verse, the following aspects emerge prominently: (a) the garden is the home for both the bulbul and the blossom, and the three share a tripartite relationship in love (b) in the relationship between the bulbul and the blossom, the perennial predicament of the lover as sufferer is projected with pathos (c) ironically, the bulbul does not even realize that it is being laughed at (d) it appears that the blossom considers the bulbul's love as nothing but a folly of its mind (e) the bulbul thus emerges as a pitiable figure and represents, symbolically, the predicament of all lovers as sufferers.

The two lines of the verse are logically bound with each other where two words—*kaar-o baar* (labour) and *KHalal* (folly)—strengthen each other and portray the figure and the fate of the bulbul. Both the words belittle the bulbul and mark the irony of its irreversible fortune. In yet another verse, Ghalib portrays the lover in a similar vein: *'ishq ne Ghalib nikamma kar diyaa / varna ham bhii aadmii the kaam ke.* Mir too pictures this lover who considers love as suffering and says so in a state of exasperation like other lovers: *kyaa kahuu.n tum se mai.n ke kyaa hai 'ishq / jaan ka rog hai balaa hai 'ishq.*

38

زندگی یوں بھی گزر ہی جاتی
کیوں ترا راہ گزر یاد آیا

ज़िंदगी यूँ भी गुज़र ही जाती
क्यूँ तिरा राह-गुज़र याद आया

zindagii yuu.n bhii guzar hii jaatii
kyu.n tiraa raahguzar yaad aayaa

(*raahguzar*—path, passage, way)

This life would have passed on, anyway
Why did I remember your path, anyway

Life knows no stopping midway and completes its course as charted out. Nothing could be put as plainly and as meaningfully as Ghalib puts his thoughts here in this verse. The speaker in this verse questions himself that he would have lived this life and reached his end anyway, but why did he remember the path that led to the beloved? One wonders if it is a case of unrequited love, or failure in love, that makes the speaker say so. In either case, the lover has to live his life in a mundane manner now. While putting this question apparently to himself, the speaker, who is clearly a lover, also seems to answer that he has no other way but to reconcile with his fate and bear the tedium of life, but only helplessly.

This verse may be read in multiple ways: (a) the lover may be posing a question to himself without expecting an answer (b) he may also be wondering about himself and complaining against himself in a state of sadness (c) he may be speculating as to why he fell in love at all (d) he may be indulging in wry reflection on his failure in love, and it also appears as if (e) he will have to live with a dull ache for all his life as he would never completely get rid of his beloved's memories.

The emphasis on—*yuu.n bhii* (just so)—imparts an ironic touch to the verse and underlines the lover's reconciliatory attitude with his lot. The rhyme of *bhii* and *hii* also adds to the precise impact that the verse creates. Incidentally, *guzar* (passing on) and *raahguzar* (path), representing two ideas, also rhyme well and impart a rhythmic design to the verse. Curiously, in another verse of this very ghazal, Ghalib refers to the lane leading to the beloved with the same passion in spite of all his disappointments: *phir tire kuuche ko jaataa hai KHayaal / dil-e gum-gashta magar yaad aayaa*. This shows how Ghalib can render the lover's experiences in multiple manners, and each time with its own appeal. This idea is well expressed in Firaq Gorakhpuri's verse as well: *Gharaz ke kaat diye zindagii ke din ai dost / vo terii yaad mei.n ho.n yaa tujhe bhulaane mei.n*.

39

کوئی ویرانی سی ویرانی ہے
دشت کو دیکھ کے گھر یاد آیا

कोई वीरानी-सी वीरानी है
दश्त को देख के घर याद आया

koii viiraanii sii viiraanii hai
dasht ko dekh ke ghar yaad aayaa

(*viiraanii*—barrenness, desolation, ruin;
dasht—desert, arid plain)

What barrenness! What do I see, as I roam
I look at the desert; I remember home

Imagine a person seeking relief from the tedium of life and his failure to find a way to sustain himself. This verse is a reconstruction of such an experience of deprivation. Looking at the desert, the speaker exclaims, and also questions, if desolation itself could be more intense than this. Subsequently, he compares the desert with home and expresses the pathos of life lived in such a vacuum.

This apparently simple and self-addressing verse reveals more layers of meaning than those that come to us at the first reading: (a) it defines barrenness and desolation as lived experiences, rather than as mere thoughts (b) it is writ large on the vast expanse of the desert, as well as within the confines of the home (c) the act of remembering a desolate home at the sight of a desolate desert is acutely associational and evidently psychological, and (d) the speaker's soft gesture of moaning without complaining, defines his own desolation, something that his home, too, signifies.

Like many other verses, this is yet another example of Ghalib's artless art. Two seminal words—*dasht* (desert) and *viiraanii* (desolation)—match each other while they also work as similes that mature into metaphors. The repetitive use of—*viiraanii*—with two different tones of expression in the same line (*koii viiraanii sii viiraanii hai*) makes for a rhetorical question which also works well as an expression of regretful wondering. For comparative purposes, a fascinating perspective on desolation may be seen in a verse by Zeb Ghauri: *aa ke kabhii viiraani-i dil ka tamaasha kar / is jungle mei.n naach rahe hai.n more bahut.*

40

پکڑے جاتے ہیں فرشتوں کے لکھے پر نا حق
آدمی کوئی ہمارا دم تحریر بھی تھا

पकड़े जाते हैं फ़रिश्तों के लिखे पर ना-हक़
आदमी कोई हमारा दम-ए तहरीर भी था

*pakRe jaate hai.n farishto.n ke likhe per naahaq
aadmii koii hamaaraa dam-e tahriir bhi thaa*

(*naahaq*—unjust;
dam-e tahriir—at the time of writing/inscription)

I'm unjustly caught for what the angels
recorded of me
Was there someone for me to see
what they reported of me

For creative writers and poets, irreverence has often been a favourite way of thinking and living. If there is an amazing way to announce this irreverence, it is here in this characteristic verse by Ghalib. According to the Islamic faith, all the actions of the faithful are recorded by an angel and it is believed that people will be rewarded or punished according to these records. Ghalib's speaker puts up an insolent posture that he is unjustly being caught as there was no witness to testify to the recordings being made against his name.

There is an unmistakable note of impudence here and it has the following implications: (a) catching anyone on the basis of a recording, not verified by a witness, is unjust (b) the presence of a witness is imperative if an account of actions is being prepared (c) one cannot be charged without showing the chargesheet (d) the charged one cannot be either punished or rewarded without giving them a chance of defence (e) the defendant interrogates the divine law and presents his own terms for objective assessment (f) he further pronounces that he is unjustly being caught because there was no witness to ascertain the authenticity of the angel's recordings, so (g) the case is openly presented in God's and people's court.

The tone of the verse is defined by some seminal expressions—*pakRe jaate hain* (I am being caught), *naahaq* (unjustly), *aadmii* (standing witness to watch the recording) and *hamaaraa* (mine/our). The one who has been charged is obviously not speaking only on his own behalf, but also on behalf of everyone else who is charged. These expressions also add up to the intent and tone of the verse that Ghalib adopts here which makes it worthy of critical attention. One wonders if Ghalib is being irreverent, or naughty, or simply amusing to tickle the readers' imagination, or genuinely expressing his anguish.

41

آئینہ دیکھ اپنا سا منہ لے کے رہ گئے
صاحب کو دل نہ دینے پہ کتنا غرور تھا

आईना देख अपना सा मुँह ले के रह गए
साहब को दिल न देने पे कितना ग़ुरूर था

aaiina dekh apnaa saa mu.nh le ke rah gae
saahib ko dil na dene pe kitnaa Ghuruur thaa

(*Ghuruur*—vanity, vainglory, ego)

She saw a mirror, got ashamed
at what she could see
How proud she had been
of not giving her heart to me

Mischievous lovers may sometimes act jovially and emerge as fascinating characters in the saga of love. This verse is a glowing example of the speaker's mischievousness against the beloved. Her 'majesty' is infatuated with her own self and is subsumed by her own complex of superiority. This is how she does not consider the lover fit enough to earn her heart. However, she finds herself at a complete loss when she looks in the mirror which does not testify to her assumed beauty. With her pride proven false by the mirror, the naughty speaker turns mocking, even revengeful. He enjoys himself at her defeat and chuckles at his victory.

There are a few interesting implications that lie under the surface of this verse: (a) while the lover is proud in the first line, the beloved is humbled (b) he mocks her and leaves her cornered in the second line (c) the mirror stands as a truthful witness and does not lie even to the beloved (d) narcissism only leads to losing face at the end, and finally, (e) her vanity proves a vice that shows the lady her place.

Three key phrases—*apnaa saa mu.nh* (feel small of oneself), *saahib* (used ironically in the sense of 'majesty'), and the gestural expression *kitnaa Ghuruur* (how much of false pride)—are full of ironical implications. They also unravel the jubilant mood of the lover who has taken his revenge and feels proud. Essentially, all these expressions account for the sunny mood of the speaker, as also of the verse. The vanity of human desire, as this verse represents, finds its expression in Muztar Khairabadi's verse in an interesting manner: *aaiina dekh kar Ghuruur fuzuul / baat vo kar jo duusra na kare.*

42

گو میں رہا رہین ستم ہائے روزگار
لیکن ترے خیال سے غافل نہیں رہا

गो मैं रहा रहीन-ए-सितम-हा-ए रोज़गार
लेकिन तिरे ख़याल से ग़ाफ़िल नहीं रहा

*go mai.n rahaa rahiin-e sitam-haae rozgaar
lekin tire KHayaal se Ghaafil nahii.n rahaa*

(*rahiin*—mortgaged, under obligation, subjected;
sitam—cruelty, tyranny, oppression;
rozgaar—livelihood, fortune;
Ghaafil—neglectful, unmindful, inattentive)

Though by the tyrannies of living,
I was ever caught
But I didn't ever remain unmindful
of you, your thought

Can a lover be unmindful of the beloved ever? This is the seminal idea that this verse is developed around. Although he has been subjected to the miseries of living, the lover tells himself, and presumably the beloved too, that he has never been forgetful of her. Even while the speaker seems to address the beloved, he might also be addressing God. This double-edged verse expresses his romantic thought, as well as his Sufi leaning.

The underlying implications in this double-edged verse include: (a) the lover has ever suffered the cruelties of life and living (b) he has never been unthankful or complaining about his lot (c) he has instead been reconciliatory without ever complaining (d) he has found his solace in remembering the beloved, or God, who too is a loved one (e) this reconciliation has brought him his solace, and (f) he has had both his will and strength to stand against his perennial predicament.

Stylistically, three words in the first line with the predominant sound of 'r'—*rahaa* (remained), *rahiin* (subjected) and *rozgaar* (fortune)—create a pleasant musical condition that combine together to represent the thematic burden of the verse. The lover's condition is then summed up in an extended three-letter construction—*rahiin-e sitam-haae rozgaar* (subjected to the tyrannies of fortune)—which embodies the extent of his long suffering. This matches well with his sense of sorrow that too has extended without an end and conditioned his life. The other line is composed of single easy-going words that work to elucidate his consistent state. While the first line is causative in nature, the second one is complementary to that. Together, they complete a circle of thought and appeal to the reader for their precision. An echo of this verse may well be heard in Firaq Gorakhpuri, who engages with this idea in a reflective manner that typifies his verses generally: *ek muddat se tiri yaad bhii aaii na hamei.n / aur ham bhuul gae ho.n tujhe aisaa bhii nahii.n.*

43

ذرہ ذرہ ساغر مے خانۂ نیرنگ ہے
گردش مجنوں بہ چشمک ہائے لیلیٰ آشنا

ज़र्रा ज़र्रा साग़र-ए मै-ख़ाना-ए नैरंग है
गर्दिश-ए मजनूँ ब चशमकहा-ए लैला आशना

zarra zarra saaGhar-e mai KHaana-i naira.ng hai
gardish-e Majnuu.n ba-chashmak-haai Laila aashnaa

(*zarra zarra*—each speck/particle;
saaGhar-e mai—glass of wine;
KHaana-i naira.ng—house of magic/fascination/many hues;
gardish-e Majnuu.n—Majnuu.n's whirling;
ba-chashmak-haai Laila—from the eyes of Laila;
aashnaa—aware, acquainted)

Each speck of the wine glass
is a house of magical spell
Majnuu.n's whirling is known to
the glances of Laila well

The wine-cup is a world unto itself that only drinkers know best. This verse moves around this idea. Literally, it means that each particle of the wine-cup is a fascinating house of magic and that each movement of Majnun's dance is reflective of Laila's desire. In connecting the two ideas together, one may infer that just as Majnuu.n whirls on the signs of Laila's eyes, each speck of this world recognizes the magic of the maker and moves rhythmically on a given tune. This verse, however, calls for a deeper exploration of its meaning.

Different implicational meanings may be traced here: (a) each speck and particle of the wine-cup makes for a world of wonders (b) this world of wonders is a small tavern, on the one hand, and a vast world, on the other (c) every particle of the wine-cup stands enthralled by its own magic, just as each manifestation of the world is mesmerized by its own wonders (d) The glint of Laila's eyes moves Majnuu.n, just as God's will moves the world (e) both the wine-cup and Laila's eyes reflect the glory of the maker, and (f) both the cup and the world are in movement, one inspired by Laila and the other commanded by God.

The most striking poetical merit of the verse lies in how each word is tightly knit into a complex pattern of meaning created by multiple metaphors. *Zarra* (speck) stands for a nucleus of larger manifestations, *saaGhar* (cup) for the world, *mai* (wine) for propelling the movement, *KHaana-i naira.ng* (house of magic) for the phenomenon, *Majnuu.n* for the wild seeker and Laila for the sought after. Consider how magnificently Ghalib creates a universe of his poetic magic.

44

ذکر اس پری وش کا اور پھر بیاں اپنا
بن گیا رقیب آخر تھا جو رازداں اپنا

ज़िक्र उस परी-वश का और फिर बयाँ अपना
बन गया रक़ीब आख़िर था जो राज़-दाँ अपना

zikr us parii-vash kaa aur phir bayaa.n apnaa
ban gayaa raqiib aaKHir thaa jo raazdaa.n apnaa

(*parii-vash*—fairy-like, angel-faced, elfin;
exquisitely beautiful;
raqiib—rival, competitor;
raazdaa.n—confidant, insider, one in the know)

An account of that fairy-like—
that too, in my own way
He, who was a confidant—
is now a rival at bay

Love lands lovers in curious conditions. Here is one such lover and his strange condition that is presented in this verse. This lover has indulged in magical descriptions of his fairy-faced beloved with such elan that he has earned a rival for himself, who, ironically enough, had been his confidant. Even while he praises himself for portraying her gloriously, he suffers loss for his own doing. This verse unravels the mysterious ways of love where the difference between a lover and his rival is delicately balanced and it grows thin too easily.

Some underlying layers of meaning may be found as follows: (a) the speaker praises both the beloved and himself in one breath—the beloved for her fairy-like appearance and himself for his magical portrayal of her (b) both seem to match each other with their individual merits (c) the stock figures of the rival and the confidant are counterbalanced against each other to impart the verse its beauty (d) ironically, the rival becomes the lover, leaving the real lover behind to muse over his sad predicament (e) the lover thus becomes an innocent victim of his own doing, and (f) his frank admission of his pitiable lot leaves us making sense of irony and self-pity writ large in the verse.

Stylistically, by playing upon two sets of stock figures of Urdu ghazal—*raqiib* (rival) and *raazdaa.n* (confidant)—and two phrases—*zikr* (mention) and *bayaa.n* (description)—Ghalib exemplifies his poetical skill of using his counters of expression with fine distinction. Other significant words that lend immediacy of appeal and deserve our attention are *phir* (over and above that) and *aaKHir* (at last). In yet another meritorious move, he also personifies *parii* (fairy) and brings her down from her lofty station to a mundane existence in flesh and blood. In relation to this verse, we may profitably refer to another verse by Ghalib where he reconstructs the figure of the rival and imparts him a layered identity: *mai.n muztarib huu.n vasl mei.n KHauf-e raqiib se / Daalaa hai tum ko vahm ne kis pech-o taab mei.n*

45

منظر اک بلندی پر اور ہم بنا سکتے
عرش سے ادھر ہوتا کاش کے مکاں اپنا

मंज़र इक बुलंदी पर और हम बना सकते
अर्श से उधर होता काश के मकाँ अपना

manzar ik bulandii per aur ham banaa sakte
'arsh se udhar hotaa kaash-ke makaa.n apnaa

(*'arsh*—sky, empyrean canopy, the ninth sphere)

I could create yet another view at the highs
How I wish I had a home beyond the skies

Human yearning knows no bounds. One desires the impossible sometimes, but poetry makes such desires eminently plausible. This verse poeticizes desire that typically characterizes human nature. The speaker ruminates here that he could create yet another scenario of his own beyond the skies. He speaks both for himself and man's infinite desire to discover wonderful horizons beyond the known spaces, and thus finds a way to assuage himself.

The verse unravels richly ambiguous layers of meaning: (a) there is an implied reference to three different spheres—the earth, the sky and the world beyond the skies (b) we are left wondering whether he looks from the earth to the skies or from the skies to the earth—that is from this sphere to that or vice-versa (c) there is a utopian desire to discover a new sphere since the present sphere is limiting and insufficient (d) this desire for limitless space has an air of inclusivity about it and it underlines the human hankering to acquire more and more, and finally (e) if we consider earth as representing reality and sky as representing desire, the verse acquires a philosophical halo.

Considering the linguistic aspect, it could be posited that although Ghalib does not put *farsh* (earth) against *'arsh* (sky) in the verse, he only underlines the eternal dichotomy between the two. A remarkable expression that holds the key to the primal import of desire in the verse is *kaash-ke* (if at all) and it serves as the crucial expression qualifying the element of longing in the verse. This verse is one of the finest examples of Ghalib's imagination verging on the mythical, rather than religious utopia, which turns him into a typically modernist poet who engaged with its problematic in critically creative manners.

46

بم کہاں کے دانا تھے کس ہنر میں یکتا تھے
بے سبب ہوا غالبؔ دشمن آسماں اپنا

हम कहाँ के दाना थे किस हुनर में यकता थे
बे-सबब हुआ 'ग़ालिब' दुश्मन आसमाँ अपना

ham kahaa.n ke daana the kis hunar mei.n yaktaa the
be-sabab huaa Ghalib dushman aasmaa.n apnaa

(*daana*—wise, intelligent;
yaktaa—matchless, incomparable, singular, unique)

I wasn't that wise, nor even unique
in any device
For no reason Ghalib, I found a foe
in the high skies

In a moment of illuminating realization, man may assess his own failings. This gives him a way to ponder over his potential and consider what he received as a prize, or punishment, from the kingdom of God in the high skies. The speaker here remorsefully contemplates his own destiny. He seems to lament that he was neither a wise person, nor unique in any art, which makes him wonder if there was any reason for God to turn inimical to him. More easily said than understood, this verse underlines the speaker's bad fortune as he is victimized for none of his own doings.

The possibilities of implied meaning in this seemingly simple verse are more than one: (a) apparently, the speaker admits his limitations in a humble way, but he also suggests the contrary—that he is both wise and unique (b) a man of means and merit often attracts enemies, as he does here (c) this feeling of superiority, which he seems to nourish, makes even providence turn hostile to him (d) as he directly interrogates God, he also underlines the fact that human worth is not always valued (e) in fact, he is one of those able beings whose potentiality is far more than can be easily comprehended.

Stylistically speaking, the first line of this verse presents a picture of the speaker's wistful resignation, the second line makes a caustic comment against the Almighty. Two adjectives in the first line—*daana* (wise) and *yaktaa* (unique)—not only rhyme together but also underline two prime features of the speaker and qualify him as a man of substance. The second line works as a sequel to the first, and reflects the poet's feeling of both remorse and helplessness which is well borne out by a single word *be-sabab* (for no reason). The irony of his fate is further highlighted with yet another word, *dushman* (enemy), used for God which adds a shade of irony to the verse. The idea of the sky acting as an enemy is poeticized differently by Ghalib in another verse which may offer us a comparative perspective on the divine dispensation: *ye fitna aadmii kii KHaana viiraanii ko kyaa kam hai / huve tum dost jis ke dushman uskaa aasmaa.n kyu.n ho.*

47

رات دن گردش میں ہیں سات آسماں
ہو رہے گا کچھ نہ کچھ گھبرائیں کیا

रात दिन गर्दिश में हैं सात आस्माँ
हो रहेगा कुछ न कुछ घबराएं क्या

raat din gardish mei.n hai saat aasmaa.n
ho rahegaa kuchh na kuchh ghabraaei.n kyaa

(*gardish*—circulation, rotation, course)

The seven skies keep rotating,
all day and night
What's to happen, will surely happen;
why nurse a fright

Destiny must play its role and man must submit to what is destined. Ghalib's speaker draws wistfully upon the proverbial movement of the seven *samaavaat* (skies, heavens, celestial spheres)—*Jannat al-Adan, Jannat al-Firdaus, Jannat an-Naiim, Jannat al-Maava, Daar-ul KHuld, Daar-ul Maqaam,* and *Daar-us Salaam*—and suggests that they inevitably impact human destiny and the same cannot be reversed. He intends saying that the seven heavens/skies keep moving day and night, and they bring what they bring to human beings naturally. If that be so, why should one worry, because whatever has to happen will happen in any case.

In reflecting broadly on the irreversibility of human fate, the speaker seems to suggest: (a) nature is on the move constantly and it unveils our individual predicaments to us (b) man only needs to accept God's will which will reflect his humility (c) he further asserts his forbearance and faith in the divine (d) in addition, he echoes his sense of resignation and bleakness as well, and (d) while he seems to argue for cultivating temperance and shunning anxiety, he also appears as a fatalist who must accept the destined moment without a grudge.

The typically poetic appeal of the verse comes to the reader in the second line with a rhetorical question—why bother, when all that has to happen will happen in any case? This comes out with emphatic assertions—*ho rahegaa* (will certainly happen) and *ghabraaei.n kyaa* (why worry). It must also be marked that while the first line is only an assertive and a causative assertion, the second line is a characteristically poetic utterance marked by a gesture of hope and faith. It should also be interesting to mark how Ghalib's fatalist approach here finds its echo in a verse by Munir Niazi: *kyu.n Munir apnii tabaahii kaa ye kaisaa shikva / jitnaa taqdiir mei.n likkhaa hai adaa hotaa hai.*

48

پوچھتے ہیں وہ کہ غالبؔ کون ہے
کوئی بتلاؤ کہ ہم بتلائیں کیا

पूछते हैं वो कि ग़ालिब कौन है
कोई बतलाओ कि हम बतलाएं क्या

puuchhte hai.n vo ke Ghalib kaun hai
koii batlaao ke ham batlaaei.n kyaa

They ask Ghalib—Ghalib who?
Let someone say, I've no clue

Men nourish the desire to be known for what they are, or what they would like to be known for. This is a natural urge, but it takes curious turns and manifests itself in different men in different ways. In the case of a poet, this desire finds its manifestation in ironical terms as well—as it appears here. This apparently simple verse is Ghalib's introduction to his own self, both as a man and a poet, but only in a veiled manner. This is one of the finest examples of simplicity made complex and complexity made simple.

This verse has multiple implications: (a) one who puts forth this question may be a stranger, an admirer, a rival, or even a resilient lover (b) there is an uncertainty about who the inquirer wants to know about Ghalib—the man or the poet (c) the answer is known, but the act of asking shows the speaker's feigned ignorance (d) there is a sense of hurt, playfulness, even boasting on the poet's part (e) the person referred to as *vo* (he/she) is an imagined admirer who has known him already but also represents those who admire him, and (f) the second line—*Koi batlaao ke ham batlaaei.n kyaa* (let someone say; I have no clue)—has two entirely different implications: first, Ghalib is not even worth a mention and, second, I cannot properly praise him as he is beyond all praise.

From the stylistic angle, while the first line comes as a question to a supposed addressee, the second line strikes a note that is both serious and amusing in one stroke. There is a play on three words—*vo* (he/she) *koii* (anyone) and *ham* (me)—where the first one is an inquirer, the second one is an answerer and the third one is the poet himself, who stays behind the scenes watching the response. The three together make a company of his admirers, of which Ghalib himself is one. The play on *batlaao* and *batlaaei.n* is also remarkable for the use of language as gesture and gesture as language. The cumulative elements of drama and gestural implications enrich the verse potentially and make it appealing to us. In another verse, presumably on his own self, Ghalib offers yet another perspective on his disposition: *be-KHudii be-sabab nahii.n Ghalib / kuchh to hai jis kii parda-daarii hai.*

49

عشرت قطرہ ہے دریا میں فنا ہو جانا
درد کا حد سے گزرنا ہے دوا ہو جانا

इशरत-ए क़तरा है दरिया में फ़ना हो जाना
दर्द का हद से गुज़रना है दवा हो जाना

'ishart-e-qatra hai dariyaa mei.n fanaa ho jaanaa
dard ka had se guzarnaa hai davaa ho jaanaa

(*'ishrat*—joy, mirth, delight;
qatra—drop, very little quantity;
fanaa—mortality, destruction, death, obliteration)

The drop's luxury is to join the ocean
When pain exceeds, pain becomes a potion

P ain has been one of the perennial points of discourse in poetry. It has had its literal and metaphorical configurations as a source of suffering, as much as of philosophical sustenance. Ghalib develops his discourse around this idea and proposes that just as the drop's joy is to perish in the ocean, pain's joy is to become a potion. With the symbolism of drop and ocean, pain and potion, Ghalib develops a metaphysical perspective on the idea of suffering and redemption which are indeed entwined together and make way for each other.

This typical Ghalib verse, marked by complexity of thought and simplicity of expression, opens up different possibilities of meaning: (a) pain is not a permanent condition as it is curable, paradoxically enough, by the excess of pain itself (b) pain is neither avoidable nor deniable, as it is an inevitable condition of life and living (c) pleasure comes only after passing through pain and penance (d) the state of pleasure may be achieved by annihilating oneself, and (e) as the specks of dust meet the soil, a drop meets the ocean, and both return to their homes and enjoy their blissful merging.

The thematic design of this verse rests on the metaphoric value of *qatra* (drop) and *dariyaa* (river), representing the part and the whole in the first line, and *dard* (pain) and *davaa* (cure), representing the opposites in the second line. There is a close interactive relationship between the metaphors in each set, just as there is a close sequential relationship between the first and the second line of the verse. Ghalib prioritizes *'ishrat* (luxury) and *fanaa* (mortality) as the two key words to suggest that a drop's luxury lies in joining the sea as pain's luxury lies in getting a cure which amounts to sacrificing, or annihilating, one state of baser existence to achieve another state of higher existence. This is what imparts a mystical dimension to this verse. In yet another celebrated verse, Ghalib engages with the nature of pain in a similar manner: *ra.nj se KHuugar huaa insaa.n to mit jaataa hai ra.nj / mushkilei.n mujh per padii.n itnii ke aasaa.n ho gaei.n.*

50

بخشے ہے جلوۂ گل ذوق تماشا غالبؔ
چشم کو چاہیے ہر رنگ میں وا ہو جانا

बख़्शो है जल्वा-ए-गुल ज़ौक़-ए तमाशा 'ग़ालिब'
चश्म को चाहिए हर रंग में वा हो जाना

baKHshe hai jalva-i gul zauq-e tamaasha Ghalib
chashm ko chaahiye har ra.ng mei.n vaa ho jaanaa

(*baKHsh*—gift, grant;
jalva-i gul—show/splendour of blossoms;
zauq-e tamaasha—taste for show/splendour/spectacle;
chashm—eye;
vaa—open)

Blossom's beauty brings the taste
to watch a lovely bloom
The eyes must open to see
all tones and tints abloom

The manifestations of beauty in the world around us are numerous and they make numerous demands on us. Ghalib engages here with the objects of seeing, the taste for seeing and the pleasures of seeing. Every beauteous object invites onlookers to have a look and enjoy the spectacle. This is such an enriching experience that the eyes must welcome every scene that comes their way. This idea is developed in this verse with the metaphor of a blossom, and how and why it calls for the viewers' attention.

This verse may be appreciated in different contexts, each different from the other: (a) blossoms are wondrous and they graciously offer the viewer a taste for adoring their spectacle (b) eyes must open to each hue of nature's manifestation (c) each manifestation of nature is immense and is meant essentially for seeing (d) there is an intimate relationship between the spectator and the spectacle, and (e) all manifestations bear witness to God's glory, which enriches the verse with a mystical meaning.

Gul (blossom) is the central metaphor in this verse that represents the beauty of nature. Two key interlaced expressions in the first line—*jalva-i gul* (blossom's splendour) and *zauq-e tamaasha* (taste for splendour)—bear the central thematic burden of the verse. The cycle of meaning is completed with the eye's willingness and need to see the beauty of nature in all tints and tones. The three semantically interrelated words *jalva* (splendour), *tamaasha* (spectacle) and *chashm* (eye) deserve particular attention as they embody the entire phenomenon as a show of different colours offering a wondrous spectacle. Ghalib's genius finds multiple ways to express an idea, and each time with an added charm and perspective, as we may discover here: *shaq ho gayaa hai siina KHushaa lazzat-e faraaGh / takliif-e parda-daari-e zaKHm-e jigar gaii.*

51

شمع بجھتی ہے تو اس میں سے دھواں اٹھتا ہے
شعلۂ عشق سیہ پوش ہوا میرے بعد

शम्अ' बुझती है तो उस में से धुआँ उठता है
शो'ला-ए इश्क़ सियह-पोश हुआ मेरे बा'द

sham'a bujhtii hai to us mei.n se dhuaa.n uThtaa hai
sh'ola-i 'ishq siyah-posh huaa mere baad

(*sh'ola-i 'ishq*—flame/fire/blaze/flash of love;
siyah-posh—cloaked in black/darkness/gloom)

When the lamp puts out,
smoke rises from the lamp
After me, this love's raging flame
turned dark and damp

What does love mean and how does a lover enjoy being in love, or endure its onslaughts? Ghalib engages with this idea in intimate terms, but in a symbolic framework. His lover states a universal truth in the first line—when the candle goes out, it leaves some smoke behind. After creating a base in the first line, he delves deeper in the second line to say that with his disappearance, the blaze of love hid itself in darkness. With this, he implies that he was an ideal lover, unlike anyone else, and love reached its apex and its end with his disappearance from the scene for good.

This verse is an example of Ghalib's imaginative vitality in the way he creates a net of multiple meanings: (a) he links the idea of the flame's perishing with the lover's disappearance from the scene (b) both the flame and the lover have a limited span of life to live and both are destined to perish (c) as long as the flame lives, it spreads light, just as a lover does (d) the fading out of a flame and the lover's life drawing to a close create a sense of sorrow, and (e) the flame of love got cloaked in darkness for good after the speaker disappeared from the scene, just as the flame found its home in the smoke rising from the quenched flame.

Like an astute craftsman, Ghalib chose to put *sham'a* (lamp), *sh'ola* (blaze) and *dhuaa.n* (smoke) together to represent the central idea of burning and quenching followed by the rising of smoke. Together, they present a process whereby life meets death for good and it finally disappears in a cloak of gloom. With the personification of love with *siyah-posh* (cloaked in darkness), an exceptional physicality is attributed to love which adds to the unique appeal of the verse. This idea finds another distinguished expression in a verse by Mir: *aag the ibtidaa-i 'ishq mei.n ham / ab jo hai.n KHaak intihaa ye hai.*

52

بلا سے ہیں جو یہ پیشِ نظر در و دیوار
نگاہِ شوق کو ہیں بال و پر در و دیوار

बला से हैं जो ये पेश-ए-नज़र दर-ओ-दीवार
निगाह-ए-शौक़ को हैं बाल-ओ-पर दर-ओ-दीवार

balaa se hai.n jo ba pesh-e nazar dar-o diivaar
nigaah-e shauq ko hai.n baal-o par dar-o diivaar

(*balaa se*—who cares;
pesh-e nazar—before the eyes;
nigaah-e shauq—yearning looks;
baal-o par—feathers and wings)

Who cares if I have before me—
these doors and walls
For yearning looks, feathers and wings
are doors and walls

Confinement and freedom symbolize two states of human existence. Doors and walls in their physical form can only bring confinement and deny freedom. This idea finds a space in Ghalib's imagination and he develops it in a complex but poetically appealing manner in this verse. He intends to suggest that love defies the bounds of doors and walls; the same doors and walls magically turn into feathers and wings to help the lover fly beyond all confines. This is, however, possible only if there is a loving look around.

This verse unfolds layers of meaning in a novel manner: (a) doors and walls obstruct vision and prevent eyes from reaching out to enjoy the spectacle beyond the threshold of a home (b) doors and walls thus symbolize constraints, while feathers and wings symbolize freedom (c) there are no barriers that can ever keep lovers in confinement (d) with these metaphors, a distinct discourse is developed on the bliss of freedom and the constraints of confinement (d) it puts premium on imagination over reason in Blakean terms of mysticism and underlines it as a defining principle of life (e) there is a sense of derision for the constraining doors and walls in physical terms, which ultimately turn into icons of liberation in emotive terms.

The expression, *balaa se* (who cares) sets the tone of the verse at the very beginning. The artistic merits of this verse may, however, be marked in the contrastive use of the metaphors of *dar-o diivaar* (doors and walls) as against those of *baal-o par* (feathers and wings). Another striking phrase which qualifies the verse is *nigaah-e shauq* (yearning looks), and marks the superiority of vision and turns the verse into a philosophical statement in poetic terms.

53

وفور اشک نے کاشانے کا کیا یہ رنگ
کہ ہو گئے مرے دیوار و در در و دیوار

वुफ़ूर-ए अश्क ने काशाने का किया ये रंग
कि हो गए मिरे दीवार-ओ-दर दर-ओ-दीवार

vufuur-e ashk ne kaashaane kaa kiyaa ye ra.ng
ke ho gae mire diivaar-o dar dar-o diivaar

(*vufuur*—excess, abundance;
ashk—tears;
kaashaana—dwelling, abode;
dar—door)

Tears' excess turned my abode—
as it took the calls
My walls and doors turned, but
to my doors and walls

Grief can affect human beings in the most unusual ways. It makes them incapable of seeing things in their right shape and form. The lover, too, is overpowered here by pain and suffering in love. As such, he has lost control over himself and cannot identify things rightly as a sane human being would normally do. Ghalib develops a novel pattern of meaning in this quizzical verse by using his images in unexpected ways and turning them upside down, like the grief-stricken lover's vision itself.

Ghalib complicates the evolution of meaning in this verse and leaves the reader to decipher them in multiple ways: (a) the lover's excessive grief has rendered him incapable of seeing even his own abode as it exists (b) his house fell to pieces and he could not even tell the wall apart from the door (c) he was so possessed by his overwhelming grief and wept so much that his vision got blurred and he could not distinguish the wall from the door as one turned into the other (d) he turned utterly helpless because he was over-possessed by his own sentiments, and most, importantly (e) he lost all distinctions in love and every image appeared differently to him.

The most vital expression in this verse is *vufuur* (abundance) itself which contains a variety of associated meanings. Combined with *ashk* (tears), it embodies and qualifies the figure of the lover further. The magic of the verse lies additionally in the use of two complementary words, *diivaar* (wall) and *dar* (door), in two different constructions, first as *diivaar-o dar* and then turning it inversely as *dar-o diivaar* to weave a pattern of implicated meaning.

54

بر چند ہو مشاہدۂ حق کی گفتگو
بنتی نہیں ہے بادہ و ساغر کہے بغیر

हर-चंद हो मुशाहदा-ए हक़ की गुफ़्त-गू
बनती नहीं है बादा-ओ-साग़र कहे बग़ैर

harchand ho mushaahida-i haq kii guftuguu
bantii nahii.n hai baada-o saaGhar kahe baGhair

(*harchand*—howsoever;
mushaahida-i haq—observation/witness/testimony of truth;
baada-o saaGhar—wine and glass)

Howsoever much you talk of
the testimonies of truth, alas!
You can't indeed make it good
without going for wine and glass

Wine, wine-cup, and wine house appear frequently in ghazals as potential metaphors. This verse also draws upon this stock subject. Ghalib, however, imparts his own touch to it by introducing a human character who personalizes the experience of drinking which helps him recognize himself. He does this by placing it in an entirely different context by taking it closer to man's effort towards developing a discourse on truth.

The significance of this verse can be traced in the levels of meaning it creates: (a) at one level, wine is an intoxicating drink and wine-cup a physical object (b) at another level, wine is a metaphor of transportation to a different state and wine-cup a microcosm that contains a macrocosm in itself (c) the discourse on truth intoxicates the believer as wine intoxicates the drinker (d) this implies that both wine and discourse intoxicate in two different ways (e) truth is revealed in a heightened state of intoxication, which is indeed a heightened moment of consciousness and exaltation.

In terms of the verbal merit of the verse, *harchand* (howsoever) holds an ironic meaning of helplessness on the part of the speaker. This condition is explored further in the word *haq* (truth), which is strengthened by *mushahida* (testimony). A deft choice of words adds strength to the verse. Wine, being a frequent reference in Ghalib's poetry gets an entirely novel perspective in yet another verse: *go haath mei.n ju.nbish nahii.n aankho.n mei.n to dam hai / rahne do abhii saaGhar-o miinaa mire aage.*

55

ان آبلوں سے پانو کے گھبرا گیا تھا میں
جی خوش ہوا ہے راہ کو پرخار دیکھ کر

इन आबलों से पाँव के घबरा गया था मैं
जी ख़ुश हुआ है राह को पुर-ख़ार देख कर

in aablo.n se paao.n ke ghabraa gayaa thaa mai.n
jii KHush huaa hai raah ko pur-KHaar dekh kar

(*aabla*—blister;
pur-KHaar—full of thorns)

I had grown nervous looking at the blisters on my feet
I'm happy now looking at the thorns filling the street

Love and suffering have been bosom friends in ghazals. Ghalib constructs the image of a lover who finds his panacea in suffering. If there were only blisters on the feet without a way to cure them, he muses, they would have driven men irretrievably disheartened. He finds a way to get rid of this suffering by going through another painful experience of addressing them. By personalizing a general human condition, he makes his idea more appealing and turns it into a meaningful discourse on pain and man's capacity to negotiate with it.

This seemingly simple verse implies more than it states so plainly: (a) it reads like an intimate personal narrative of suffering that characterizes a typical lover of Ghalib's make, but it represents a larger condition (b) the desire to bring pain to its end is reflective of human nature that seeks relief when in pain (c) while blisters represent life's suffering, the path strewn with thorns symbolizes the path of life that has suffering spread the entire way (d) the idea of suffering blisters on the soles and the thorns puncturing them exemplifies that one pain is sometimes relieved by another pain itself (e) pain redeeming pain is at its core a philosophical idea unto itself, and (f) there is a stamp of irony here in how he finds his relief by undergoing yet another suffering (g) this enables him to fulfil his desire to walk the road of life further.

Two vital words—*aabla* (blister) and *KHaar* (thorn)—juxtaposed against each other and consecutively placed in the first and the second line of the verse, create a whole scenario and bear out the essential import of the verse marked by a sense of sarcasm, on the one hand, and pleasure, on the other. The images of blisters and thorns appear in a Ghalib verse once again but they work differently here and create a contrastive situation: *kaa.nto.n kii zabaa.n suukh gaii pyaas se yaa Rab / ik aabla-paa vaadii-e pur-KHaar mei.n aave.*

56

فنا تعلیم درس بے خودی ہوں اس زمانے سے
کہ مجنوں لام الف لکھتا تھا دیوار دبستاں پر

फ़ना-तालीम-ए दरस-ए बे-ख़ुदी हूँ उस ज़माने से
कि मजनूँ लाम अलिफ़ लिखता था दीवार-ए दबिस्ताँ पर

*fanaa taaliim-e dars-e be-KHudii huu.n us zamaane se
ke Majnuu.n laam alif likhtaa thaa divaar-e dabistaa.n per*

(*fanaa*—oblivious;
taalim-e dars-e be-KHudii—education in
the lessons of selflessness;
laam alif—two letters of Arabic alphabet;
dabistaa.n—school)

I'm fervent-taught in selflessness --
ever since that age
When Majnuu.n used to write LA --
on the school wall's page

Self and selflessness have been the oft-discussed themes of the Urdu ghazal in all ages. In one of the strongest expressions of this theme, Ghalib configures a speaker here who takes pride in his commitment towards exploring the blessings of selflessness. Strangely, but uniquely enough, he thinks of Majnuu.n asserting his individual superiority. He declares that he had been fervently devoted to educating himself in selflessness for ages, while Majnuu.n, that idolized lover, was still learning to write the alphabets on the walls of his schoolhouse.

There are several implications in this verse: (a) both the speaker and Majnuu.n are exceedingly passionate about their concerns with mystical thought and love respectively (b) both are committed to creating and retaining their unique identities (c) but the speaker asserts his superiority, as he had already been devoted to his quest, while Majnuu.n was still learning his first lessons in his school (d) only those intensely passionate in love and mysticism learn the secrets of selflessness and reach the highest states of this condition (e) the two Arabic letters, *laam* and *alif*, combined together, make *laa*, which is a word of negation, and the speaker here has chosen to negate stereotypical learning that Majnuu.n accepted for himself.

Fanaa (oblivion) and *dars* (lesson) are two seminal words here. The word *fanaa*, however, carries dual meanings of mortality, on the one hand, and being fervently lost in a pursuit, on the other. In the context of this verse, *fanaa* is used to qualify the complete submission of the speaker in his pursuit of selflessness. *Dars* (lesson) is also double-edged, as it applies to both of them who get their education from two different schools of love and mysticism. Apart from Ghalib, a classic example of how the idea and experience of selflessness can be presented in a verse may be seen in an iconic verse by Siraj Aurangabadi: *shah-e be-KHudii ne 'ataa kiyaa mujhe vo libaas-e barahnagii / na KHirad kii baKHiyaagarii rahii na junuu.n kii parda darii rahii.*

57

مجھے اب دیکھ کر ابر شفق آلودہ یاد آیا
کہ فرقت میں تری آتش برستی تھی گلستاں پر

मुझे अब देख कर अब्र-ए शफ़क़-आलूदा याद आया
कि फ़ुरक़त में तिरी आतिश बरसती थी गुलिस्ताँ पर

mujhe ab dekh kar abr-e shafaq-aaluuda yaad aayaa
ke furqat mei.n tiri aatish barastii thii gulistaa.n per

(*abr*—cloud;
shafaq-aaluuda—horizon covered with redness at sunset;
furqat—separation, parting;
aatish—fire)

When I looked at the evening's red-lit cloud, I recalled
How in your separation, fire on the gardens sprawled

Separation from the beloved is a major theme in ghazals which all poets have drawn upon incessantly. Here too, Ghalib narrates in metaphorical terms a lover's ill luck, who has been separated from the beloved. Looking at the evening cloud bearing the redness of the horizon at sunset, the lover gets reminded of how, in his separation from the beloved, the blossoms and petals of the garden, too, burnt red. This implies that not only the garden, but the lover, too, burnt in separation from the beloved.

The implications of this verse include: (a) clouds lose their normal hue when covered with redness in the evening, just as a lover loses his natural glow when separated from the beloved (b) separation from the beloved burns the lover (c) the burning of the lover is equal to the burning of his garden of love (d) nature is reflective of the lover's condition (e) rather than making a statement in general, the speaker is narrating his suffering to the beloved after meeting her and suggests, by implication, that his separation from her put him in a state of burning.

There is a cause-effect relationship between the two lines of the verse where the word *ab* (now) plays a vital role by underlining the two conditions of then and now. Here, 'then' is marked by suffering in separation, while 'now' is marked by pleasure in union with the beloved. Importantly enough, we may read *shafaq-aaluuda* (horizon covered with redness at sunset) along with *aatish* (fire) to appreciate how the common redness of the two turns into a blaze and burns the garden of love. Irony reaches its height when we realize that this loss happens in separation, suggesting thereby that separation has metaphorically burnt both the lover and the garden of love. Ghalib constructs this condition of separation in a picturesque frame in another verse as well: *hai mujhe abr-e bahaarii kaa baras kar khulnaa / rote rote Gham-e furqat mei.n fanaa ho jaana.*

58

نہ لڑ ناصح سے غالبؔ کیا ہوا گر اس نے شدت کی
ہمارا بھی تو آخر زور چلتا ہے گریباں پر

न लड़ नासेह से 'ग़ालिब' क्या हुआ गर उस ने शिद्दत की
हमारा भी तो आख़िर ज़ोर चलता है गरेबाँ पर

na laR naaseh se Ghalib kyaa huaa gar us ne shiddat kii
hamaaraa bhii to aaKHir zore chaltaa hai garebaa.n per

(*naaseh*—preacher;
shiddat—extremity, severity;
garebaa.n—collar, collar opening)

Don't fight with the preacher, Ghalib,
what if he is severe on you
After all, I too may reach my collar,
if I choose to do

Lovers can get crazy and act crazily when pushed beyond a point. This verse presents an unusual situation before us. Instead of Ghalib addressing the lover, the lover addresses Ghalib here and advises him not to pick up a fight with the preacher because he is too oppressive in imposing his diktats. Since he is so strongly opinionated, he would not yield in any case. As such, he says that he has his own way of dealing with him. After all, he is a lover and he can reach his collar and tear it apart if it comes to that, and if he wishes to do so. He comes up as if with a challenge to the preacher, whom he would face in the typical image of a lover with collars torn apart.

This verse opens certain interesting aspects for the reader to ponder over: (a) the preacher is too intolerant and follows the beaten path of his own make (b) the lover, on the other hand, is liberal and is advised not to unfruitfully engage with the preacher's persistent doggedness (c) the lover can register his protest in his own way and can tear his collars apart, although it would make no difference to the preacher (d) this self-chosen action on the part of the lover would bring consolation to him (e) most importantly, he offers a liberal discourse as opposed to the one preached and practised by the preacher, and finally (f) he asserts his protest through his independence to act according to his own wishes.

The *naaseh* (preacher) is a stock figure of Urdu poetry. The word *shiddat* (severity) in this verse typically characterizes him and what he represents as an institution. In the three characters that emerge here, the lover and poet are on one side, and the preacher on the other, against whom the speaker advises the lover with *na laR* (don't pick up a fight) since he is an incorrigible one and cannot see any reason. In a playful but logical manner, Dagh Dehlavi represents this experience in his verse thus: *tuu KHudaa to nahii.n ai naaseh-e naadaa.n meraa / kyaa KHataa kii jo mai.n ne na maanaa teraa.*

59

بے بسکہ ہر اک ان کے اشارے میں نشاں اور
کرتے ہیں محبت تو گزرتا ہے گماں اور

है बसकि हर इक उन के इशारे में निशाँ और
करते हैं मुहब्बत तो गुज़रता है गुमाँ और

hai bas-ke har ik un ke ishaare mei.n nishaa.n aur
karte hai.n mohabbat to guzartaa hai gumaa.n aur

(*bas-ke*—although;
gumaa.n—conjecture, guess, presumption)

In each of her gestures, there's a sign beyond a sign
She indulges in love, I guess it's some other sign

Beloveds defy a definite identity. They have as many appearances as they have of behaviours. Ghalib's lover constructs the image of the beloved along this line and considers her as one who does not always shower love, and if she does, she does it in queer ways. What he expects from the beloved remains unrealized and what really happens is unexpected. In effect, it is a queer experience for the lover and he expresses this with a sense of enjoyment.

This verse is a unique example of image-making with respect to the beloved and makes these suggestions: (a) the image of the beloved as constructed here is neither unusual nor impossible (b) she can be dearly loving, slyly mischievous, craftily coquettish and pleasantly playful by turns, and can always hide her real intention in expressing her love (c) the ways and manners of the beloved are such that her love appears like artifice or deceit (d) the lover is an innocent prey who does not necessarily achieve what he expects, and (e) most importantly, the lover cannot really trust her as a genuine beloved as she is a smart manoeuverer whose real intentions remain unfathomable.

The real fun of this verse lies in two words, *gumaa.n* (conjecture) and *aur* (something else). The first word carries two meanings—of doubt, on the one hand, and presumption, on the other. The second word, which is as simple as simple can be, is indeed replete with mixed senses of hope, faith as well as apprehension. *Ishaara* (gesture) and *nishaa.n* (sign) are two other words that make a compatible pair and spell out the queer nature of the beloved.

60

یارب وہ نہ سمجھے ہیں نہ سمجھیں گے مری بات
دے اور دل ان کو جو نہ دے مجھ کو زباں اور

या रब वो न समझे हैं न सम्झेंगे मिरी बात
दे और दिल उन को जो न दे मुझ को ज़बाँ और

yaa Rab na vo samjhei.n hai.n na samjhe.nge mirii baat
de aur dil un ko jo na de mujh ko zabaa.n aur

O God! She hasn't got my intent,
nor will ever do;
Give her heart a little more,
if not a tongue to me, to woo

Lovers complain to no end, and the fun of loving lies in listening to their complaints and attending to them as true lovers. Ghalib presents this act with a difference. His lover portrays his beloved as one who has not yet appreciated his pleas nor would ever do in the future. So, he addresses God, who alone can make his love easier for him to enjoy. May she have a kind and loving heart, he implores, if he is not given a tongue to implore more, because no imploring can help any further.

The verse opens up the poet's intent in interesting ways: (a) the lover makes an unusual and innocent entreaty to God to make his beloved kind so that she may understand his expressed and unexpressed desires of union (b) a sense of abiding despair characterizes the lover's persona (c) in spite of that despair, his love for the beloved does not wane and remains constant (d) this is how the lover-beloved relationship continues, with hope and despair punctuating each other, and (e) interestingly enough, the verse may also be read as an expression of the hostility, or insensitivity, that some of Ghalib's contemporaries had shown towards him, although he wished that they showed better understanding towards him.

The verse appeals to us for its logical relationship between the two lines. It also appeals for the rich ambiguity that the word *vo* (he/they) represents, as it refers to both his beloved and his contemporaries. It is important to note further that the expressions *samjhei.n hai.n* (has understood) and *samjhe.nge* (will understand) do not literally imply an understanding of the matter, but an appreciation of his imploring. Similarly, the expression *aur dil* (more of a heart, or a different heart) does not imply another heart but a heart with greater sympathy which reflects the emotional state of the lover more suitably.

61

تم شہر میں ہو تو ہمیں کیا غم جب اٹھیں گے
لے آئیں گے بازار سے جا کر دل و جاں اور

तुम शह्र में हो तो हमें क्या ग़म जब उठेंगे
ले आएंगे बाज़ार से जा कर दिल-ओ-जाँ और

tum shahr mei.n ho to hamei.n kyaa Gham jab uThe.nge
le aae.nge bazaar se jaa kar dil-o jaa.n aur

Why worry if you're in town, I'll get up and go
To get myself another love, if that be so

Tiffs and expressions of anger are common in love. Here is a lover who is apparently sick and tired of his beloved, and says in a moment of exasperation that he will get up one day and go out to get another beloved from the market. His saying that he will get another beloved from the market does suggest that they are readily available there for an asking (which is not the reality at all). It also suggests that there are many heartbroken lovers around who too can, and would, do the same.

The speaker in this verse addresses the beloved in an unusual way and makes two possible suggestions: (b) first, he is angry and expresses himself ruthlessly without any control over himself, and that (b) he is a lusty male who has tired too soon of his beloved and is seeking a new one (c) second, he is a light-hearted and playful lover who does not really mean what he says, and that (d) he is an amiable kind and loves his beloved by teasing her; (e) a third idea also makes its way here that there are beloveds available in the market like dolls and wares which is not true and defies any comment.

The key expressions that compose the special mood of the verse are *Gham* (grief), *uThe.nge* (will wake up/will walk up), *le aae.nge* (will get in) and *aur* (yet another). *GHam* is used here more like a casual and throwaway remark than an expression of sorrow. The two other nasal-sounding words—*uThe.nge* and *le aae.nge*—spell out the speaker's casual tone towards the beloved who listens to him but only mutely.

62

ہیں اور بھی دنیا میں سخن ور بہت اچھے
کہتے ہیں کہ غالبؔ کا ہے بے انداز بیاں اور

हैं और भी दुनिया में सुख़न-वर बहुत अच्छे
कहते हैं कि 'ग़ालिब' का है अंदाज़-ए-बयाँ और

hai.n aur bhii duniyaa me.in suKHanvar bahut achhe
kahte hai.n ke Ghalib ka hai andaaz-e-bayaa.n aur

(*suKHanvar*—the eloquent one, poet;
andaaz-e bayaa.n—style of expression, way of eloquence)

Many other poets in the world, there are many, who sway
But Ghalib, they say, has a different way to say a say

Poets are known for taking pride in themselves and their poetry, but more importantly they get their appreciation from their genuine readers and critics. Ghalib gets a speaker for himself in this verse who applauds him for his worth. The speaker distinctly marks Ghalib's individual style, which distinguishes him from all other poets. Although he admits that there are many other poets in this world who are quite good, he asserts that people praise him for writing differently with distinction.

The beauty of this verse may be appreciated along the following lines of argument: (a) the speaker seems to speak to himself, but he actually speaks to Ghalib's admirers, or even his detractors who are around (b) interestingly, he also makes others say what he says about Ghalib—that he has a different way of writing poetry (c) this recognition of Ghalib comes as a certification of his genius which is a real compliment to him (d) he places Ghalib as a poet of greater substance in the larger context of other poets, who may be of both the past and the present (e) this exudes a sense of confidence in Ghalib's genius with a sense of pleasure and pride.

The use of the word *aur* (many more) twice with two different meanings distinguishes this verse quite clearly. The first one in the first line refers to other good poets, but in the second line it refers to his unique style which no one else has. This is one of his several other verses where Ghalib's worth is glorified with pride and pleasure. Indeed, Ghalib has himself written verses of *t'allii* (self-praise) like other poets, which is an accepted poetic tradition of the ghazal. A parallel of his *t'allii* may be found in a verse by Mir Taqi Mir: *saare 'aalam per huu.n mai.n chhayaa huaa / mustanad hai meraa farmaayaa huaa.*

63

ناداں ہو جو کہتے ہو کہ کیوں جیتے ہیں غالبؔ
قسمت میں ہے مرنے کی تمنا کوئی دن اور

नादाँ हो जो कहते हो कि क्यूँ जीते हैं ग़ालिब
क़िस्मत में है मरने की तमन्ना कोई दिन और

naadaa.n ho jo kahte ho ke kyu.n jiite hai.n Ghalib
qismat me.in hai marne kii tamanna koii din aur

(*tamanna*—desire, yearning)

You must be naïve to say: why are you alive, Ghalib, why
Who wants to live; I only yearn to die, you know why

The desire for dying surfaces in poetry in different contexts and in different ways. This is Ghalib's last verse (*maqta*) of an elegy he wrote in the form of a ghazal on the death of young Arif, his dear nephew. Since he had adopted him as a son, as none of his seven sons survived beyond their childhood, he was deeply pained and perturbed by his passing. The sense of loss and subsequent suffering comes out quite clearly in these two lines that reflect his sentiments on Arif's premature death and his own pathetic survival after that.

Ghalib puts this verse in perspective and points towards some perennial questions about life and death: (a) he ruefully says that he, who puts forth a question as to why he lives on even after Arif's passing away, does not realize what he means by putting such a question to him (b) because he himself cannot die before the appointed day, he is only destined to long for his death a few days more—that is, as long as he has to survive (c) life and death are beyond human control, and he is a prisoner of life even after Arif's passing away (d) he also hints rather indirectly that a reconciliation has to be struck with the eternal truth of death that arrives only at the appointed hour, and (e) the desire for his own death draws him closer to his dear departed one.

Some of the vital expressions that qualify this verse as a passionate expression of grief include *naadaa.n* (innocent), *tamanna* (longing), and *koii din aur* (some other day). These phrases are imbued with deep ironical implications and impart an edge to the verse that is essentially remorseful in nature. We may also consider this verse by Ghalib in this perspective: *kahuu.n kis se mai.n ke kyaa hai shab-e Gham burii balaa hai / mujhe kyaa buraa thaa marnaa agar ek baar hotaa.*

64

حریف مطلب مشکل نہیں فسون نیاز
دعا قبول ہو یا رب کہ عمر خضر دراز

हरिफ़-ए मतलब-ए मुश्किल नहीं फ़ुसून-ए नियाज़
दुआ क़ुबूल हो या रब कि उम्र-ए ख़िज़्र दराज़

hariif-e matlab-e mushkil nahii.n fusuun-e niyaaz
du'aa qubuul ho ya Rab ke 'umr-e KHizr daraaz

(*hariif*—rival, opponent, competitor, adversary;
matlab-e mushkil—difficult intent, grey word;
fusuun-e niyaaz—magic of prayer/humility;
daraaz—long, lengthy)

The magic of a prayer heard
is no rival to the grey word
May Khizr live for long, O God,
may my prayer be now heard

P rayer and humility are no aliens to human desire; they indeed are the causes of human strength. Yet, all human prayers are not easily granted. This idea reminds the speaker of Khizr, the eternal path finder and spiritual guide of Moses and Alexander, whose prayers may be accepted with far greater certainty as compared with others. The speaker thus evokes Khizr to get his prayers answered.

This verse is complex as it projects an indirect relationship between the two lines. However, it may be read in these possible ways: (a) humility and prayer can act magically towards the acceptance of even a difficult desire (*matlab-e mushkil*) but this does not happen always (b) the speaker's desire remains unfulfilled in spite of his prayers and entreating (c) it is better, therefore, for the speaker to submit to God for granting a still longer life to Khizr, who could unknot complexities and find the answer—that is, show the right path to lost ones (d) this prayer for Khizr who had already drunk the water of life (which grants immortality to the path finder and helps them guide people who have lost their path in life, for eternity) underlines the speaker's faith in his exceptional skills and prayers (e) getting a prayer granted is equal to getting the right answer and the right path, which Khizr alone may do for all the disappointed ones until the day of judgement.

The first line of the verse comes to us as a gentle statement, while the second line comes as a prayer. The word *hariif* (rival) incorporates a tinge of irony, *matlab-e mushkil* (difficult intent) acts as a creative expression for desire and *fusuun-e niyaaz* (the magic of prayer) as a compliment to the magic of a human entreating before God. This deftly chosen set of words creates a philosophical halo around the verse. This verse may be read further along with another verse by Ghalib: *Khizr sultaa.n ko rakhe Khaliq-e akbar sar-sabz / shah ke baagh mei.n ye taaza nihaal achha hai.* Shad Azimabadi echoes these sentiments: *raahrau tujh saa kahaa.n ai Khizr-e shauq / kaun terii KHaak-e paa ko paaegaa.*

65

نہ گل نغمہ ہوں نہ پردۂ ساز
میں ہوں اپنی شکست کی آواز

न गुल-ए नग़्मा हूँ न पर्दा-ए साज़
मैं हूँ अपनी शिकस्त की आवाज़

na gul-e naGhma huu.n na parda-i saaz
mai.n huu.n apnii shikast kii aavaaz

(*gul-e naGhma*—blossom/spirit of melody;
parda-i saaz—veil of music instrument, source of music;
shikast—defeat, failure, breaking, fall)

Neither the blossom of music nor the instrument's veil
If at all, I am the voice of my own defeat, my own wail

Poets are known to have come up with many worthy philosophical expositions in moments of reflection over their own self. Ghalib ponders over life in a larger context and opens a discourse on existence itself. He reflects that he is neither the joy that melody creates nor a string that produces music. He speaks to us in the first person and asserts that he is, at best, a discordant voice or a sound of his own defeat. These expositions about his own self open avenues for larger meditations on life.

The levels of meaning here are numerous: (a) the speaker addresses us in the garb of the poet himself to objectify his idea (b) instead of lamenting over what he is not, he regretfully says what he is indeed (c) he creates a binary of illusion and reality, and associates himself with the latter (d) the two sets of adjectives qualify life as a song and rhythm, but subsequently it is contrasted with the voice of defeat, and (e) finally, life cannot be apprehended in absolute terms as it is a curious combination of success and failure.

Two sets of adjectival constructions—*gul-e naGhma* (blossom of melody) and *parda-i saaz* (veil of music instrument)—act as exquisite and positive metaphors of life and they mark the high point of Ghalib's creativity. The third metaphor for life—*shikast kii aavaaz* (voice of defeat, or sound of breaking)—is figurative, and represents the sad music of life and works towards imparting a dramatic aura to Ghalib's expression. It is in this contrast that we may situate the artistic merit of this verse. This must also be appreciated that one who addresses us in the first person emerges ultimately as the voice of a man whose voyage of life is challenging but also rewarding in terms of acquiring a deeper understanding of life. A larger perspective on this verse emerges further in another verse by Ghalib: *mudda'aa mahv-e tamaashaae shikast-e dil hai / aaiina KHaane mei.n koii liye jaataa hai mujhe.*

66

زخم پر چھڑکیں کہاں طفلانِ بے پروا نمک
کیا مزہ ہوتا اگر پتھر میں بھی ہوتا نمک

ज़ख़्म पर छिड़कें कहाँ तिफ़्लान-ए बे-परवा नमक
क्या मज़ा होता अगर पत्थर में भी होता नमक

zaKHm per chhiRkei.n kahaa.n tiflaan-e be-parvaa namak
kyaa maza hotaa agar pathhar mei.n bhii hotaa namak

(*tiflaan-e be-parvaa*—careless lads)

But why, on the wounds, the careless lads
should spray salt
What fun would that be,
if the stones, too, had salt

Careless kids indulge in strange acts; they throw stones and cause pain to the crazy ones like Majnuu.n. Here, these kids may spray salt on the wounds of their victim, but they also wonder as to why and how long should they do this without getting enough pleasure. The speaker then comments that if the stones, too, had salt in them, these kids would throw those stones on them to cause double the pain to their victims and bring greater joy to themselves.

This act by the careless kids acquires deeper meanings than what appears on the surface. The layers of meaning may be identified as follows: (a) those who spray salt on wounds could be wanton boys doing it typically for their mischievous sport, reminding us of Shakespeare's, 'As flies to wanton boys are we to the gods; they kill us for their sport' from *King Lear* (b) they could also be the social rivals who get sadistic pleasure in causing damage to their foes (c) they might be the beloveds who take the same pleasure in bringing pain to their lovers (d) or even the jealous lovers putting other lovers to agony, and finally, (e) in all these cases, the sufferer is ironically the one who has done no damage to anyone, and yet he has to bear all the onslaughts.

The verse finds its edge in the phrase *kahaa.n* (what for/but why) which intensifies the idea of needless rubbing of salt on the wound. The two words *maza* (taste/enjoyment) and *namak* (salt) that complement each other, visualize a stone with salt in it which could cause greater pain to the victims when thrown at them. By implication, throwing stones without salt in them would be akin to serving/tasting food without salt. The idea of salt in stone is indeed a novel one that only an ingenious poet like Ghalib could have imagined and poeticized. Ghalib executes the metaphor of salt as a cause for suffering in another verse in an equally creative manner: *shor-e pand-e naaseh ne zaKHm per namak chhiRkaa / aap se koii puchhe tum ne kyaa maza paayaa.*

67

آہ کو چاہیے اک عمر اثر ہوتے تک
کون جیتا ہے تری زلف کے سر ہوتے تک

आह को चाहिए इक उम्र असर होते तक
कौन जीता है तिरी ज़ुल्फ़ के सर होते तक

aah ko chaahiye ik 'umr asar hote tak
kaun jiitaa hai tiri zulf ke sar hote tak

(*sar*—(be)coming)

My wails need a lifetime to reach
the heart, wait, O wait
But who lives that long enough
to see it reach, wait, O wait

Human beings wail when in pain; unfortunately for the wailers, it takes long to reach sympathetic ears. In spite of this, man keeps expecting that his wail would bear fruit, sooner or later. This verse is the wailing of a lover seeking the beloved's favour, but sadly enough, he fails to get it. He moans, therefore, that it would take a lifetime for his wail to reach her and get her favour. He is disheartened and speaks in metaphorical terms that he may not live that long to see the beloved's graceful tresses becoming a soothing shade for him. The lover speaks in a voice that is decidedly one of despondency.

Even this seemingly simple verse has some interesting aspects that deserve our critical attention: (a) wailing is inevitable in love with which lovers have ever been identified (b) favour in love does not come easily to the lover, as it makes tough demands (c) it takes longer than imagined, and tests and tries the lover's patience (d) the life of the lover is shorter than the period of wait involved, and finally, (e) the lover may not live that long to see his wailings of disappointment bearing fruit and turning into the pleasures of union.

It is important to mark that Ghalib turns the visual image of the beloved's long tresses into a metaphor to represent the long stretch of the lover's waiting. Also, tresses may be appreciated as shades that may bring relief to the lover from the odd weathers of life. He also employs an idiomatic expression of *sar hote tak* (until accomplished) to express the idea of a tedious wait that knows no end. Instead of *hone tak*, Ghalib uses *hote tak* which is yet another linguistic innovation, characteristic of his creative imagination. Compared with Ghalib, this condition of suffering while waiting for the beloved's favour is represented rather scathingly in a verse by Momin Khan Momin: *asar us ko zaraa nahii.n hotaa / ra.nj raahat-fazaa nahii.n hotaa.*

68

عاشقی صبر طلب اور تمنا بیتاب
دل کا کیا رنگ کروں خون جگر ہوتے تک

आशिक़ी सब्र-तलब और तमन्ना बेताब
दिल का क्या रंग करूँ ख़ून-ए जिगर होते तक

'aashiqii sabr talab aur tamanna be-taab
dil ka kyaa ran.g karuu.n KHuun-e jigar hote tak

(*sabr talab*—seeking patience, asking for endurance)

Love demands patience; desire takes no plea
How to tend this heart till it breathes its last for thee

In love, human desires are uncontrollable, but love expects endurance and serenity from the lover. Here is Ghalib's realistic portrayal of a lover's state of impatience in waiting when he falls in love. He authenticates an axiom that love demands patience, but unfortunately for the lover, desires defy all kinds of patience. As the lover's desires are uncontrollable, Ghalib wonders as to how the lover may possibly contain his heart until it gets vanquished finally.

This verse unveils the plight that a lover typically confronts and negotiates with in his love life: (a) as he suffers in love, he poses a rhetorical question to himself about how he would sustain his heart till it is finally vanquished (b) this also accounts for the pain he would have to bear in a waiting which may be endless (c) while sharing his own plight, he typically underlines the plight of all lovers who suffer helplessly (d) helplessness is a condition of being in love and there is no escape from it, and (e) finally, the lover is destined to find the answer to his rhetorical question in his vanquishing only.

Two squarely juxtaposed conditions reflected in the words *sabr* (patience) and *be-taab* (impatience) hold the basic thematic structure of this verse. Two other corresponding words—*ra.ng* (condition/colour) and *KHuun-e jigar* (heart's blood)—draw our attention further to the symbolism of red colour which represents the idea of dying by shedding one's own blood. *KHuun-e jigar* is also a traditional reference in the ghazal tradition that lovers shed blood in love. Close to Ghalib's verse, Khwaja Mir Dard constructs the condition of impatience with a touch of pathos in his verse that also accounts for the beloved's crankiness: *KHudaa jaane kyaa hogaa anjaam us kaa / mai.n be-sabr itnaa huu.n vo tund-KHuu hai.*

69

ہم نے مانا کہ تغافل نہ کرو گے لیکن
خاک ہو جائیں گے ہم تم کو خبر ہوتے تک

हम ने माना कि तग़ाफ़ुल न करोगे लेकिन
ख़ाक हो जाएंगे हम तुम को ख़बर होते तक

ham ne maanaa ke taGhaaful na karoge lekin
KHaak ho jaae.nge hum tum ko KHabar hote tak

(*taGhaaful*—negligence, indifference, inadvertence;
KHaak—ashes, dust)

You would not be negligent, I agree,
you would not be
But I would be all dust till you knew
what happened to me

Waiting for favours from the beloved is a traditional subject in ghazals. Some beloveds are kind and they do not test and try the lover's patience, as even the small periods of waiting may put the lover in distress, and even claim his life. Here is a moaning lover addressing his beloved. He agrees that his beloved would not be negligent of his condition, but, by the time she would get to know of his state, he would be vanquished and would have turned to ashes. He understands that he would surely receive favours but fate would not give him a wink more to restore himself.

This verse offers some interesting aspects to ponder over: (a) the lover enjoys the beloved's confidence in him and hopes that she would not be negligent if he fell prey to adversity (b) but he ruminates rather regretfully that it would be too late by the time she would get to know of his suffering and disappearance from the face of this earth (c) this confidence in the beloved's kindness is peculiarly different from the traditional attitude depicted in ghazals (d) the idea of the lover turning to ashes in separation from the beloved also marks the state of his misery which adds deep pathos to the verse (e) apart from reflecting upon the fate of the lover, this verse may also be considered as a reflection on the miserable state of a sufferer who seeks justice from the powers that be and laments the delay in the dispensation of justice to him.

Ghalib imparts a bleak shade to the neutral word *KHabar* (information) in the context of this verse. The sense of the lover's loss is further intensified through a similar sounding word—*KHaak* (soil)—which invokes the idea of meeting the end and turning into dust, never to be retrieved in any possible way. However, the expression *ham ne maanaa* (I accept and appreciate) presents the lover in a positive light and distinguishes him from the ever-complaining conventional lovers or seekers of favour. The consequence of the beloved's indifference leading to the lover's vanquishing as constructed by Ghalib acquires an added layer of meaning in a verse by Siraj Aurangabadi: *nazar-e taGhaaful-e yaar kaa gila kis zabaa.n sii.n bayaa.n karuu.n / ke sharaab-e sad-qadah aarzuu KHum-e dil mei.n thii so bharii rahii.*

70

غم ہستی کا اسدؔ کس سے ہو جز مرگ علاج
شمع ہر رنگ میں جلتی ہے سحر ہوتے تک

ग़म-ए हस्ती का असद किस से हो जुज़ मर्ग इलाज
शमा हर रंग में जलती है सहर होते तक

Gham-e hastii kaa Asad kis se ho juz marg 'ilaaj
sham'a har ra.ng mei.n jaltii hai sahar hote tak

(*hastii*—existence, being, life;
juz—other than, besides, except;
marg—death, demise, decease;
sahar—dawn of day, daybreak)

Who can cure, Asad, the pains of life for life's sake
The lamp burns in every hue until the dawn's break

Suffering is an eternal condition of life and is meant to be borne by men endowed with exceptional power of forbearance. Ghalib proposes a philosophical point to himself here, but he also addresses anyone who would care to listen to him. He wonders if there is someone who can bring cure to life's miseries as they are endless and they should, justifiably, come to an end at some stage. Finding no answer from his own conscience, or from anywhere else, he reconciles with the idea that until the end arrives, life has to run its full course with suffering alongside.

This verse makes several suggestions: (a) life and suffering are born companions that go hand-in-hand in a larger philosophical order (b) death is inevitable as per the Qur'an (50:19) and it works as a separator between the worldly life and the afterlife (c) death alone can bring human miseries to an end, which is akin to the idea of *moksha* in Hindu philosophy (c) just as human beings get redemption in death, the lamp gets its redemption in burning itself out, which comes close to the Christian idea of redemptive suffering (d) as such, human beings have to continue suffering till the dusk of life arrives, just as a flame has to keep alive until the first rays of the day appear (e) no one knows what the lamp suffers as it burns all night, just as no one can guess what happens to human beings as long as they live, which reflects upon the inscrutability of the human predicament, and (f) symbolically, Ghalib conceives night as suffering, dawn as cure and death as a deliverer into the zone of light.

Ghalib juxtaposes two vital symbols—*sham'a* (lamp) and *sahar* (daybreak)—to represent two phases of life. The lamp dispels the darkness of night as does the dawn, but ironically enough, they do not dispel the gloom from human life, which implies that they have to suffer both day and night. A clear note of affirmation in man's essential spirit comes through the phrase *har ra.ng mei.n* (in every hue), which asserts man's capacity to live through every state, being a noble creation of God. Ghalib reminds of Sheikh Ibrahim Zauq, who also ponders over this idea of transitoriness by executing the metaphor of lamp for life: *ai sham'a terii 'umr-e tabi'ii hai ek raat / ha.ns kar guzaar yaa ise ro kar guzaar de.*

71

خوش حال اس حریف سیہ مست کا کہ جو
رکھتا ہو مثل سایۂ گل سر بہ پائے گل

ख़ुश-हाल उस हरीफ़-ए सियह-मस्त का कि जो
रखता हो मिस्ल-ए साया-ए गुल सर ब पा-ए गुल

KHush-haal us hariif-e siyah-mast kaa ke jo
rakhtaa ho misl-e saaya-i gul sar ba paae-gul

(*hariif-e siyah mast*—heavily drunk rival/competitor, adversary;
misl-e saaya-i gul—like the shadow of blossoms;
paae-gul—blossom's feet)

Blessed be the rival, drunk to the brim,
who puts his head on her feet,
Like the likening shadow of a blossom
at the blossom's feet

Love has many shades and lovers have many moods. In their different moods, they enjoy, suffer, cajole, complain and pass through a variety of pains and pleasures in love. Here is Ghalib's unique pen-portrayal of a drunken lover who is in a state of utter intoxication and puts his head at the beloved's feet, which presents an exceptional scene. To turn this scene into one of rare distinction, Ghalib likens this to a scene where the shadow of the blossom is seen at the blossom's feet.

In its unusual complexion, this verse opens up very interesting shades of meaning to us: (a) the lover who lays his head at his beloved's feet in a state of inebriation is worthy of praise (b) his gesture represents complete and unconditional submission (c) in putting his head at her feet, he resembles the rose's shadow that bends towards the rose's feet (d) in the comparison of the beloved with the blossom and the drunken lover with the shadow of the blossom's bough, both the beloved and the lover are venerated, and (e) there is a sense of supplication here which is expressed through a sense of amazement at the lover's gesture.

The expression—*hariif-e siyah-mast* (heavily-drunk rival) works as a compound adjective to portray the lover as one who is just 'black drunk'. The expression *hariif* (rival) is not used here in the traditional sense to identify a rival in love, but to mark the lover himself who is his own rival and wishes to surpass his own self in his devotion to his beloved. Two other expressions—*saaya-i gul* (blossom's shadow) and *paae-gul* (blossom's base/feet)—work as mixed metaphors to represent a grandiose romantic condition. This is heightened with the magic of rhyme that creates a soulful condition of music. The verse gains its unique transcendental appeal with the auditory effect it creates, especially in the second line. It is in this context that the lover is presented as *KHush-haal* (fortunate)—that is, being drunk to the brim on the wine of love.

72

غم نہیں ہوتا ہے آزادوں کو بیش از یک نفس
برق سے کرتے ہیں روشن شمع ماتم خانہ ہم

ग़म नहीं होता है आज़ादों को बेश अज़ यक नफ़स
बर्क़ से करते हैं रौशन शम्-ए मातम-ख़ाना हम

Gham nahii.n hotaa hai aazaado.n ko besh az yak nafas
barq se karte hai.n raushan shamm-'e maatam KHaana ham

(*besh az yak nafas*—not beyond a moment;
barq—lightening;
maatam—lamentation, mourning, grieving)

The liberated ones don't grieve for more than
a moment's buzz
I lit up the lamp of my grieving abode,
just as lightening does

Human beings have infinite capacity to bear pain, as also to wage war against the outrageous fortune and release themselves from suffering. Here is a verse mythicizing man's unparalleled prowess. It works as a paean to human potential, especially of the liberated ones who emerge as noble beings. Such men do not believe in mourning and remaining in gloom even for a moment. Instead, they light the lamp of their grieving house with lightning itself which fills up the surroundings with its radiance.

There are multiple layers of interspersed meanings in this verse: (a) the noble ones negate grief and don't allow the grief to overpower them (b) such men keep their grieving abodes aglow with lightning itself, as they themselves are like lightning (c) when the mourning house acquires its glow, it sparkles with celestial light, which is far superior to the lamps lit up by human hands (d) the house here also serves as a metaphor for the bright hearts of the noble beings that negate gloom and welcome light (e) the verse clearly negates pessimism and underlines the spirit of optimism that the noble ones represent.

The adjective *aazaado.n* (the liberated ones) contains several layers of meaning. Literally, it signifies free human beings, but it stands here for the noble, the enlightened and the potentially empowered ones. They represent hope and faith which this verse is all about. Two nouns—*barq* (lightning) and *maatam KHaana* (grieving house)—cut across each other and validate the thematic burden of the verse. The idea of illuminating the lamp of the mourning house with lightning is one of the brightest examples of Ghalib's stupendous flights of imagination. This imagination is as strong as the extraordinary potential of human beings themselves. From a different literary tradition, one is reminded of Prince Hamlet's monologue in Shakespeare's *Hamlet* which highlights man's infinite capacities: 'What a piece of work is Man! how noble in reason, / how infinite in faculty ...'

73

مہرباں ہو کے بلا لو مجھے چاہو جس وقت
میں گیا وقت نہیں ہوں کہ پھر آ بھی نہ سکوں

मेहरबाँ हो के बुला लो मुझे चाहो जिस वक़्त
मैं गया वक़्त नहीं हूँ कि फिर आ भी न सकूँ

mehrbaa.n ho ke bulaa lo mujhe chaaho jis vaqt
mai.n gayaa vaqt nahii.n huu.n ke phir aa bhii na sakuu.n

Be kind and call me—whenever you wish to regain
I'm not a moment gone—that cannot come again

Kindness is one of the most prominent human virtues, but not easily experienced by everyone in life. The best human beings are necessarily kind; they share pain and impart pleasure to the sufferer. Ghalib strikes a note of sympathy for a supposed listener who is evidently in pain. Significantly enough, he persuades that listener to be kind and respond when called in times of misery. He convinces him that he is, after all, a kind human being and not like unheeding time that he cannot come back when called. Essentially, this verse celebrates kindness as the prime human virtue.

The speaker in this verse opens up different levels of meaning: (a) he speaks with humility to his addressee, as a kind human being would do (b) he asks his addressee to be kind and reciprocate with his kindness (c) the best quality of kindness is that it begets kindness (d) the speaker is unlike the cruel and unheeding time that does not ever return (e) conversely, he defines time as cruel that brings suffering to human beings (f) the speaker seems to be missing his companion, may be his beloved, who might also be missing him and needs sympathizing.

The key expression in this verse—*mehrbaa.n* (kind)—appears as a persona representing larger human sympathies. It should be rewarding to notice the interesting play on the word *vaqt* (time) used twice in the verse with two different connotations. While the first one refers to an unqualified and neutral moment of time, the second one is qualified and characterized as one that is unheeding, even cruel. The phrase *chaaho jis vaqt* (whenever you wish) further characterizes the speaker who makes an open offer without any conditions attached to it. Developing a different perspective on the beloved's possibility of being kind, Ghalib comes up with a more scathing verse that offers a comparative perspective: *nikaalaa chaahtaa hai kaam kyaa t'aano.n se tuu Ghalib / tire be-mehr kahne se vo tujh per mehrbaa.n kyu.n ho.*

74

ہم سے کھل جاؤ بوقتِ مے پرستی ایک دن
ورنہ ہم چھیڑیں گے رکھ کر عذر مستی ایک دن

हम से खुल जाओ ब-वक़्त-ए मय-परस्ती एक दिन
वर्ना हम छेड़ेंगे रख कर उज़्र-ए मस्ती एक दिन

ham se khul jaao ba-vaqt-e mai-parastii ek din
varna ham chhede.nge rakh kar 'uzr-e mastii ek din

(*mai-parastii*—the act of consuming wine;
'uzr-e mastii—excuse/pretext for teasing)

Open up to me once when we
drink together one day
Else, I'll tease you, blaming
on my frenzy, you'll see, one day

Light moments in love bring special pleasures to lovers. Moments of teasing, coaxing and cajoling have caught the attention of ghazal poets quite often, as it has engrossed Ghalib's attention in novel ways. In this uniquely amusing verse, a lover addresses his beloved, and wants her to confide in him and share her secrets while sharing a drink with him one fine day. The situation is enlivened when he says that if she does not do that, he will tease her on the pretext of his intoxication to get her secrets out, and, if that happens, she would not be able to help herself out of this situation.

This is one of Ghalib's more playful verses which makes us think that (a) the lover and the beloved are not just lover and beloved; they are jovial partners who tease each other sportingly (b) this teasing is purely for the sake of fun and not for blaming, which makes their relationship very special (c) the lover does not expect a reply nor does he get one, but his one-sided address to her turns the scene delightfully dramatic (d) this delightful drama could happen in a session of drinks alone when secrets come out naturally in the state of sheer intoxication.

The phrase *khul jaao* (open up) is an informal beckoning to share secrets which suits the funny nature of this verse. The rhyming phrases—*mai-parastii* (wine drinking) and *'uzr-e mastii* (excuse for teasing)—lighten the mood of the verse further. The expression *ek din* (one day/someday), used as *radiif* (end rhyme) in both the lines, contains two shades of implication of 'this day' when the secret has to be shared and 'that day' when she would be teased if she did not share her secrets. Above all, the phrase *mai-parastii* (literally wine worship, but otherwise the act of consuming wine) underlines their unending appetite and love for drink and sessions of drink. Ghalib's playfulness with the beloved finds another manifestation in his verse: *yaar se chheR chalii jaae Asad / gar nahii.n vasl to hasrat hii sahii.*

75

قرض کی پیتے تھے مے لیکن سمجھتے تھے کہ ہاں
رنگ لاوے گی ہماری فاقہ مستی ایک دن

क़र्ज़ की पीते थे मय लेकिन समझते थे कि हाँ
रंग लावेगी हमारी फ़ाक़ा-मस्ती एक दिन

qarz kii piite the mai lekin samajhte the ke haa.n
ra.ng laavegii hamaarii faaqa-mastii ek din

(*faaqa-mastii*—cheerfulness in adversity, blissful thirst)

I got my wine on credit, I drank
and thought, someday
My blissful thirst will bear its colours
for sure, someday

One of the prominent images in the picture gallery of the Urdu ghazal is that of the mythical drinker. He emerges as an iconic figure representing various states of his being. This is yet another verse where the sad lot of the drinker is presented with wry humour. The speaker admits that he borrowed money and drank his wine, but more importantly, he thought that his joviality in a state of adversity would surely do wonders one day. Even if he does not say what that wonder would possibly be, he suggests that his habit of drinking would show its colours in literal terms one fine day.

What are the shades of implication here, one wonders, but these points come out clearly: (a) the drinker, possibly Ghalib himself as his biographical details testify, is completely sane and not drunk at all when he says this to himself, or to his listeners (b) he enjoys his drink, as much as he enjoys his carelessness, which turns him into a reckless raconteur (c) he knew well that he would have to pay for his act one day but he chose to remain an epicurean and a blessed one even in a state of deprivation (d) he could not care less for what might happen to him someday—that is, he might be either humiliated by the creditors, or even forgiven by them considering his status (e) his attitude of carelessness turns him into some kind of an aberrant Sufi, drunk on himself and his pride.

Three phrases *ra.ng laavegii* (would bear fruit), *faaqa-mastii* (blissful thirst) and *ek din* (one day/someday) constitute the verbal design of this verse and represent its core thematic content. The first phrase is playfully ironic, but the second one suggests three things: (i) the speaker's ability to remain intoxicated even in want and keep drinking on borrowed money (ii) his habit of buying wine on borrowed money, and (iii) his looking forward to an imminent day that might come sooner or later.

76

دھول دھپا اس سراپا ناز کا شیوہ نہیں
ہم ہی کر بیٹھے تھے غالبؔ پیش دستی ایک دن

धौल-धप्पा उस सरापा-नाज़ का शेवा नहीं
हम ही कर बैठे थे ग़ालिब पेश-दस्ती एक दिन

*dhaul-dhappaa us saraapaa naaz ka sheva nahii.n
ham hii kar baiTthe the Ghalib pesh-dastii ek din*

(*dhaul-dhappaa*—mutual cuffing, thumping and slapping;
saraapaa naaz—gracefulness incarnate;
pesh-dastii—making advance, transgression)

That dainty love did not go thumping,
slapping any day
It was me who made advances
earned that treat one day

The astounding varieties of the beloved's mood and behaviour have been variously represented in the ghazal tradition. Ghalib himself is a master in portraying such situations with his seemingly juvenile, but actually clever characters. Here is once more a naughty verse, by all means. It dramatizes a funny moment in love. That beauteous being was not the one to have indulged in hitting him, Ghalib makes his lover say, but it is only he who made advances to her and got what he deserved. The element of hilarity can be hardly missed in the situation that he creates for his own embarrassment.

The verse makes interesting suggestions: (a) the lover is far from being lecherous; he is simply naughty and enjoys being so (b) his advances gave that lady the courage to punish him, the way she did (c) even while he is hit by the beloved, he treats her respectfully, like a devoted lover, and (d) he willingly puts himself in the dock for being a frisky wrongdoer that he surely appears to be.

The phrase *dhaul-dhappaa* (thumping and slapping) does not go with *saraapaa naaz* (gracefulness incarnate), but she indulges in this act against the lover only because he exceeded his limits of decency and made indecent advances and got, in return, what he deserved. In spite of this, her gracefulness remains unblemished. The most compelling phrase, however, is *pesh-dastii* (making an advance) which underlines the lover's loss of control over himself in a passionate moment and, appropriately, represents his waywardness as well as the mood of the verse.

77

ہم کو ستم عزیز ستم گر کو ہم عزیز
نا مہرباں نہیں ہے اگر مہرباں نہیں

हम को सितम अज़ीज़ सितमगर को हम अज़ीज़
ना-मेहरबाँ नहीं है अगर मेहरबाँ नहीं

ham ko sitam aziiz sitam-gar ko ham aziiz
naa-mehrbaa.n nahii.n hai agar mehrbaa.n nahii.n

(*sitam*—cruelty, tyranny, coercion, oppression;
sitamgar—cruel, tyrant, oppressor;
aziiz—dear, favourite;
naa-mehrbaa.n—unkind, harsh, mean;
mehrbaa.n—benign, malevolent, kind)

I love being oppressed; my oppressor loves me
She isn't unkind to me; if she isn't kind to me

There are certain moments in love and romance when the lover and the beloved share a pleasurable relationship, even though they coerce each other at times. Here is an exquisite portrayal of a unique relationship between the lover and the beloved. The speaker asserts that the beloved's oppression is as dear to him as he is to his oppressor. The punch lies in his richly ambiguous statement that she is not unkind to him, even if she is not kind to him.

A technically well-constructed verse like this may be appreciated in these terms: (a) the lover is quite unambiguous about his relationship with the beloved as he has developed complete affinity with her and accepts her oppression as a token of love from her (b) he does not either question, or complain, about what the beloved does to him (c) their oppressions over each other are welcome because both are basically kind to each other (d) she oppresses him because he is himself desirous of her oppression, and (e) her oppression is a sign of her kindness which implies that she is not unkind if not kind, and not unkind if kind.

Each line is a fine and delicate blend of two strands of thought that are balanced rhythmically in *ham ko sitam aziiz* (I love coercion) and *sitamgar ko ham aziiz* (I am dear to the oppressor) in the first line, and *naa-mehrbaa.n nahii.n hai* (she is not unkind) and *agar mehrbaa.n nahii.n* (if not kind) in the second line. By employing the technique of inverting ideas and playing with words, Ghalib creates a design of meaning. In this act, Ghalib grows sportive with *sitam* and *sitamgar* in the first line and *naa-mehrbaa.n* and *mehrbaa.n* in the second line. A fine craftsman and an artist of remarkable distinction, Ghalib's ingenuity lies in his witticism. On this idea of the beloved being kind or unkind, Firaq Gorakhpuri develops a clinical perspective: *husn ko ik husn hii samjhe nahii.n aur ai Firaq / mehrbaa.n na-mehrbaa.n kyaa kyaa samajh baiThe the ham*

78

نقصاں نہیں جنوں میں بلا سے ہو گھر خراب
سو گز زمیں کے بدلے بیاباں گراں نہیں

नुक़्साँ नहीं जुनूँ में बला से हो घर ख़राब
सौ गज़ ज़मीं के बदले बयाबाँ गिराँ नहीं

nuqsaa.n nahii.n junuu.n mei.n balaa se ho ghar KHaraab
sau gaz zamii.n ke badle bayabaa.n giraa.n nahii.n

(*junuu.n*—frenzy; madness;
bayaabaa.n—wilderness, desert;
giraa.n—expensive, costly)

Damn the house, lost in a lunatic frenzy, why repeal
For a hundred yards of land, wilderness is no bad deal

Spectacular imagination is one of the hallmarks of great poetry. Here is an example of how Ghalib's imagination can take a leap, and how he proposes something irrational from the worldly point of view, yet so pleasantly startling from the non-worldly perspective. The speaker makes a wild claim here and proposes that getting a larger area of land, even if that be wilderness, in lieu of a small a piece of land measuring hundred yards is not a bad deal. This idea keeps us wondering about the unusual perception he tries to develop and give us a shock of recognition.

The speaker's unusual position points towards multiple implications in the verse: (a) he hardly cares if his house is wrecked because of his frenzy, since he is getting a far bigger space in exchange for a house on a hundred yards of land (b) he has gone wild and doesn't give a damn about the consequences (c) he may be a lunatic to have such a stance, or be in a state of queer exaltation to think so irrationally (d) he relates better with nature and the freedom it provides (e) the second line which offers a reason for the speaker's wild choice also proves, quite interestingly, that he is capable of weighing his choice in terms of loss and gain, which implies that he is not in a wild state, and equally important, (f) the entire rumination of the speaker is of a philosophical nature and marks him as one who has risen above mundane considerations.

As in many other verses, Ghalib once again develops a scheme of meaning by creating an antinomy of ideas and images. He does this by juxtaposing the images of *bayaabaa.n* (wilderness) and *ghar* (home) against each other. The person who makes this irrational choice is best qualified with the word *junnuu.n* (madness), which is both a heightened state of consciousness and frenzy that Ghalib wants to underline in particular. In several of his verses, he has developed discourses on the idea of home and wilderness. Here are two examples to develop a comparative perspective: *ghar hamaaraa jo na rote bhii to viiraa.n hotaa / bahr gar bahr na hotaa to bayaabaa.n hotaa* and *ug rahaa hai dar -o diivaar se sabza Ghalib / ham bayaabaa.n mei.n hai.n aur ghar mei.n bahaar aaii hai.*

79

جہاں تیرا نقش قدم دیکھتے ہیں
خیاباں خیاباں ارم دیکھتے ہیں

जहाँ तेरा नक़्श-ए क़दम देखते हैं
ख़याबाँ ख़याबाँ इरम देखते हैं

jahaa.n teraa naqsh-e qadam dekhte hai.n
KHiyaabaa.n KHiyaabaa.n iram dekhte hai.n

(*naqsh-e-qadam*—footprints;
KHiyaabaa.n—flower-bed, garden;
iram—paradise)

Wherever I find your footprints,
I'm taken by surprise
From flowerbed to flowerbed,
I see a paradise

In ghazals, the image of the beloved's footprint is often represented as an emblematic one. Lovers adore them, idealize them, follow them and bow before them, as if in a state of romantic obeisance. The lover in this verse affirms that wherever he looks at his beloved's footprints, he sees in each one a flowerbed of paradise. Ghalib draws upon this popular image of the beloved's fabled footprints and configures it with novelty to bestow all praise on the beloved.

Two important perspectives emerge quite clearly here: (a) these are the footprints of the beloved that open up tracts of paradise before the lover (b) on the other hand, these footprints are of a divine being—say, Prophet Mohammad, the redeemer on the day of judgement—that reflect the images of the paradise (c) in both the conditions, there is a heaven that appears before the lover, and finally, (d) there is a mythicization of the lover and the beloved in two different ways which adds a rich ambiguity to the verse.

Three visual images—*naqsh-e qadam* (footprints), *KHiyaabaa.n* (garden) and *iram* (paradise)—lay out the scenic context and grandeur of the verse. They form a class of homogenous images that act as sources of delight, abundance and fulfilment for the omniscient lover, who remains perennially obliged to one who may be a lady love or a spiritual master. The word *jahaa.n* (wherever) is also significant as it encompasses all spaces and places where the sought-after persona has left the stamp of his or her feet. An amazing construction of the footprints may be seen in a verse by Siraj Aurangabadi: *naqsh-e qadam huaa huu.n mohabbat kii raah kaa / kyaa dil kushaa makaa.n hai mirii sajda-gaah kaa.*

80

بنا کر فقیروں کا ہم بھیس غالبؔ
تماشائے اہل کرم دیکھتے ہیں

बना कर फ़क़ीरों का हम भेस ग़ालिब
तमाशा-ए अहल-ए करम देखते हैं

banaa kar faqiiro.n ka ham bhes Ghalib
tamaashaa-i ahle-e karam dekhte hai.n

(*ahl-e karam*—kind person, generous ones)

I don the guise of a faqiir, Ghalib; I only observe
The games of the generous ones and their verve

The phenomenon known as the world is full of such manifestations that strongly hold the attention of keen observers. One who walks this earthly terrain even in the guise of a *faqiir* comes across both the odd and the even manifestations of God. Ghalib projects a character here who walks around in a guise, concealing his real identity. Speaking in his own voice, or that of Ghalib himself, he puts the generous people to test as he acts out a role and watches how the generous ones act out their own roles of kindness, if they choose to.

The verse offers rich possibilities of meaning: (a) the speaker is neither a beggar nor does he expect any generosity from the kind and the generous ones (b) he has donned the garb of a beggar by design only to watch how the generous ones bestow favours or how they shy away from any kind of generosity (c) this beggar is indeed a *faqiir* who is far more empowered and endowed in spiritual terms, than the supposedly kind and generous persons (d) this act on the part of the speaker underlines the difference between pretence and reality, and, in sum, (e) the *faqiir* appears as a stock figure who observes the worldly manifestations that are more of illusion than of reality.

The two lines are thickly populated with four highly impregnated words—*faqiir* (beggar), *bhes* (guise), *tamaasha* (spectacle) and *ahl-e karam* (the kind ones). While *faqiir* and *ahl-e karam* are made to stand against each other in holistic terms for their respective merits and demerits, *bhes* and *tamaasha* join hands to create a scene of pretence. Together, all these words representing characters and conditions configure a delicate balance between the absolute and non-absolute manifestations of creation. A *faqiir*, being an image of a far superior entity as reflected in Ghalib's verse here, finds a closer replica in a verse by Seemab Akbarabadi as well: *KHud biin-o KHud shanaas milaa KHud numaa milaa / insaa.n ke bhes mei.n mujhe aksar KHudaa milaa.*

81

میں اور حظ وصل خدا ساز بات ہے
جاں نذر دینی بھول گیا اضطراب میں

मैं और हज़्ज़-ए वस्ल ख़ुदा-साज़ बात है
जाँ नज़्र देनी भूल गया इज़्तिराब में

mai.n aur hazz-e vasl KHudaa saaz-baat hai
jaa.n nazr denii bhuul gayaa iztiraab mei.n

(*h*azz-e vasl—joy of union;
vasl—union;
KHudaa-saaz—God's gift;
nazr—offering;
iztiraab—restlessness, perplexity)

Me and the joy of union! that's a gift of God, if at all
I was in a flurry; I forgot to offer my life, if at all

The idealization of the beloved to the point of exaggeration is not uncommon in the ghazal tradition. However, only those verses that demand a willing suspension of disbelief in Coleridgean terms stand out with their meaningfulness and appeal. The speaker's sense of gratitude is too apparent here. He shows a sense of fulfilment as God has been kind to him in bringing him to cross the line of separation and be in union with his beloved. He is thus in such a state of excitement that he forgets offering his life to the beloved in gratitude, but he does not hesitate to admit this in all frankness.

What are the possible interpretations of this unusual verse, one wonders, but justifiably these: (a) the speaker did not consider himself lucky enough to be in union with the beloved (b) if he had his union with the beloved, it was surely a gift from God to the lover as the beloved was not too kind and condescending to him (c) his sense of excitement is so deep that it drove him out of his senses and he could not thank her enough, and (d) what he wished to offer to her in benediction and missed doing so was his life itself, which, in any case, was devoted to her (e) the idea of offering life to the beloved in gratitude is hardly short of poetic exaggeration, but it imparts certain poetic credibility to the verse.

The curious combination of consequential nouns—*hazz* (joy), *vasl* (union), *nazr* (offer) and *iztiraab* (restlessness)—spell out the essential spirit of the verse. *Vasl* is qualified by *hazz* and *nazr* by *iztiraab*. These conditions typically characterize the lover. It is interesting to note that *nazr*, which is usually associated with religious or ritualistic offering or sacrifice, is well appropriated here in a romantic context. This is exceptionally impactful as it portrays the lover in a new role of a sacrificial being in relationship with the beloved. The idea of union being so precious and dear also drives the fear of its loss which Ghalib expresses brilliantly in another verse to present a study in contrast: *vasl mei.n hijr kaa Dar yaad aayaa / 'ain jannat mei.n saqar yaad aayaa.*

82

وہ سحر مدعا طلبی میں نہ کام آئے
جس سحر سے سفینہ رواں ہو سراب میں

वो सेहर मुद्दआ-तलबी में न काम आए
जिस सेहर से सफ़ीना रवाँ हो सराब में

*vo sehr mudda'aa-talabii mei.n na kaam aae
jis sehr se safiina ravaa.n ho saraab mei.n*

(*sehr*—magic, enchantment;
mudda'aa-talabii—looking for the claimant, plaintiff;
safiina—vessel, boat;
ravaa.n—flowing, fluent;
saraab—mirage, illusion)

May not that magic be of use
in making a plea for a gain
The magic that makes the vessel float in
the mirage yet again

Some men are endowed with magical powers. They may use those powers to seek their aim and satisfy themselves, but they must be critical enough about how to use them and for what purpose. A master in implicating intentions in highly imaginative ways, Ghalib makes a plea here that there is a magic which may be used to seek a favour of any kind. However, it is better not to use it for mean purposes but for better ones like making the vessel float in a mirage, which in itself is no less than a magical phenomenon.

The complexity of this verse may be negotiated with reference to these points: (a) it must be some magic that makes things happen both in love and life (b) this magic should not be used merely to seek a favour or to get a wish fulfilled in love (c) instead, that magic should be used to make a vessel float in a mirage—that is, to achieve the seemingly impossible (d) this implies that love is a mirage and it is not possible to make a vessel float in a mirage without magic, and (e) the lover wants to sail forth in love in magical ways which will naturally lead towards the fulfilment of all desires.

The key word *sehr* (magic) used twice in the verse acquires its real character in the second line and is far superior in the volume of meaning to the one used in the first line. The two other words, *safiina* (vessel) and *saraab* (mirage), symbolize love and illusion respectively. Even while they deny each other, the magic of love may turn them friendly. to help the vessel of love float in the mirage of lovelessness.

83

رو میں ہے رخش عمر کہاں دیکھیے تھمے
نے ہاتھ باگ پر ہے نہ پا ہے رکاب میں

रौ में है रख़्श-ए उम्र कहाँ देखिए थमे
ने हाथ बाग पर है न पा है रिकाब में

rau mei.n hai raKHsh-e 'umr kahaa.n dekhiye thame
ne haath baag per hai na paa hai rakaab mei.n

(raKHsh—horse, stallion;
baag—bridle, reins;
rakaab—stirrup, pedal)

The stallion of time and age fares fast ahead,
see where it stops
Neither hands on the reins nor feet on the pedals
to check the hops

Movement is the order of time that rolls out in terms of past, present and future. Man, a subject to time, knows not where his movement will stop as the Marvellian 'time's winged chariot' is on the move even while the rider does not have his hands on the reins and feet in the pedals. Here is yet another philosophical discourse on human life which is in a continuous state of flux and flow. Human beings have set life's stallion free to run its course and there is an uncertainty about when it would stop and what it would possibly bring to human beings.

The prominent implications of this verse include: (a) life's stallion runs galloping; it knows no stopping even as the rider risks his life without clasping the reins and holding on to the pedals (b) the rider is either unable or unwilling, powerless or helpless, to control its speed and chooses to put his life to risk (c) life is characterized by speed but also by a perilous present and an uncertain future for the rider (d) importantly, the rider does not emerge here as a controlling figure, but is presented only as one who is subject to the speed of life's stallion, and finally, (e) life, being a larger reality, is greater than man who lives this life, but remains subservient to it.

Ghalib establishes his discourse on life in terms of three metaphors—*raKHsh* (stallion), representing speed, and *baag* (reins) and *rakaab* (pedal),—symbolizing control. The idiomatic expression *kahaa.n dekhiye thame* (see where it stops) underlines a certain sense of wonder and the uncertainty about life's end. The verse is a metaphysical exposé on life and man, and the reality of their seemingly intimate relationship that proves trivial at the end. A variation on this theme of speed may be seen in another verse by Ghalib: *'umr harchand ke hai barq-KHaraam / dil ke KHuu.n karne kii fursat hii sahii.*

84

اصل شہود و شاہد و مشہود ایک ہے
حیراں ہوں پھر مشاہدہ ہے کس حساب میں

अस्ल-ए शुहूद-ओ-शाहिद-ओ-मश्हूद एक है
हैराँ हूँ फिर मुशाहदा है किस हिसाब में

asl-e shuhuud-o shaahid-o mash'huud ek hai
hairaa.n huu.n phir mushaahada hai kis hisaab mei.n

(*asl-e shuhuud*—reality of being present/witnessed/seen;
shaahid—eyewitness, observer, seer;
mash'huud—witnessed, observed, seen;
mushaahada—observation, witnessing/act of witnessing)

The reality of the being, the seer and the seen
are one, no doubt
I am thus amazed; what is this
seeing and the seen all about

The essence of the phenomenon, the seer and the seen are three different manifestations of one reality; although they have had different identities. Rising up and understanding this reality is too demanding and it keeps man challenged. Such metaphysical concerns figure in all literatures and literary traditions. Ghalib, who often develops philosophical discourses around these issues with exceptional skill, engages with these matters in this verse of a purely philosophical complexion. It underlines the reality of witnessing, the witness and the witnessed, and engages with the mystery of creation and man's ability, or inability, to unravel it.

The discourse projected here may be appreciated in these terms: (a) there are three major references here—the essence of being, the witness himself and the reality of what is witnessed (b) all three represent only one entity who is behind all the creations (c) that one entity has kept his creation mysteriously enfolded only to convey that all mysteries are not for human beings to unravel (d) all observations and all witnesses by human beings are thus of little value, but (e) as human beings are born as eternal questers, they will keep their quest going.

Four heavily sibilant sounds emanating from the words *shuhuud* (essence of witness), *shaahid* (witness), *mash'huud* (witnessed) and *mushaahada* (witnessing/act of witnessing) create an auditory condition in the verse. Making distinctions among them is as demanding as realizing that all these cumulatively point towards one entity, the omnipotent God, or Brahma, who is the creator of all. Man's inability to distinguish the real from the unreal is most appropriately expressed in *hairaa.n huu.n* (I wonder) that creates a sense of amazement and sorts out the intricacy of meaning to help us arrive at a point of resolution. It is pertinent to remember how Imam Bakhsh Nasikh also responds to the problematic of witness and witnessing in one of his verses: *sivaae ahl-e suKHan ho mushaahada kis ko / nihaa.n hai shaahid-e m'anii suKHan ke parde mei.n.*

85

ہے غیب غیب جس کو سمجھتے ہیں ہم شہود
ہیں خواب میں ہنوز جو جاگے ہیں خواب میں

है ग़ैब-ए ग़ैब जिस को समझते हैं हम शुहूद
हैं ख़्वाब में हुनूज़ जो जागे हैं ख़्वाब में

hai GHaib-e GHaib jis ko samajhte hai.n ham shuhuud
hai.n KHvaab mei.n hanuuz jo jaage hai.n KHvaab mei.n

(*GHaib-e Ghaib*—absent, unseen, unknown;
shuhuud—being present, witnessed, seen;
hanuuz—still, so far, as yet)

What we know as revealed
is truly hidden within a hiding;
When awake, I am still in a dream,
still abiding

The human dilemma to distinguish between illusion and reality, and the inability to do so, has been a subject of sermons, metaphysical treatises and literary texts. Here is a verse of a philosophical nature yet again which addresses these intellectual complexities with reference to the distinction between the real, the supposedly real, and the surreal. It also asserts that man leads his life in the states of dreaming and non-dreaming, while trying to apprehend the real which evades man quite often.

Playing sportingly with his words, Ghalib creates complex levels of meaning through his speaker: (a) what we consider as the real and the seen is indeed hidden and absent (b) we are still in a state of dreaming while we have woken up in a dream, which is yet another manifestation of a life lived (c) images and ideas appear involuntarily in dreams and reflect the states of the subconscious, since being in a state of a dream is being concealed within concealment (d) in both the states of dreaming and being awake within a dream, it is the shadow of the divine that remains all-pervasive, and (e) man spends his life in dreaming and dreaming within a dream, but without ever catching the glimpse of the real, which indeed is the divine entity.

The phrase *Ghaib-e GHaib* (unseen) is Ghalib's most creative construction to double-stress the condition of absence and hiding. The condition of being in a dream, even while awake in a dream, appears amusing first, but turns out to be a philosophical condition of being which reflects richly upon the vitality of Ghalib's creative imagination.

86

حیراں ہوں دل کو روؤں کہ پیٹوں جگر کو میں
مقدور ہو تو ساتھ رکھوں نوحہ گر کو میں

हैराँ हूँ दिल को रोऊँ कि पीटूँ जिगर को मैं
मक़दूर हो तो साथ रखूँ नौहा-गर को मैं

hairaa.n huu.n dil ko ro'uu.n ke piiTuu.n jigar ko mai.n
maqduur ho to saath rakhuu.n nauha-gar ko mai.n

(*maqduur*—means, resources, power, authority;
nauha-gar—mourner, lamenter, griever)

Pity my heart or mourn over it;
I wonder what to do
If possible, I would keep a lamenter;
by my side, too

How do we address and sustain our sorrows and sufferings? This perpetual question has ever remained at the root of man's consciousness. Too oppressed by the miseries of life, the speaker knows not whether he should cry for his heart. The heart that bears and carries all human griefs, are ultimately kept and sustained by the grieving man himself. In order to negotiate with his pain and suffering, the speaker believes that it would help a man to have a mourner by his side to wail for his losses, but he wonders if he could possibly have one for himself.

The underlying threads of meaning in this apparently straight narrative of suffering may be traced as follows: (a) bearing pain all by oneself is much too demanding and well-nigh impossible for man (b) the loss of heart, which is the home of all dreams, desires and disappointments, is the loss of spirit and life force, and it can be mourned only with sympathizers and mourners around (c) mourners offer psychological support even if they do so only ritually (d) the speaker remorsefully wonders if he may really have a mourner with himself to sustain him through all his miseries (e) the verse also substantiates a psychological truism that human beings need words of solace in times of misery, which only true sympathizers and mourners provide.

Dil and *jigar*, used frequently in Urdu romantic poetry, stand for heart which is mostly in a state of distress. Ghalib also appropriates the proverbial expression of *ronaa piitnaa* (crying and mourning), but it does not sound like a cliché as he supplements it with another idea of having a *nauha-gar* (mourner) by his side in the next line which adds a dramatic dimension to his suffering. Further, the figure of the *nauha-gar* also brings to mind the institution of *nauha-garii* (reciting elegies/dirges) which is meant to share grief and seek solace.

87

جانا پڑا رقیب کے در پر ہزار بار
اے کاش جانتا نہ ترے رہگزر کو میں

जाना पड़ा रक़ीब के दर पर हज़ार बार
ऐ काश जानता न तिरे रह-गुज़र को मैं

*jaanaa paRaa raqiib ke dar per hazaar baar
ai kaash jaantaa na tire rahguzar ko mai.n*

(*raqiib*—rival, competitor, adversary;
rahguzar—path, way, passage)

A thousand times, I had to go to my rival's door
I wish I had not known the way to you, I abhor

Rivals are archetypal figures in the dramatis personae of Urdu ghazals. They enliven the plot of love and make it move in strange directions. Between the lover and the rival is the beloved, who watches both of them pursuing their interests that clearly clash with each other. Ghalib capitalizes upon this tripartite plot of the Urdu ghazal and presents a typical situation in love, where the lover, the rival and the beloved remain in an odd and helplessly inseparable relationship together. Pathetically, the lover emerges as a greater sufferer than the two others.

This verse is richly ambiguous and it has several implications: (a) the lover visited the rival's house because the beloved used to go there, and this irked and worried him (b) the rival visited the beloved's house, so the lover had to go there because that, too, was worrying for him (c) the rival was at the beloved's house, so visiting her was visiting a rival's house, which posed a queer situation and appeared unacceptable to him (d) in all these situations, it was the lover who suffered and who is narrating his strange plight here, and (e) there is a sense of exasperation in the lover, who seems to consider it bad luck to have known and loved her since this love brought him more of suffering than pleasure.

The *raqiib* (rival) and his *dar* (door), along with the *rahguzar* (way), symbolize alien and hostile zones for the lover. The expression *ai kaash* (I wish) echoes the lover's sentiments of disappointment and sense of failure. These expressions together determine the mood of the verse and reflect the lover's sense of despair. For a different treatment of this experience, we may refer to a fascinating verse by Momin Khan Momin: *us naqsh-e paa ke sajde ne kyaa kyaa kiyaa zaliil / mai.n kuucha-i raqiib mei.n bhii sark e bal gayaa.*

88

چلتا ہوں تھوڑی دور ہر اک تیزرو کے ساتھ
پہچانتا نہیں ہوں ابھی راہ بر کو میں

चलता हूँ थोड़ी दूर हर इक तेज़-रौ के साथ
पहचानता नहीं हूँ अभी राह-बर को मैं

chaltaa huu.n thoRii duur har ik tez-rau ke saath
pahchaantaa nahii.n huu.n abhii raahbar ko mai.n

(*tez-rau*—fast traveller;
raahbar—path finder, guide, conductor)

With every swift mover, a few steps I sweat
I do not recognize my real guide, yet

If life is a journey and man a traveller, he must seek a guide to lead and help him reach his destination. The big philosophical question, however, is whether there is a guide anywhere. Ghalib's speaker makes an unassuming statement here about how one may fare forward in the journey of life. He confesses that he walks a short distance with every fast-moving traveller, considering him to be the guide, but he still does not know who the real guide is. As such, he moves on, but without a real guide and a destination in sight, which makes his travelling a challenge.

We may locate the possible implications of this verse as follows: (a) there are three persons involved here—while the fast movers and the wayfarer are projected in real terms, the real guide remains invisible (b) the wayfarer chooses to walk with the fast-moving persons, one after another, thinking they must be the guides to his destination (c) after walking a short distance, he realizes that those fast movers may indeed be the chasers of their selfish goals on the path of life, which does not make them guides (d) this means, by implication, that even one who walks with patience and care, without moving fast, could possibly be the real guide (e) it also implies that it is not easy to find a guide and that every traveller has to find a guide on his own, and (f) that every traveller on the path of life needs to distinguish between appearance and reality to be able to recognize the real guide who may help them arrive safely at a destination.

Ghalib seems to institutionalize the visible *tez-rau* (fast traveller), the invisible *raahbar* (guide) and the actual wayfarer, who is projected as a keen but unassuming commentator on the scene. The commentator, being naïve enough, is not yet able to recognize the real guide. The verse must be appreciated as a deft construction of a situation through institutionalized symbols to unravel life as a journey, the traveller as an explorer and the guide as an elusive figure whose presence or absence makes all the difference. The traveller reminds us of the quintessential traveller in Robert Frost's poem 'Stopping by Woods on a Snowy Evening', who walks at his own pace, and meditates on the mysteries of life and death in his intensely individual way.

89

قطرہ اپنا بھی حقیقت میں ہے دریا لیکن
ہم کو تقلید تنک ظرفی منصور نہیں

क़तरा अपना भी हक़ीक़त में है दरिया लेकिन
हम को तक़लीद-ए तुनुक-ज़फ़ीं-ए मंसूर नहीं

qatra apnaa bhii haqiiqat mei.n hai dariyaa lekin
ham ko taqliid-e tunuk-zarfii-i Mansur nahii.n

(*haqiiqat*—reality;
taqliid—toeing, following, conformity;
tunuk-zarfii—irritable nature, of small capacity)

My drop, in reality, is a river, but I must say
I cannot ever accept toeing Mansur's edgy way

Man, being man, is often possessed by a sense of superiority. He places himself on a high pedestal and thinks of himself as the prime mover (who believes that everything moves because of them). Ghalib's speaker defines that self-proclaiming man, who proudly thinks that if he holds a drop in his hand, he actually holds the river. His pride takes him to an exalted state but he cannot follow Mansur Al-Hallaj who chanted *Ana-al Haq* (I am the truth/I am the God) and was punished by hanging for being a heretic.

Drawing upon the allusion of Mansur, Ghalib unravels deeper reams of meaning: (a) the speaker asserts that his own drop, an incarnation of his self, is a river in reality (b) he does not say so in personal terms by using 'I' but by using an impersonal term 'we' (c) this imparts a holistic identity to him and adds a mystical halo around his existence quite unlike Mansur, who, instead of appreciating the larger and the ultimate reality, asserted his own superiority by proclaiming that he was the ultimate mover, the real God (d) by doing so, the speaker emerges as an entity of far greater worth who can visualize the entire world through its tiny constituents, than proclaim himself to be the driving force behind everything, without appreciating the reality of the phenomenon.

The word *haqiiqat* (reality) in the first line incorporates the core message of this verse through the tiniest manifestation of *qatra* (drop). This brings us to the Blakean mystic vision of seeing the 'world in a grain of sand/ and a heaven in a wild flower'. The adjective *tunuk-zarfii* (irritability of human nature) characterizes Mansur's lack of a larger vision which cannot lead anyone to his *taqliid* (toeing). This suggests that merely following a line without a penetrative understanding of the phenomenon is meaningless. It is this philosophical aura that Ghalib creates around this verse, which distinguishes it prominently. Another representation of Mansur and his *An-al Haq* may also be seen in Sheikh Zahuruddin Hatim's verse: *An-al Haq kii haqiiqat ko jo ho Mansur so jaane / ke us ko aasmaa.n chaRne se chaRnaa daar behtar thaa.*

90

یہ ہم جو ہجر میں دیوار و در کو دیکھتے ہیں
کبھی صبا کو کبھی نامہ بر کو دیکھتے ہیں

ये हम जो हिज्र में दीवार-ओ-दर को देखते हैं
कभी सबा को कभी नामा-बर को देखते हैं

ye ham jo hijr mei.n diivaar-o dar ko dekhte hai.n
kabhii sabaa ko kabhii naamaa-bar ko dekkhte hai.n

(*hijr*—separation;
dar—door;
sabaa—breeze;
naamaa-bar—messenger)

In separation, I look at the walls and doors,
that you may see
Now the breeze, now the messenger, is what
I see; you may see

Despair in love can sometimes bring unbearable pain to the lover. Ghalib presents here the image of a despaired lover who wears a vacant look and lingers in a state of complete desolation. He portrays this lover as one who has suffered in separation from his beloved and needs to be comforted with a word from the beloved, albeit through a messenger. As he is disappointed, he can only stare vacantly and silently at the walls and doors, watch the breeze blowing, and wait for the messenger who might be on his way to him.

The portrayal of separation and the resultant despair is replete with many suggestions: (a) separation does not make the lover only lonely and silent; it drives him to brooding (b) he looks at the door and the walls with philosophical detachment, and finds himself in a state of despair (c) his despair is heightened further because neither the breeze nor the messenger bring any news from the beloved (d) this state of despair, disappointment and silence turns into a perpetual condition for him (e) he partakes in, as if, the purity and holiness of silence, which Rumi believes takes man to the core of life and helps him listen to it in the absence of the beloved (f) this despair and silence of the speaker could have been ruptured with the presence of the beloved and brought him to experience the bliss of love which does not happen here.

Hijr (separation), being a stock condition of the archetypal lover in the ghazal, is constructed here with the absence of the beloved, but more importantly with the four stock symbols—*diivaar* (wall), *dar* (door), *sabaa* (breeze) and *naamaa-bar* (messenger)— that are befittingly characterized by silence. Silence, as such, emerges as the condition with which the lover negotiates, but only in his state of misery. Mir Taqi Mir's personalized depiction of this experience is worth attention in this verse by him: *be-qaraarii jo koii dekhe hai so kahtaa hai / kuchh to hai Mir jo ik dam tujhe aaraam nahii.n*

91

وہ آئے گھر میں ہمارے خدا کی قدرت ہے
کبھی ہم ان کو کبھی اپنے گھر کو دیکھتے ہیں

वो आए घर में हमारे ख़ुदा की क़ुदरत है
कभी हम उन को कभी अपने घर को देखते हैं

vo aae ghar mei.n hamaare KHudaa kii qudrat hai
kabhii ham un ko kabhii apne ghar ko dekhte hai.n

(*qudrat*—power, divine magic)

That's God's command indeed; she's here at my abode
Well, I look at her now, now at my humble abode

The coming of the beloved to the lover's home is a matter of celebration for the lover. It does not, however, happen as often as desired. Ghalib's lover, too, expects the arrival of his beloved to his abode. Although he never expected it to happen, it did happen one fine day. So, he looks like a picture of amazement and wonders if what he sees is real indeed. He presupposes in this process that he is too insignificant to expect such a surprising thing to happen, but since this has happened, he finds himself in a state of exaltation.

Here are the possible suggestions that this verse makes to the reader: (a) it must be divine power that brings the beloved to the lover's abode (b) on her unexpected arrival, he looks at her now, now at his abode both of which are real but appear like fantasy to him in this moment of exaltation (c) the lover is too modest as he thinks that she is too extraordinary to have thought of coming to him (d) he also wonders whether this is she who has come to him or is it his humble abode where she has come, and in sum, (e) there is a unique pleasure writ large on his face, but it also reflects his surprise and disbelief which allegorizes the beloved and turns her into an icon of love.

The word *qudrat* has multiple meanings of power, divine magic, authority, control, command and prowess. Generally used to represent divine power, Ghalib appropriates this word here, to his great advantage, in the romantic context of this verse and considers her coming to his abode as a result of divine intervention. By portraying the condition of a lonely lover in this manner, Ghalib imparts a different character to this word which fills the verse with pleasant surprise for the reader.

92

نظر لگے نہ کہیں اس کے دست و بازو کو
یہ لوگ کیوں مرے زخم جگر کو دیکھتے ہیں

नज़र लगे न कहीं उस के दस्त-ओ-बाज़ू को
ये लोग क्यूँ मिरे ज़ख़्म-ए जिगर को देखते हैं

nazar lage na kahii.n us ke dast-o-baazuu ko
ye log kyu.n mere zaKHm-e jigar ko dekhte hai.n

(*dast-o-baazuu*—hands and shoulders, strength of arm)

On her hands and shoulders,
may no evil look be cast
Why do these people look
at my heart's wounds, aghast

Those in love always wish the best for their beloveds. Ghalib's lover in this verse is one of a kind, who expresses his deep concern and commitment to the beloved. His heart has had wounds and he has suffered much, but he does not want the beloved to be blamed for whatever has happened to him.

The lover's sentiments for the beloved have these underpinnings that enrich the verse: (a) the lover accepts that he has had wounds, but wonders why should people think that the beloved has caused them (b) he artfully conceals his suffering only to save her from any blaming or embarrassment (c) he does this because she is also the one who brings the pleasures of love to him, even in his suffering (d) this is why he prays that no evil eye should fall on her or her hands and arms that are traditionally known for inflicting injuries, and, in this manner (e) he turns the beloved into a fabled being.

Ghalib appropriates a proverb—*nazar lage na* (may no evil eye be cast)—and uses it in a poetic context to make it more appealing to the common imagination. Another expression—*dast-o baazuu* (hands and shoulders)—represents the agents of injury, but they also appear as the soothing ones here, which makes the lover pray that no evil eyes may ever fall on her or her hands and arms.

93

قید ہستی سے رہائی معلوم
اشک کو بے سر و پا باندھتے ہیں

क़ैद-ए हस्ती से रिहाई मालूम
अश्क को बे सर-ओ-पा बांधते हैं

qaid-e hastii se rihaaii m'aaluum
ashk ko be-sar-o paa baa.ndhte hain

(*ashk*—tears;
be-sar-o paa—helpless, baseless)

No release from the prison of life, I know, none
In none of the saner ways, I bind my tears, none

Both life and death are realities that balance against each other. Once life is awarded to man, it must reach its end in death. Ghalib represents this idea in a far more creative manner and turns the idea of death from abstraction to reality. There is no release from the bonds of life before one reaches the destined moment of death, his speaker asserts firmly, but he also adds that as long as that does not happen, one has to shed tears without an end and without any excuse.

Complicated layers of meaning can be marked here: (a) existence is broadly viewed and problematized as three periods of pre-existence, existence and post-existence (b) human predicament is marked by eternal suffering in all the three stages of existence (c) there is no escape from any of them, as one succeeds the other (d) since pain has an eternal presence in all the stages, man ever remains powerless and suffers only helplessly (e) man, as such, has to sustain his predicament without any chance of deliverance.

There is a clear tinge of irony in *m'aaluum* (knowing), which actually implies that there is no release from the constraints of existence. The most creative expression, *be sar-o paa baa.ndhte hai.n* (binding in no saner way possible), does not literally mean the act of binding tears (which does not make any sense), but it implies doing something only helplessly where the act of making an effort itself is highlighted.

94

اہل تدبیر کی واماندگیاں
آبلوں پر بھی حنا باندھتے ہیں

अहल-ए तदबीर की वा-मांदगियाँ
आबलों पर भी हिना बाँधते हैं

ahl-e tadbiir kii vaamaa.ndgiiyaa.n
aablo.n per bhii hinaa baa.ndhte hai.n

(*ahl-e tadbiir*—resourceful person;
vaamaa.ndgii—lagging behind, weary, fatigued;
aabla—blister)

Ah, the ingenious beings, their weary ways
With henna, they bind the blisters, and amaze

Man is born resourceful, but he sometimes fails in achieving his goal, in spite of all his resourcefulness. Ghalib speaks on behalf of all those who experience this failure. Their spirit is eulogized subsequently as they make efforts to live their lives with optimism. This is like applying henna even on blisters, which hides the real colour of blisters and supposedly offers relief, but that does not, in any case, alleviate his suffering.

In a broad commentary on the human predicament, this verse suggests that: (a) although man is created in the image of God, he is pitiably incapacitated in struggling against what is already scripted for him (b) in spite of this, man considers himself highly resourceful and makes all efforts for redressal (c) he does not accept his failure and goes even to the extent of feigning—that is, applying henna on blisters (d) this is essentially an act of pretension to hide his inability and negate the divine design (e) as opposed to this, and by implication, are the lovers, or those people charged with passion, who walk thorny paths with blisters on their soles and reach their goals ultimately.

Two expressions—*ahl-e tadbiir* (resourceful person) and *vaamaa.ndgii* (weariness)—draw our attention to two incompatible conditions. The fact that the resourceful person is fatigued is ironical. His act of applying henna on blisters underlines his pretentious nature. This is well brought out by another equally powerful expression— *hinaa baa.ndhte hai.n* (bind henna on blisters)—used with a touch of creativity. This distinguishes Ghalib as a master who could refine and define his diction to suit the pithy and precise space of the ghazal.

95

دائم پڑا ہوا ترے در پر نہیں ہوں میں
خاک ایسی زندگی پہ کہ پتھر نہیں ہوں میں

दाइम पड़ा हुआ तिरे दर पर नहीं हूँ मैं
ख़ाक ऐसी ज़िंदगी पे कि पत्थर नहीं हूँ मैं

daaim paRaa huaa tire dar per nahii.n huu.n mai.n
KHaak aisii zindagii pe ke pathhar nahii.n huu.n mai.n

(*daaim*—permanent, perpetual, eternal;
dar—door, doorstep, doorway)

Alas, I'm not lying at your doorsteps, for ever
Damn this life, I'm not even a stone, for ever

Human desires find strange manifestations and they appear incredible quite often. These desires turn stranger in the case of lovers pining endlessly for their beloveds. Here is a first-person narrative of Ghalib's lover, who wishes, strangely enough, to be a stone lying at the beloved's doorstep. Had he been in such a state, he ruminates, he would be near her all the time—even as a lifeless object, which he already is in separation from her.

There are fascinating layers of meaning hidden in the lover's expostulation: (a) had he been a stone lying at his beloved's doorstep, he would kiss her feet at every exit and entry (b) a stone is lifeless but her touch would infuse life into it (c) he would be trampled by her feet when she moved in and out, which is the lover's fate in any case (d) lying unattended at a spot creates the picture of a *faqiir* who cares little for whatever goes around, but remains steadfast in his commitment, and sadly, (e) in spite of being a human, and a kind and a true lover, he has no access to her quarters.

The real charm of this verse lies in the word *daaim* (permanently), which represents a condition of perpetuity that the lover desires to be in for all times. Further, the inability or impossibility of being in that condition takes him to curse his own self, which could not have been expressed better than in the phrase *KHaak aisii zindagii pe* (may such a life be damned).

96

کیوں گردش مدام سے گھبرا نہ جائے دل
انسان ہوں پیالہ و ساغر نہیں ہوں میں

क्यूँ गर्दिश-ए मुदाम से घबरा न जाए दिल
इंसान हूँ पियाला-ओ-साग़र नहीं हूँ मैं

kyu.n gardish-e-mudaam se ghabraa na jaae dil
insaan huu.n pyaala-o saaGhar nahii.n huu.n mai.n

(*gardish*—circulation, rotation, vicissitude;
mudaam—eternal, perpetual, continual;
saaGhar—cup, bowl, goblet)

Why shouldn't my heart be upset
with this endless swirl, forever
I am a human, not a wine cup,
or a cask, forever

Man is a social being and gregarious by nature. Living a perpetually monotonous life makes him sick. Ghalib's speaker finds himself in a state of despair and expresses his condition with a rhetorical question as to why a man should not get tired of negotiating with this endless monotony. He justifies himself by asserting that he is a human being after all, not a wine-cup that remains in perpetual circulation to please others and remain neglected later.

We may decode the speaker's confessional statement in these terms: (a) being in an eternal state of playing stereotypical roles, he is tired of the mundane ways of his life (b) a wine-cup that moves from person to person and lip to lip is not liked for what it is but what it contains (c) the wine-cup is lifeless, but the speaker is a human being who cannot be used for a given purpose and set aside like the wine-cup (d) there is a sense of annoyance and frustration since he cannot enjoy his freedom and his status as a human being, and ultimately, (e) the speaker indirectly and sardonically comments on the futility of his existence and the improbability of bettering his prospects, which is a philosophical exposé on his life in a broader perspective (f) this sense of futility is a hallmark of modernist literature, and reminds of the works by Samuel Beckett and Albert Camus in the Western literary tradition.

The spirit of this verse is well captured in the phrase *gardish-e mudaam* (constant circulation), which characterizes the kind of monotonous life the speaker is subjected to live. In addition, the constant circulation of *pyaala* (cup) and *saaGhar* (goblet), which act as two visual similes, adequately represent the tedium of his life and add strength to the verse.

97

یارب زمانہ مجھ کو مٹاتا ہے کس لیے
لوحِ جہاں پہ حرفِ مکرر نہیں ہوں میں

या-रब ज़माना मुझ को मिटाता है किस लिए
लौह-ए जहाँ पे हर्फ़-ए मुकर्रर नहीं हूँ मैं

yaa Rab zamaana mujh ko miTaataa hai kis liye
lauh-e jahaa.n pe harf-e mukarrar nahii.n huu.n mai.n

(*lauh-e jahaa.n*—world's tablet/plant/ board;
harf-e mukarrar—repeated or recurring word)

O God, why should the world rub me out
from my base
I'm not a repeated word on the world's tablet,
why erase

Perishing into oblivion is the ultimate destiny of a man who prospered in life, as also of one who lived but only marginally. This is one of Ghalib's many questioning verses, where his speaker addresses God directly to ask why does the world want to erase him from the earth's tablet. He submits that he is not a script, after all, that is written in repetition, but he lives only in his individual image which is ephemeral in any case. As such he, too, would have to perish like others with the individual mark of his individuality.

Now, consider the suggestions that the speaker makes here: (a) he marks two states of human existence that comprise here and hereafter (b) speaking for the larger entity of man, he argues that time should not erase his name from the world's tablet as he is not a word that deserves erasing (c) since life here is purely ephemeral, erasing a name would amount to erasing life itself (d) human beings have to bear the world's cruelties, in spite of all their abilities, and face the threats of erasure (e) the relationship between life here and hereafter is essentially adversarial, which suggests that there is no ultimate script that the world here can offer to the world hereafter, and finally, (f) the speaker is qualified here as a seeker of truth through the question he asks, which is too often discoursed in the Persian Sufi poetry of Rumi, Hafez, Saadi and Attar.

The sense of entreaty in the phrase *yaa Rab* (O God!) is a passionate plea which carries the real spirit of the verse. The word *harf* (letter) represents the idea of a script which is life itself in symbolic terms and the expression *harf-e mukarrar* (repeated letter) represents life's continuity in a cycle.

98

غالبؔ وظیفہ خوار ہو دو شاہ کو دعا
وہ دن گئے کہ کہتے تھے نوکر نہیں ہوں میں

ग़ालिब वज़ीफ़ा-ख़्वार हो दो शाह को दुआ
वो दिन गए जो कहते थे नौकर नहीं हूँ मैं

Ghalib vaziifa-KHvaar ho do shaah ko du'aa
vo din gae ke kehte thhe naukar nahii.n huu.n mai.n

(*vaziifa-KHvaar*—pensioner, scholarship holder)

Bless the emperor, Ghalib;
you are a pensioner now
Gone are the days you said
I'm not there to serve or bow

Pride sustains man and enriches him as a human being. This pride is, however, subject to certain negotiations at times. In this self-reflective verse, Ghalib uses the first-person narrative to talk of his baffling personality. May the emperor stay blessed, he asserts unreservedly, since he is indebted to him as a pensioner now. He admits frankly, and without remorse, that gone are the days when he took pride in not being at anyone's service, as he is now. Pitiably enough, there is much more that remains unsaid in this account of his self.

The layers of implication in this verse are interesting to take note of: (a) his statement is clearly double-edged as he expresses his gratitude to the emperor, on the one hand, but also comments on his own deprivation of independence, on the other (c) he does not express his gratitude only, he also blesses the emperor which shows his total allegiance to him (d) he confesses, but only in a quizzical and ironical manner, that he is no longer as proud of himself as ever—that is, after his affiliation with the royalty (e) this clearly implies that he is now a servant and a subject of the emperor at the cost of his ego, in which he notoriously took pride all his life, and finally, (f) he expresses a sense of his ironical pride, on the one hand, as well as his feigned individuality, on the other.

There are two expressions—*vaziifa-KHvaar* (pensioner) and *naukar* (servant)—that are closely synonymous and self-identificatory. The ironical turn in the verse, however, comes with the phrase *vo din gae* (gone are the days), which reflects on his proud past and spells out his servile present when he is at the service of the emperor.

99

سب کہاں کچھ لالہ و گل میں نمایاں ہو گئیں
خاک میں کیا صورتیں ہوں گی کہ پنہاں ہو گئیں

सब कहाँ कुछ लाला-ओ-गुल में नुमायाँ हो गईं
ख़ाक में क्या सूरतें होंगी कि पिंहाँ हो गईं

sab kahaa.n kuchh laala-o gul mei.n numaayaa.n ho gaei.n
KHaak mei.n kyaa suuratei.n ho.ngii ke pinhaa.n ho gaei.n

(*laala-o-gul*—tulips and flowers, beauty, greenery, freshness;
numaayaa.n—apparent, conspicuous, visible;
pinhaa.n—hidden, secret, concealed)

Not all, only a few, manifested
as blossoms in trust
What splendid faces were those
that went to hide in dust

Man is God's noble creature and is created in God's image. He is also God's vicegerent on the earth, as per the Qur'an (6:165). However, all men are not alike. Ghalib develops a philosophical discourse on the idea of man's superiority. He is beauteous like a rare blossom and also a rare phenomenon that finds its manifestation in the form of noble human beings. However, this beauty remains concealed mostly and finds its home only in the soil which is its final abode.

There are manifold levels of meanings here: (a) only a few faces appear and reappear as tulips and roses that represent exceptional beauty, while others, being ordinary, remain consigned to dust (b) these may be human faces, or the manifestations of noble beings (c) only true incarnations of beauty find their reincarnation (d) the beautiful blossoms emerge from the soil of the beautiful ones only, and finally (e) it is beauty alone that is the incarnation of truth and truth alone that incarnates beauty, as in Keatsian terms, 'beauty is truth, truth beauty, that's all/ye know on earth, and all ye need to know.'

Almost all counters of expression in this verse hold our attention. The compact expression *sab kahaa.n kuchh* (not all, but a few) represents a sense of awe and astonishment, and *laala-o gul* (tulips and flowers) symbolizes the truly beauteous entities. Four other words hold our attention for their symbolic implications: *numaayaa.n* (conspicuous) embodies the idea of incarnation and reincarnation, *KHaak* (dust) holds the eternal meaning of dust from which man rises and to which he goes back ultimately, *suuratei.n* (faces and manifestations) picturizes the images of beauty and, finally, *pinhaa.n* (concealed) of their perishing. There are not many verses even in Ghalib that are as tightly knit, in linguistic and implicational terms, as this one.

100

نیند اس کی ہے دماغ اس کا ہے راتیں اس کی ہیں
تیری زلفیں جس کے بازو پر پریشاں ہو گئیں

नींद उस की है दिमाग़ उस का है रातें उस की हैं
तेरी ज़ुल्फ़ें जिस के बाज़ू पर परेशाँ हो गईं

nii.nd us kii hai dimaaGh us kaa hai raatei.n us kii hai.n
terii zulfei.n jis ke baazuu per pareshaa.n ho gaei.n

(*baazuu*—arms;
pareshaa.n—spread out, scattered, dispersed)

Sleep is his, the pride his, the nights too
On whose lucky arms your tresses blew

The beloved of the Urdu ghazal has a thousand faces and a thousand forms. One with her long tresses, sometimes provides the cool shade of love and comfort to the lover. The lovers who have this luxury are blessed. Ghalib presents a well-carved romantic scene here that has a beauteous beloved with her long tresses and her lucky lover by her side. The lover slumbers in delight; his mind self-possessed and his night blissful because he has her mythic tresses spread over his arms.

Some eminently possible explanations of this condition could be: (a) the lover and the beloved, presented graphically in the first and the second lines respectively, create a condition of romantic bliss together (b) they constitute this scene of dream-like ecstasy in their states of splendid privacy (c) the only other person who watches this is the poet himself, who is probably jealous, as the tone of his narration suggests, and (d) in spite of that, he portrays this scene with pride and pleasure.

There is an amazing internal unity in the lexical units of *nii.nd* (slumber), *dimaaGh* (pride), *raatei.n* (nights), *zulf* (tresses) and *baazuu* (arms). Out of all these, *zulf* and *baazuu* have had fabled identity in the ghazal tradition. However, all the images together configure the verse as a picture of ecstasy since they act as intoxicants and portray the lover in his state of trance. The word *pareshaa.n* (dispersed) is used here in the positive sense of the spreading out of tresses, which is equivalent to the spreading of bliss rather than of misery, which the word *pareshaa.n* usually and typically means.

101

هم موحد ہیں ہمارا کیش ہے ترک رسوم
ملتیں جب مٹ گئیں اجزائے ایماں ہو گئیں

हम मुवह्हिद हैं हमारा केश है तर्क-ए रुसूम
मिल्लतें जब मिट गईं अजज़ा-ए ईमाँ हो गईं

ham movahhid hai.n hamaaraa kesh hai tark-e rusuum
millatei.n jab mit gaei.n ajzaa-i iimma.n ho gae.in

(*movahhid*—monotheist;
kesh—customs, rituals;
tark-e rusuum—abandonment of rituals;
millat—communities;
ajzaa-i iimma.n—parts of faith)

My way is to abandon rituals;
I am surely a monotheist
They became the parts of faith,
when communities vanished from our midst

Matters of faith find a prominent place in poetry in different ways and with various shades of implications. Ghalib, too, has developed his individual understanding of these issues, both directly and by suggestion. Here, he proposes a serious discourse on the merits of believing in one and only God as the prime mover of all that is revealed and concealed. It implicates further that when communities disappeared from the scene, they became the parts of an all-pervasive faith themselves.

Ghalib sets up a homily here which underlines that: (a) those who are monotheists and believe in one God shed all customs aside by holding them irrelevant to the mainstay of their faith, as practised in the Abrahamic religions—Christianity, Judaism and Islam (b) customs do not hold good for them as customs contravene the essential spirit of the monotheistic faith (c) all communities have their presence in a historical period and all of them make way for succeeding communities (d) once they do so, they subsume all differences and come to repose faith in one God, and finally, (e) the spirit of faith lies in unity than in diversity.

There are four seminal words drawn here from the vocabulary of religious faiths—*movahhid* (monotheist), *rusuum* (rituals), *millat* (communities) and *iimma.n* (faith)—that construct the thematic pattern of this verse. The understanding of the term *movahhid*, as against a polytheist, an atheist and an agnostic, is central to the appreciation of this verse. Another word, *rusuum*, qualifies the monotheist in his denial of rituals. The word *millat* connotes the communities of believers that ultimately takes all faiths and followers into its fold to constitute a single community after shedding all customs and rituals. This brings us to the Upanishadic proclamation of *tat tvam asi,* which implies 'you are that' in which 'that' refers to one supreme entity.

102

رنج سے خوگر ہوا انساں تو مٹ جاتا ہے رنج
مشکلیں مجھ پر پڑیں اتنی کہ آساں ہو گئیں

रंज से ख़ूगर हुआ इंसाँ तो मिट जाता है रंज
मुश्किलें मुझ पर पड़ीं इतनी कि आसाँ हो गईं

ra.nj se KHuugar huaa insaa.n to mit jaataa hai ra.nj
mushkilei.n mujh per padii.n itnii ke aasaa.n ho gaei.n

(*ra.nj* = sorrow, grief, sadness, distress;
KHuugar = accustomed, habituated, used)

When man is used to sorrows,
sorrows leave man for good
So many hardships I suffered,
so very well I stood

If pleasure is a short season in life, sorrows and sufferings, too, come to an end at one point of time. In return, they turn men much more patient and forbearing. Ghalib's speaker, who has already been seasoned with suffering, speaks here in a lucid way about living his life with positivity. He proclaims with remarkable ease that if man gets used to sorrows and sufferings, they do not really matter beyond a point. He admits that he suffered so many hardships that it became easier for him to put up with them.

Ghalib's enlightened speaker makes a keen comment on man and man's capacity to negotiate with adversities by suggesting that: (a) man has the infinite capacity to bear adversities and he does not break easily (b) he does this by bringing two opposite conditions in a good embrace in the second line, which sounds paradoxical, but only on the surface (c) he does this to creatively substantiate that suffering, strengthened by itself, is the cure for suffering which gives it a proverbial halo, and (d) it echoes the Nietzschean view that the will to power lies at the root of all human happiness, and suffering is the source of all strength in life.

The key words that bear out the central import of the verse are *ra.nj* (sorrow), *KHuugar* (getting used), *mushkilei.n* (adversities) and *aasaa.n* (easy). While the first two words represent man's habit to absorb pain, the next two construct meaning by posing the opposites against each other. So, *mushkil* multiplied by *mushkil* finds its resolution in *mushkil* itself, which is truly paradoxical as well as paradoxically true, and amounts to establishing a plausible poetic statement.

103

یوں ہی گر روتا رہا غاؔلب تو اے اہل جہاں
دیکھنا ان بستیوں کو تم کہ ویراں ہو گئیں

यूँ ही गर रोता रहा 'ग़ालिब' तो ऐ अहल-ए जहाँ
देखना इन बस्तियों को तुम कि वीराँ हो गईं

yuu.n hi gar rotaa rahaa Ghalib to ai ahl-e jahaa.n
dekhnaa in bastiyo.n ko tum ke viiraa.n ho gaei.n

(*ahle-jahaa.n*—people of the world, world's inhabitants;
viiraa.n—deserted, desolate, abandoned)

If Ghalib keeps on crying like this,
O you all—all around
Would see these habitats getting deserted,
and go aground

An individual's suffering may sometimes destroy everything around. In other words, if a man suffers, he does not suffer individually because more and more people bear its onslaughts. So, with every individual's suffering, a script for the larger suffering is writ symbolically. Here is Ghalib speaking in the first person about his pitiable lot, which could well be the lot of any other individual who has suffered. If this is how Ghalib keeps on weeping, he despairingly says, you would see these habitations go desolate one day.

What does he intend to say by drawing upon his own condition, we might ask. The possible answers could be: (a) he does not appear here as an individual but as a stock figure who represents the eternal human predicament conditioned and caused by the dire dynamics of time (b) it also comes out that if human beings live in misery, the world would have no reason to survive (c) this means, by implication, that both men and the world around must live in peace with each other, but that is not how nature has designed their mutual relationship, and further, (d) the element of apparent self-pity, which appears to be hidden within the verse, also compels and empowers an individual to encounter the world as it is.

Ghalib addresses the people of this world in defiance which is quite well borne out by his address to them as *ai ahl-e jahaa.n* (you, the people of the world). To add an edge to his aggressive comment, he brings in two expressions—*bastiyo.n* (habitats) and *viiraa.n* (deserted)—that stand in opposition to each other and construct the intent of his complaint. After all, desolate habitats would announce the disappearance of its inhabitants of which he, too, would be one.

104

شوریدگی کے ہاتھ سے ہے سر وبال دوش
صحرا میں اے خدا کوئی دیوار بھی نہیں

शोरिदगी के हाथ से है सर वबाल-ए दोश
सहरा में ऐ ख़ुदा कोई दीवार भी नहीं

shoriidagii ke haath se hai sar vabaal-e dosh
sahraa mei.n ai KHuda koii divaar bhii nahii.n

(*shoriidagii*—disturbance, tumult, commotion;
vabaal—burdensome, vexatious;
dosh—shoulder;
sahraa—wilderness)

I'm in commotion, my head a burden
on my shoulders, O God
There is not even a wall in the wilderness,
O God, my God

Poets astonish us with their extremely unusual ways of apprehending various phenomena and their astonishing manifestations. Here is an example of how a poet like Ghalib creates a world of astounding proportions, even in a state of loss and desertion. His speaker is in commotion; he has gone berserk and thinks that even his head sits like a burden on his shoulders. He is in the wilderness, which is a world unto itself, but it has no walls which we associate with the world of human habitations. He is, therefore, perturbed that he does not have a wall against which he could smash his head to take his revenge against his ill luck.

The inferences that we might draw from this verse are numerous: (a) the speaker, a lover by all signs, has been totally shaken by what he has suffered in love (b) he cannot stand his own head that is heavy with worries and sits heavily on his shoulders (c) instead of being a blessing, the head is now a burden (d) in such an upsetting state, he has found his refuge in the wilderness, which is a typical refuge for disappointed lovers (e) in such a state of utter commotion, he can only think of smashing his head against a wall, but, pitiably for him, the wilderness does not have any walls (f) it is ironical that one who loved and lived in bliss once is now in the wilderness with no one around, not even a wall to offer him safety, but only his wailings to go with him.

Shoriidagii (commotion) and *vabaal* (burdensome) are the two words that accompany each other to portray the figure of the dishevelled lover. As opposed to this, there are two other words—*sahraa* (wilderness) and *diivaar* (wall)—which stand as aliens to each other and construct the central meaning of the verse. In addition, the pressing memory of a protective *diivaar* makes the lover all the more helpless and miserable. Equally important are three contiguous words—*sar* (head), *haath* (hand) and *dosh* (shoulder)— that configure together a tormented lover, but none of them is of any worth to him any longer. By employing one of his most favoured techniques, Ghalib brings together similar sets of words, in terms of their meaning, to construct the essential intent of the verse.

105

نہیں ہے زخم کوئی بخیے کے در خور مرے تن میں
ہوا ہے تار اشک یاس رشتہ چشم سوزن میں

नहीं है ज़ख़्म कोई बख़िये के दर-ख़ुर मिरे तन में
हुआ है तार-ए अश्क-ए-यास रिश्ता चश्म-ए सोज़न में

nahii.n hai zaKHm koii baKHya ke dar-KHur mire tan mei.n
huaa hai taar-e ashk-e yaas rishta chashm-e sozaa.n mei.n

(*dar-KHur*—agreeable, suitable;
taar-e ashk-e yaas—line of despaired tears;
chashm-e sozaa.n—burning eyes)

There is not even a wound on my body
now worth a stitch
The thread in a needle's eye, a string of tears,
is a bond of twitch

P oets are extraordinarily endowed with the capacity to create their allegories of belonging and unbelonging. Ghalib's speaker here is too miserable, both emotionally and physically. There is not a wound on his body that may possibly be stitched, but it so appears that his sad tears have found a friend in his burning eyes. Ghalib finds a metaphorical way to suggest that every suffering finds a home ultimately, as tears find their place here in the burning eyes.

The speaker in this verse, who is arguably a lover, opens the following possibilities of meaning before us: (a) his body is an abode of untreatable wounds which turn him miserable (b) this is such a desperate state that the thread in the needle's eye itself appears like a string of tears, which implies that even the needle is tearful about his condition (c) there is an empathetic bond between the string of sad tears, the needle and his own burning eyes, where the tears find a home, and finally, (d) suffering does not perish, but it is metamorphosed in yet another form.

A verse of this kind may be expressed best through metaphoric configurations than through bare statements. The metaphors of *zaKHm* (wound), *tan* (body), *ashk* (tears) and *chashm* (eyes) that appear consecutively represent the misery of the lover in terms of his body, which is full of wounds already.

106

ہزاروں دل دیے جوش جنون عشق نے مجھ کو
سیہ ہو کر سویدا ہو گیا ہر قطرۂ خوں تن میں

हज़ारों दिल दिये जोश-ए जुनून-ए इश्क़ ने मुझ को
सियह हो कर सुवैदा हो गया हर क़तरा-ए-ख़ूँ तन में

hazaaro.n dil diye josh-e junuu.n-e 'ishq ne mujh ko
siyah ho kar suvaidaa ho gayaa har qatra-i KHuu.n tan mei.n

(*josh-e junuu.n*—wildness of passion, frenzy;
suvaidaa—black dots, heart's core)

My passion, my frenzy in love,
gave me a thousand hearts
My blood-drops turned black,
then to heart's core in my body parts

Love that can put a lover in agony can also bring him to a state of bliss. The frenzy of his passion gave him a thousand hearts to rejoice, says the wonderstruck lover. He adds further that it so enriched him that the drops of blood in his body became black first, and then turned into the cores of his heart and body. This is how the lover considers love to be an enabling phenomenon that transported him from a baser state to a nobler state.

That the power of love is magical is expressed here with greater precision and creativity: (a) the frenzy of love is a nobler state for the lover to be in (b) it can turn one heart into thousands and reward the lover immensely (c) it may go to the extent of transforming the red drops of heart's blood into little, shining black diamonds, and then become the noble cores of the heart and body (d) the drops of blood becoming black could also imply, alternatively, that it became so with suffering in love, but remained precious even in that state (e) in a broader perspective, thus, love is realized as a purifying passion and transforms human hearts into noble material (f) it is amazing to note how Ghalib spells out a scientific truth that, over a period of time, the spilled blood that was red earlier turns black as it dries up and its haemoglobin breaks down into a compound known as methaemoglobin.

Ghalib presents the idea of blood's transformation from red to black, and then to a noble material with two words—*siyah* (black) and *suvaidaa* (black dot constituting the heart's core). These two words that construct the core of meaning, represent Ghalib's imaginative brilliance that can configure images in the stages of their appearance and their implication in a context.

107

دل ہی تو ہے نہ سنگ و خشت درد سے بھر نہ آئے کیوں
روئیں گے ہم ہزار بار کوئی ہمیں ستائے کیوں

दिल ही तो है न संग-ओ-ख़िश्त दर्द से भर न आए क्यूँ
रोएंगे हम हज़ार बार कोई हमें सताए क्यूँ

dil hi to hai na sa.ng-o KHisht dard se bhar na aae kyu.n
roe.nge ham hazaar baar koii hame.in sataae kyu.n

(*sa.ng*—stone, pebble, rock;
KHisht—brick, tile)

This is a heart, not a stone or brick;
why shouldn't this be moved with pain
I'll cry a thousand times;
why should anyone make me suffer in vain

People in pain are sometimes best left to themselves. A moment of complete privacy is a moment of bliss to those who need to address themselves in complete seclusion. Here is an entirely personal and idiosyncratic way of addressing people regarding their interference in others' matters. It should not matter to anyone if someone, including a disappointed lover, keeps shedding tears or engages with one's self in one's own way.

Giving a voice to the lover, the narrator defends himself and poses questions to people while making observations about his predilections in life and love: (a) he argues that it is his heart, after all, neither a stone nor a brick that is devoid of feeling pain; so why should it worry anyone? (b) he contends further that it is his emotion that makes him cry; so why should anyone oppress him further, even if he cried a thousand times? (c) what is evident is that he has been oppressed in love, which makes him indifferent, sulky, angry and dismissive of people and their intrusive ways (d) he does not care if the self-appointed inspectors of manners are listening to him, but he surely wishes that they listen to him (e) it is the fiercely independent assertion of his pride in his individuality that distinguishes the lover, and in sum (f) this strong assertion could be of any individual preserving his sense of personal pride.

In his characteristic style, Ghalib creates a paradigm of contiguities and antinomies to evolve a pattern of meaning. We can see how he places a sensitive and tender *dil* (heart) against the insensitive and hard *sa.ng* (stone) and *KHisht* (brick) to define what a human heart actually is and how easily it can be hurt. Then, we come across two contiguous words, *dard* (pain) and *roe.nge,* (will keep shedding tears), which suggest that if there is pain there will be tears too. This is how Ghalib finds a way to develop a discourse on human susceptibility to pain and his infinite capacity to bear pain. In another verse, Ghalib appropriately considers weeping in love as a cleansing experience: *rone se aur 'ishq mei.n be-baak ho gae / dhoye gae ham itne ke bas paak ho gae.*

108

دیر نہیں حرم نہیں در نہیں آستاں نہیں
بیٹھے ہیں رہ گزر پہ ہم غیر ہمیں اٹھائے کیوں

दैर नहीं हरम नहीं दर नहीं आसताँ नहीं
बैठे हैं रह-गुज़र पे हम ग़ैर हमें उठाए क्यूँ

dair nahii.n haram nahii.n dar nahii.n aastaa.n nahii.n
baiThe hai.n rahguzar pe ham Ghair hamei.n uThaai kyu.n

(*dair*—convent, monastery, temple, church;
haram—sanctuary in Mecca;
dar—door; doorway;
aastaa.n—abode, threshold, shrine;
rahguzar—pathway, passage)

I have neither a temple nor a mosque;
neither a door nor an abode
I sit here on the way, why should anyone
remove me, why should anyone goad

A moment of complete disassociation with everything sometimes provides people the freedom to find their own sources of emotional, or even spiritual, sustenance. Whosoever be the speaker here—a believer or a non-believer, a lover or a commoner—he addresses the populace around in anger and defiance. He asks why should anyone deprive someone who is already divested of essential sources of his sustenance.

The speaker expresses his anguish quite unambiguously that (a) he neither has a temple nor a mosque, neither a threshold nor an abode, where he could seek his emotional or spiritual solace and compose himself (b) since he has none of the four, he sits with pride on the pathway and daringly questions why should anyone remove him from there (c) in his typical style, he suggests rather plainly, but defiantly, that it matters little that those four sites of emotional sustenance are not available to him now (d) this is so because he has already claimed an open space for himself where he is rewarded far better (e) being in a state of dispossession with independence and pride is preferable than being in that of a humiliating possession, and (f) like the previous verse, this too is a declaration of man's assertion of personal strength to face the antagonistic world spread around.

Ghalib uses four locations of *dair* (convent), *haram* (sanctuary), *dar* (door) and *aastaa.n* (shrine) as metaphors to represent the two domains of faith and ordinary life. He constructs his 'self' in relation to the 'other' and inhabits a free space that may not be usurped by anyone. Importantly enough, instead of lamenting over his deprivation, he gathers courage and seeks a secular space as a sure site of his belonging. As a sublime gloss on Ghalib, a verse by Mir Taqi Mir may be read with great profit: *dair-o haram se guzre ab dil hai ghar hamaaraa / hai KHatm is aable per sair-o safar hamaaraa.*

109

قید حیات و بند غم اصل میں دونوں ایک ہیں
موت سے پہلے آدمی غم سے نجات پاے کیوں

क़ैद-ए हयात-ओ-बंद-ए ग़म अस्ल में दोनों एक हैं
मौत से पहले आदमी ग़म से नजात पाए क्यूँ

qaid-e hayaat-o band-e Gham asl mei.n dono.n ek hai.n
maut se pehle aadmii Gham se nijaat paae kyu.n

(*qaid*—imprisonment, captivity, confinement;
band—bondage, servitude;
nijaat—deliverance, release, liberation)

Life's captivity and pain's bondage,
both indeed are the same
Why should pain release a man,
before his death makes a claim

The matters of living, suffering and perishing have engaged poets and creative writers perennially. The idea of death as a redeemer is not too uncommon in the poetry that philosophizes upon human suffering and redemption. Ghalib develops his own discourse on living and suffering that go hand in hand. He posits a note of reconciliation by asserting that none can take leave of suffering before the destined moment of dying, which is a way of finding redemption as a reward.

The mysteries of life and their relationship with pain are contemplated over in this verse as follows: (a) life as a period of imprisonment and grief as a bondage of fate are indeed one and the same (b) a man cannot get deliverance before death arrives to seal the passage of life (c) so, any longing for release from life's suffering would only be in vain (d) the idea of death as deliverance is in itself a philosophical-cum-mystical idea, and (e) even as the poet unravels life's reality, he also sounds a little pessimistic, even though the Qur'an asserts that 'every soul will taste death' (3:185) and the Bible proclaims that 'it is appointed for man to die' (Hebrew 9:27).

It is difficult to miss how artfully Ghalib brings together two densely impregnated expressions—*qaid-e hayaat* (imprisonment imposed by life) and *band-e Gham* (man's servitude to grief)—to stress upon the inescapable human predicament characterized by slavery to life and enslavement to grief. It is equally important to note that the word *nijaat* (release) may more profitably be considered as deliverance, rather than release or riddance from life.

110

ہاں وہ نہیں خدا پرست جاؤ وہ بے وفا سہی
جس کو ہو دین و دل عزیز اس کی گلی میں جائے کیوں

हाँ वो नहीं ख़ुदा-परस्त जाओ वो बेवफ़ा सही
जिस को हो दीन-ओ-दिल अज़ीज़ उस की गली में जाए क्यूँ

*haa.n vo nahii.n KHudaa parast jaao vo be-vafaa sahii
jis ko ho diin-o dil aziiz us kii galii mei.n jaae kyu.n*

(*parast*—worshipper, devoted to, adorer;
diin—faith, religion;
aziiz—dear, darling, favourite)

Well, she doesn't worship God;
let her be disloyal; take a beat
He who loves his heart and soul,
why should he visit her street

The adage that love is blind is evident many times in life and poetic representations. Here is one such lover who gives latitude to his beloved. True, she does not worship God, true she is faithless, admits the lover here; but then he also asks why should one, holding one's faith and heart dear to oneself, visit her lane at all. This is a lover's exasperation with respect to the beloved, yet it strikes a note of emotional association with her which cannot be undone easily.

There are two distinct layers of meaning here: (a) the beloved may not be a believer in God and she may not be loyal to her lover, but why should these matters bother anyone (b) in spite of this, the lover cannot restrain but think of her (c) it appears as if not believing in God and not being loyal to the beloved are the same, which implies conversely that the beloved is a sort of female deity herself who is necessary for the male worshipper (d) the lover considers love a private affair and strongly disparages public gaze of any kind, and (e) those who hold their faiths, lives and hearts dear to themselves may better take care of their own selves than worry about someone else's affair.

The expressions *haa.n* (yes) and *jaao* (go away) are not merely denotative of their usual meanings; they actually have rings of defiance which are also expressed through the implied gestures that the words embody. This is intensified further in the second line when the prying person is asked rhetorically—*us kii galii mei.n jaae kyu.n* (why go to her lane at all). If that person chooses to visit her lane still, he can do so only to risk his own faith and life.

111

غالبؔ خستہ کے بغیر کون سے کام بند ہیں
روئیے زار زار کیا کیجیے ہاے ہاے کیوں

ग़ालिब'-ए ख़स्ता के बग़ैर कौन से काम बंद हैं
रोइए ज़ार ज़ार क्या कीजिए हाए हाए क्यूँ

Ghalib-e KHasta ke baGhair kaun se kaam band hai.n
roiye zaar zaar kyaa kiijiiye haai haai kyu.n

(KHasta—fragile, infirm, debilitated, broken;
zaar zaar—to wail bitterly)

Without that fragile Ghalib,
does any business come to a halt?
Why then cry one's heart out,
why then bring one's heart to assault

No one is indispensable and nothing stops in this world without anyone. This old adage finds its poetic representation in this verse that appeals better to reason than to emotion. Once again, Ghalib ponders over his own significance, or insignificance, in a queer manner and addresses us in the first person. He says that nothing would stop if he, the broken one, is no longer around and is gone forever. So, he wonders why should anyone weep or wail over his disappearance from the world.

In this seemingly straightforward verse, there are stimulating aspects to ponder over: (a) human beings come and go but the world goes on forever, as it is mightier than man which reminds of these lines from 'The Brook' by Alfred Tennyson, '... men may come and men may go/but I go on for ever' where 'I' stands for eternal nature (b) soothing his lamenters, Ghalib suggests, as if from the other world, that the world would go on even if he is gone and dead (c) he thus dispels all illusions we have about our lives and ourselves, being special and superior to others (d) more importantly, he brings out the futility of human pride and underlines a philosophical idea that no one is inevitable as the world's business goes on as usual without caring as to who lives and who dies (e) this is unlike those verses where Ghalib eulogizes man and his pride in exalted terms and offers a broader comment on his real worth.

The word *KHasta* (fragile) has the multiple connotations of weak, aged, broken and incapacitated which add to the multivalency of the verse. Two other words repeated twice—*zaar-zaar* (wail bitterly) and *haai haai* (alas)—adequately bring out the intensity of weeping and lamenting over the passing away of this person who was a poet par excellence.

112

غنچۂ ناشگفتہ کو دور سے مت دکھا کہ یوں
بوسے کو پوچھتا ہوں میں منہ سے مجھے بتا کہ یوں

गुंचा-ए ना-शिगुफ़्ता को दूर से मत दिखा कि यूँ
बोसे को पूछता हूँ मैं मुंह से मुझे बता कि यूँ

Ghuncha-i naa-shagufta ko duur se mat dikhaa ke yuu.n
bose ko puuchhtaa huu.n mai.n mu.nh se mujhe bataa ke yuu.n

(*Ghuncha*—blossom, flower bud;
naa-shagufta—not yet flowered;
bosa—kiss)

Don't show the closed bud from a distance and say,
'Well it's like this'
I'm asking for a kiss, just enact with your lips,
'Well it's like this'

Loving would be monotonous without moments of fun and frolic. As the two lovers together play out their roles in gaiety, they transform the act of loving into a blessing for each other. This is once again a light-hearted verse dramatizing a lighter moment of teasing and romancing between them. Ghalib's playful lover asks the beloved how to kiss and the beloved shows a bud with petals still unfurled to say this is how it is to kiss. But the naughty lover's demand follows: Show it to me by enacting how to kiss.

The layers of beauty in this verse may be traced keeping the following in mind: (a) Ghalib sets up a scene here with a naughty lover and his playful beloved who holds a bud in her hand (b) rather than asking bluntly for a kiss, the lover creates a drama to get that kiss (c) they play with each other through gestures and surpass each other without yielding (d) in wanting her to enact kissing, the lover seeks physical closeness, since kissing is the first step towards the bodies getting into embrace (e) the beloved does not fall prey to his enticements and remains steadfast, as beloveds have traditionally been in the ghazal tradition.

The phrase *Guncha-i naa-shagufta* (bud not yet flowered) has two distinct meanings here. It suggests a closed bud but more importantly it implies that the beloved is yet to be sexually consummated. Another expression—*duur se mat dikhaa* (don't show me from a distance)—unfolds the lover's longing to get the beloved close to him, who is only tempting and enticing him naughtily from a distance. This underlines further that the real romance of beauty, or the beauty of romance, lies in the distance involved than in closeness, or physical proximity. This reminds of Mir Taqi Mir's naughty verse, like Ghalib's, where desire and its depiction seek our attention: *bosa us butt kaa le ke mu.nh moRaa / bhaarii pathhar thaa chuum kar chhoRa.*

113

حسد سے دل اگر افسردہ ہے گرم تماشا ہو
کہ چشم تنگ شاید کثرت نظارہ سے وا ہو

हसद से दिल अगर अफ़्सुर्दा है गर्म-ए तमाशा हो
कि चश्म-ए तंग शायद कसरत-ए नज़ारा से वा हो

hasad se dil agar afsurda hai garm-e tamaasha ho
ke chashm-e ta.ng shaaed kasrat-e nazzara se vaa ho

(*hasad*—envy;
afsurda—disappointed, dejected;
garm-e tamaasha—enthusiastic about seeing;
chashm-e ta.ng—narrow eyes;
kasrat-e nazzara—abundance of manifestation)

If jealousy has made you sad,
look at the fairy faces, have fun
Fun's plenty may open your eyes
to a joyful, jolly run

Good counsel brings positivity in life. Here is Ghalib's counsel to his listeners. It comes as an easy-going address to them in the form of good guidance. Do not suffer in a state of envy, he articulates straightway, and persuades them to get around and watch the brilliant spectacle spread outside. He reasons further that this is how the narrow eyes may open up and the multitudinous world around may offer its pleasant spectacles.

Here is a verse that eulogizes the beauty of creation around and the value of a liberal outlook. It makes these suggestions: (a) the world has multiple manifestations for human beings to watch and appreciate their significance (b) envying the manifestations, rather than enjoying them, turns men into inferior beings (c) opening up and embracing the manifestations around would make human beings prolifically aware and enlightened, and (d) it is in appreciating God's manifestations on this earth that men may meet the purpose of their creation.

The word *hasad* is used here in the ordinary sense of envy, which incorporates the spirit of this verse—rather than jealousy, which carries a negative sense. As usual, Ghalib picks up opposites—*afsurda* (disappointed) and *garm* (enthusiastic) in the first line, and *tang* (narrow) and *vaa* (open) in the second line—to construct his pattern of meaning. This technique accounts for the poetic precision which distinguishes this verse and makes it appealing to ears willing to take the message.

114

طاعت میں تا رہے نہ مے و انگبیں کی لاگ
دوزخ میں ڈال دو کوئی لے کر بہشت کو

ताअत में ता रहे न मै-ओ-अंगबीं की लाग
दोज़ख़ में डाल दो कोई ले कर बिहिश्त को

taa'at mei.n taa rahe na mai-o a.ngabii.n kii laag
dozaKH mei.n daal do koi le kar bahisht ko

(*taa'at*—obedience, longing;
mai-i a.ngbii.n—limpid/clear wine;
dozaKH—hell)

Let there be no trace of obedience
to the limpid wine
Let someone pull out the heavens
and dump in hell's line

Poets speak sometimes to an imagined audience and expect a fair reception, even if the idea projected may sound alien, or even eccentric. Ghalib makes such an effort in this verse. He creates a character who can clearly distinguish between hell and heaven, and outrageously assert that heaven may be dumped into hell. Even though human beings have not seen hell or heaven for themselves, they have been told and taught about them in traditional ways. They are thus aware that heaven is a sacred place for virtuous people and hell a condemned one for the sinful ones, according to all religious faiths.

This verse lends itself to various interpretations: (a) people worship because of the temptations of houris, honey and heavenly wine that have been promised in the Qur'an (47:15) to be offered to the worshippers in heaven (b) the logic behind flinging heaven into hell lies in the fact that if all these temptations are wiped out, the worshippers will then worship genuinely in the holy precincts of heaven without any temptations (c) further, if one worships selfishly for the blessings of heaven only, the idea of obedience to God would be proved false; this is another reason why heaven should be flung into hell (d) Sufis and poets have not idealized heaven because they seek their own ways of developing intimacy with God (e) but the institutionalized religious authorities threaten everyone with the punishment of hell, even while dreaming of heaven for themselves, thus, (f) Ghalib's unusual character in this verse seems to take cudgels against the starkly committed believers and expresses his preference for liberal faith, which makes him assert himself boldly.

The word *taa'at* (obedience) has a religious connotation which has no room for any *laag* (link) with wine, or the consumption of wine. The idea of hurling heaven into hell is a startling and irreverent idea, but Ghalib offers a rationale for such a call, and helps the verse acquire its meaning and appeal in spite of its irreverence.

115

ہوں منحرف نہ کیوں رہ و رسم ثواب سے
ٹیڑھا لگا ہے قط قلم سرنوشت کو

हूँ मुंहरिफ़ न क्यूँ रह-ओ-रस्म-ए सवाब से
टेढ़ा लगा है क़त क़लम-ए सर-नविश्त को

huu.n munharif na kyu.n rah-o rasm-e savaab se
teRhaa lagaa hai qatt qalam-e sar-navisht ko

(*munharif*—person who denies;
rah-o rasm—ways and rituals;
savaab—reward, recompense;
qatt—crooked, curvy;
sar-navisht—writing on the forehead)

Why shouldn't I deny the ways that bring
the rewards straight
The pen's nib had taken a wrong curve
to write my fate

Defiance and irreverence form the staple material for poetry quite often, and open up strange ways of reaching out to reality. Here is a quirky response of a person to the question of what lies in his fate. He finds no reason to remain stuck to the established ways of worshipping and getting rewarded. He argues, therefore, that he would not walk the conventional path to attain his reward because his destiny was not written with a conventionally shaped nib.

The idea embedded in this verse is one of defiance. It finds a defiant speaker to propose his case: (a) he puts forth a rhetorical question in the first line: Why should I not deny and move away from the religious path that could otherwise bring me rewards (b) he gives his answer in the second line: I do so because the pen which wrote my destiny had a crooked nib (c) the idiosyncrasy of the speaker is borne out by the eccentric question he poses and the strange answer he proposes, (d) he interrogates God indirectly and asserts that he does not really care for the man he made because he did not write his destiny well, and finally, (e) reward and punishment remain in the mind of the speaker as the guiding principle of life, but he approaches it from an unusually independent position, which appears like a position of belligerence although truthfully expressed.

Denial has often been considered a way to arrive at affirmation. The word *munharif* (denier) in the first line defines the essential character of the speaker and creates a condition for the verse to find its way in the second line. His spirit of denial finds an echo in the word *teRHaa* (crooked) used for the pen's nib that cannot write his destiny straight.

116

ہے آدمی بجائے خود اک محشر خیال
ہم انجمن سمجھتے ہیں خلوت ہی کیوں نہ ہو

है आदमी बजाए ख़ुद इक महशर-ए ख़याल
हम अंजुमन समझते हैं ख़ल्वत ही क्यूँ न हो

hai aadmii bajaae KHud ik mahshar-KHayaal
ham anjuman samajhte hai.n KHalvat hi kyu.n na ho

(*mahshar-KHayaal*—commotion of ideas,
pandemonium of thoughts;
anjuman—coterie, congregation, assembly;
KHalvat—seclusion, isolation, privacy)

Man is surely a bedlam of thoughts unto himself
He's an assembly to me, may he be seclusion himself

Man has remained an inexhaustible subject in poetry and arts as a reservoir of ideas and thoughts. All efforts to define and develop a discourse on man have resulted in defining him but only partially, and there are possibilities for further reflection on this. This verse is Ghalib's rich tribute to man and his infinite capacities as a progenitor of ideas. More than an individual, man is God's noble piece of creation who excels in the domains of thoughtful discourses.

Ghalib acknowledges man's infinite capabilities for several reasons: (a) he reminds of the Traditions (*Al-Bukhari* 6227 and *Muslim* 2841) and the verse of the Bible (Genesis I:27) which say that God created man in his own image (b) created in such an exalted image, man has been endowed with infinite capabilities, including the capability of exercising his intellect and imagination, which puts him on the highest pedestal of divine creations (c) he is thus the cause and effect of all ideas, a potential embodiment of rational discourses, who makes things happen, and helps humanity grow (d) even in seclusion, he represents an assembly and emerges as a source of intellectual treatises (e) as such, he is God's vicegerent on earth, endowed with exceptional prowess (the Qur'an 2: 31–33).

This verse makes a statement but what makes it poetry, one might ask. It is Ghalib's capacity to evolve strong metaphors that enables him to represent man as *mahshar-e KHayaal* (commotion of ideas) and an *anjuman* (congregation) unto himself. This explains that as thoughts keep crowding man's mind even in seclusion, he is transformed into a supremely empowered being.

117

وفا داری بشرط استواری اصل ایماں ہے
مرے بت خانے میں تو کعبہ میں گاڑو برہمن کو

वफ़ा-दारी ब-शर्त-ए उस्तुवारी अस्ल ईमाँ है
मरे बुत-ख़ाने में तो काबे में गाड़ो बिरहमन को

vafaadaarii ba-shart-e ustavaarii asl-e iimaa.n hai
mare butKHaane mei.n to k'aabe mei.n gaaRo brahman ko

(*ustavaarii*—constancy, firmness, steadfastness;
asl-e iimaa.n—kernel of faith;
butKHaana—house of idols)

Loyalty, on the condition of constancy,
is the kernel of faith for sure
If the Brahmin dies in the temple,
bury him in the k'aba, just ensure

What is faith, what is truthfulness, what is steadfastness? These are not just questions essentially related to man's faith, they have their relevance in larger contexts beyond faith. Ghalib has chosen to address these questions poetically in this verse. He considers steadfastness as an essential condition of truthfulness and supplements this idea with a daring reference to the Brahmin, who may die in his temple but may well be buried in the k'aba.

The suggestions that this verse makes could be marked as follows: (a) steadfastness is an article of faith in every religion and the faithfulness of a believer is qualified by his steadfastness (b) both the Sheikh and the Brahmin are tested equally for their steadfastness in following their respective faiths (c) this implies that a Brahmin who has been steadily practising his faith in his temple is as good as the Sheikh following his own in the k'aba (d) as such, a brahmin may well be buried in the k'aba instead of being burnt elsewhere (e) this is also because both burning and burying turn the human body to ashes and soil of which all are born, irrespective of their faiths.

The first line of the verse is axiomatic in nature. The second line offers a paradigm for that axiom. The most powerfully operative expressions—*vafaadaarii* (faithfulness), *ustavaari* (constancy) and *asl-e iimaa.n* (kernel of faith)—put together in the first line, set the thematic base and dominant tone of the verse, while *butKHaana* (temple) and *k'aba* (the cube-shaped shrine in Mecca) that follow in the second line appear as the institutional sites of faith. We cannot miss noticing the significance of the mutually consenting words—*mare* (die) and *gaaRo* (bury)—that represent a sequence of action, since that is how human beings meet their end and prove that born of dust, they go back to dust.

118

نہ لٹتا دن کو تو کب رات کو یوں بے خبر سوتا
رہا کھٹکا نہ چوری کا دعا دیتا ہوں رہزن کو

न लुटता दिन को तो कब रात को यूँ बे-ख़बर सोता
रहा खटका न चोरी का दुआ देता हूँ रहज़न को

na luTtaa din ko to kab raat ko yuu.n be-KHabar sotaa
rahaa khaTkaa na chorii kaa du'aa detaa huu.n rahzan ko

(*rahzan*—robber, looter)

I wouldn't sleep carefree at night,
if not looted in day, I avow
Let me now bless the robber,
there is no fear of a theft now

Bizarre ideas sometimes lend themselves wonderfully to poetry. Here is one such example which sounds rather funny, but spells out an unusual aspect of the human experience. In this typically playful Ghalibean verse, the speaker finds himself in a queer position when he has been robbed of his possessions in daytime, but consoles himself and blesses the robber that he can now sleep in peace at night.

Interesting inferences may be drawn from this verse: (a) material possession is a boon but being robbed of it is a cause for worry (b) by implication, a carefree sleep is also a boon, but being robbed of it is a distressing experience (c) looting in the night is usual but looting in the daytime is a way of duping the victim (d) anyone may be looted any time of the day and the night (e) blessing the robber is a way of a mystical compromise with what has befallen the speaker.

Let us think of this verse as a series of four blocks: (i) *na luTtaa din ko to* (had I not been looted in the daytime, then) (ii) *kab raat ko yuu.n be-KHabar sotaa* (would I ever sleep so carefree at night) (iii) *rahaa khaTkaa na chorii ka* (there is no apprehension of theft now) and (iv) *du'aa detaa huu.n rahzan ko* (I bless the looter). Each block makes way for the other block to reach a conclusion. Furthermore, each line creates its own paradigm of meaning and both the lines together weave a full circle of meaning. The vital word, *khaTkaa* (apprehension), sums up the psychological condition only too adequately and imparts the verse its rational excuse.

119

تم جانو تم کو غیر سے جو رسم و راہ ہو
مجھ کو بھی پوچھتے رہو تو کیا گناہ ہو

तुम जानो तुम को ग़ैर से जो रस्म-ओ-राह हो
मुझ को भी पूछते रहो तो क्या गुनाह हो

tum jaano tum ko Ghair se jo rasm-o raah ho
mujh ko bhii puuchhte raho to kyaa gunaah ho

(*rasm-o raah*—friendly relations, familiarity, understanding, contact)

Whatever be your bond with the other,
that's your matter
Would that be a sin if you wooed me too,
and chose to flatter

Lovers seek favours from their beloveds in charming ways. Here is an innocent and fascinating way that Ghalib's lover finds to get what he pines for. It is for the beloved to decide with whom she would like to be friends, comments the lover without blaming her, but it would not be a sin if she remained friends with him too. Most interestingly, the lover is not possessive here—he only wants the beloved's attention, which would make him happy and fulfilled.

There are some thought-provoking aspects here that may be highlighted to help appreciate this verse: (a) the lover is obviously submissive before the beloved and speaks rather persuasively to her (b) he does not expect much from the beloved, but he cannot live without her either, which is what makes him an acquiescent lover (c) although disappointed, he still wants to be friends without claiming her as a matter of his right, or even complaining about her new-found sympathies (d) there is a muted sense of jealousy with the other lover which hangs heavily on his mind and reflects sadly on his state (e) however, this aspect is kept rather subdued in the verse to project and strengthen the lover's innocent disposition.

While the first line adds an element of irony to the verse with *Ghair* (the other), the second line enriches it with a double meaning: (i) it would not be a sin if you were cordial to me too, and (ii) would it be a sin if you were cordial to me as well? In the difference of shades of implications and intended ambiguities lies the magic of Ghalib's poetic utterances which he ably demonstrates quite often, as he does here.

120

جب مے کدہ چھٹا تو پھر اب کیا جگہ کی قید
مسجد ہو مدرسہ ہو کوئی خانقاہ ہو

जब मय-कदा छुटा तो फिर अब क्या जगह की क़ैद
मस्जिद हो मदरसा हो कोई ख़ानक़ाह हो

jab maikada chhuTaa to phir ab kyaa jagah kii qaid
masjid ho madrasa ho koii KHaanqaah ho

(*maikada*—tavern;
KHaanqaah—convent)

If the tavern became out of reach,
what matter which place now
May that be a mosque, a seminary,
or a monastery to bow

A reckless drinker may drink at any place, once he is driven out of the tavern. This verse personifies a compulsive drinker who believes more in drinking than in thinking about the place where to drink. Any wine lover, or anyone else who enjoys his drink like him, would generally say that the tavern is the best place to have a drink. But if he is deprived of his place in the tavern, it hardly matters where and how he would find a place to drink, since his drink is more important to him than his place of drink.

Ghalib takes this idea to an amazing height by drawing upon his poetic license and opening up several possibilities of meaning: (a) the speaker shows a clear sense of remorse in leaving the tavern for whatever reason, but he wryly admits that he may now drink at any other place that comes his way (b) while thinking of the mosque, seminary or convent as his new place of drinking, he liberates himself from his committed choice of a tavern (c) this also suggests his abandoning one way of life, which was plebian, and choosing another which is secular (d) in doing this, he adds a liberal dimension to his thought and extends the meaning of life and living (e) it is in this aspect that he appears as a nonconformist and discovers the value of his free will to live on his own terms (f) if wine brings intoxication in a tavern, it would do the same in religious places as well, where the drinkers are drunk on the divine wine of obeisance and submission.

In terms of an imagistic paradigm created by *maikada* (tavern), *masjid* (mosque), *madrasa* (seminary) and *KHaanqaah* (convent), Ghalib underlines the aesthetics of his speaker's peculiarly different style of showing his irreverence. The exclamatory phrase *ab kyaa jagah kii qaid* (what bother for a given place now) underlines that all places, including religious places, are alike, which carries forward the central burden of the verse. In terms of thought, this verse reminds of another verse by Ghalib: *masjid ke zer-e saaya KHaraabaat chaahiye / bhau.n paas aa.nkh qibla-i haajaat chaahiye.*

121

سنتے ہیں جو بہشت کی تعریف سب درست
لیکن خدا کرے، وہ ترا جلوہ گاہ ہو

सुनते हैं जो बहिश्त की तारीफ़ सब दुरुस्त
लेकिन ख़ुदा करे वो तिरा जल्वा-गाह हो

sunte hai.n jo bahisht kii t'aariif sab durust
lekin KHuda kare vo tiraa jalvagaah ho

(*bahisht*—heaven, paradise;
jalvagaah—house of splendour, place of display)

What all the praise, I have heard of the heavens,
all that must be right
But may God make it a dazzling site,
may that be your theatre bright

Lovers wish for the best places on the earth and the skies for their beloveds. Here is a lover who earnestly desires that the beloved's site of repose should be one of rare grandeur and glory. The lover avows that there is no denying the praise one has heard of heavens, but may that heaven be the celestial place to bear the beloved's resplendent image. In making this desire for the beloved's repose, he invokes even God's indulgence to turn his desire into reality.

Ghalib makes stimulating suggestions here: (a) the lover accepts all the praise he has heard about heaven, but he asserts that it cannot be heaven without the beloved being there (b) he extends this thought by desiring heaven to be a house of the beloved's splendour (c) in other words, he actually wants heaven to be a reflection of the beloved's beauty (d) interestingly, he wants his desire to be fulfilled by none other than God Himself (e) it also appears that he considers the beloved's site of repose and heaven as complementary to each other (f) in this manner, he wishes to eternalize the beloved, along with eternal heaven.

The first phrase—*sunte hain* (it is heard)—has the ring of hearsay about heaven's praise since nobody has seen it, but Ghalib's artless art helps it acquire a level of certainty with another phrase at the end of the same line—*sab durust* (all that is true). This is an amazing way of turning a hearsay into a certainty only by placing a simple and precise counter of expression at the right place. Similarly, another phrase—KHuda kare (may God grant)—has an intent and a ring of prayer, but more importantly, it reflects the speaker's desire. These examples of verbal artistry impart an inimitable literary merit to the verse. It should be interesting to refer here to Shah Nasir, who makes a fabulously picturesque representation in this context: *dil jalva-gaah-e suurat-e jaanaana ho gayaa / shisha ye ek dam mei.n parii KHaana ho gayaa.*

122

کسی کو دے کے دل کوئی نواسنج فغاں کیوں ہو
نہ ہو جب دل ہی سینے میں تو پھر منہ میں زباں کیوں ہو

किसी को दे के दिल कोई नवा-संज-ए फ़ुग़ाँ क्यूँ हो
न हो जब दिल ही सीने में तो फिर मुँह में ज़बाँ क्यूँ हो

*kisii ko de ke dil koii navaa-sanj-e fuGhaa.n kyu.n ho
na ho jab dil hii siine mei.n to phir mu.nh mei.n zabaa.n kyu.n ho*

(*navaa*—sound, voice, tune;
sanj-e fuGhaa.n—measurer of lamentation,
weigher of grief)

When the heart has gone after someone,
why should one lament
If no heart in the breast, why a tongue
in the mouth for an intent

A lover's entreaty in distress has the quality of holding the attention of listeners. Ghalib's lover shares his curious condition here. He does this by asking himself if he should, or could, lament the giving of his heart to the beloved. He also realizes that he has lost his heart, his will as well as his need to express his grief. He is amazed if love affords him a way to compose himself with any amount of hope to face its travails.

The prominent pointers to meaning in this verse are: (a) if the heart has gone to the beloved, there is no reason for the lover to lament now, which implies that pain is an essential condition of love (b) similarly, once the heart is surrendered to the beloved, there is no reason for the tongue to be in the mouth, which implies that the lover must suffer in silence (c) this also indicates that complaining in love is against the integrity of the lover himself (d) further, hiding one's complaint against the beloved is an act of honouring the beloved (e) in this case, the lover is destined to suffer without a heart that beats and a tongue that speaks.

With the expression *kisii* (any) the beloved has been presented as a stock figure of oppression. Then, there is a close interactive relationship between *fuGhaa.n* (lament) and *zabaa.n* (tongue) that underlines the essentiality of grief for the lover and the absence of tongue rendering him speechless. The expressions *kyu.n ho* (why should that be) used twice as a refrain sound like two rhetorical questions, but it clearly implies that no answers should be expected, as they are automatically answered in negative.

123

وفا کیسی کہاں کا عشق جب سر پھوڑنا ٹھہرا
تو پھر اے سنگ دل تیرا ہی سنگ آستاں کیوں ہو

वफ़ा कैसी कहाँ का इश्क़ जब सर फोड़ना ठहरा
तो फिर ऐ संग-दिल तेरा ही संग-ए आसताँ क्यूँ हो

vafaa kaisii kahaa.n kaa 'ishq jab sar phoRnaa Thahraa
to phir ai sa.ng dil teraa hii sa.ng-e aastaa.n kyu.n ho

(*sa.ng*—stone;
aastaa.n—abode, threshold)

What loyalty, what love, when I am destined
to break my head at last
Why then, O stone-hearted, at your stony threshold
should I ever cast

This is, once again, a sad narrative of a heartbroken lover and an unkind beloved. Jilted by her, he is destined to break his head, but he does not want to do so only at her threshold. He retains his pride even in his state of brokenness and asserts his strength in spite of his despair. This assertion, thus, distinguishes him as a lover of remarkable control, strength and pride.

The impending inferences in this verse could be appreciated in these terms: (a) what is love when faith is broken, and why should the lover worry about it when he is destined to bash his head? (b) and if that be so, why should he bother to bash it at her threshold? (c) even in putting forth these questions presumably to the beloved, the lover appears deeply despondent about his faithless love and clearly denies the very existence of such a beloved for himself (d) as he rejects the beloved, he subjects himself to a kind of suffering that comes when one is downcast—a state that is not so unusual in love.

Prone to posing questions in many of his verses, Ghalib puts forward three questions here—*kaisii* (of what kind), *kahaa.n* (of where) and *kyu.n* (why)—that define the tone and tenor of this verse with respect to *vafaa* (loyalty) and *'ishq* (love). These are not the questions that the lover poses to himself, or anyone around about her love and her loyalty to him, but these are expressions of his anger and disappointment against her, tinged with a clearly ironical overtone. The pun on the two phrases *sa.ng dil* (stone-hearted) and *sa.ng-e aastaa.n* (stone threshold) must also be noticed as the first is used for the heartbroken lover and the second for the beloved's threshold of stone, and both of them bear out each other as metaphors of obduracy and rigidity for the beloved. This condition may be compared and contrasted with a verse by Bedam Shah Varsi: *vo sar aur Ghair ke dar per jhuke tauba M'aazAllah / ke jis sar kii risaaii tere sa.ng-e aastaa.n tak hai.*

124

قفس میں مجھ سے روداد چمن کہتے نہ ڈر ہمدم
گری ہے جس پہ کل بجلی وہ میرا آشیاں کیوں ہو

क़फ़स में मुझ से रूदाद-ए चमन कहते न डर हमदम
गिरी है जिस पे कल बिजली वो मेरा आशियाँ क्यूँ हो

qafas mei.n mujh se ruudaad-e chaman kahte na dar hamdam
girii ho jis pe kal bijlii vo meraa aashiyaa.n kyu.n ho

(*qafas*—cage;
hamdam—friend, companion;
ruudaad—narration, account, story;
aashiyaa.n—bird's nest)

Don't be scared, my friend, telling me
the story of the garden in this cage
Why should that be my nest where
the lightning chose yesterday to rage

The adage that ignorance is bliss is used in different situations of life, but quite often to indicate a sense of psychological fear, that is, not knowing something helps us think that it doesn't exist/happen. This verse is a fine exposition of human psychology in an allegorical framework. It dramatizes how and why human beings are constantly apprehensive of unimaginable things happenings to them. Even while they are too close to knowing the reality, they often choose to deny or disbelieve what has happened.

This verse unravels the psychological condition of an apprehensive speaker and its implications are unveiled in these stages that unfold like a story: (a) a bird, separated from his nest, has been held captive in a cage (b) that captive bird has seen the lightning strike the garden and knows secretly that his nest was really burnt yesterday (c) this bird speaks to a friendly bird who has perched himself on a branch close to his cage and impels him to tell the truth (d) but the visiting bird who knows the truth cannot have the courage to share what happened (e) the sense of anxiety looms large in the mind of the captive bird but he would like to feign ignorance to unsuccessfully assuage himself.

This verse is quite typical in the sense that it conceals the plot of a painful story. Four visual images—*qafas* (cage), *chaman* (garden), *bijlii* (lightning) and *aashiyaa.n* (nest)— compose the plot of the verse which in itself is a *ruudaad* (account) of a bird's anxiety and apprehension. While *qafas* and *aashiyaa.n* broadly represent two images of abodes, one characterized by restriction and another by comparative freedom, they, together, constitute the archetypal composition of the *chaman*. *Bijlii* operates here as a metaphor of annihilation that brings a well-composed world to destruction. It is with this philosophical angle that this verse acquires its special significance. A pathetic strain that corresponds with Ghalib's verse, runs through this verse by Bismil Azimabadi: *sevaae daaGh milaa kyaa chaman mei.n aa ke mujhe / qafas nasiib huaa aashiyaa.n banaa ke mujhe.*

125

یہ فتنہ آدمی کی خانہ ویرانی کو کیا کم ہے
ہوئے تم دوست جس کے دشمن اس کا آسماں کیوں ہو

ये फ़ित्ना आदमी की ख़ाना-वीरानी को क्या कम है
हुए तुम दोस्त जिस के दुश्मन उस का आसमाँ क्यूँ हो

ye fitna aadmii kii KHaana-viiraanii ko kyaa kam hai
hue tum dost jis ke dushman us kaa aasmaa.n kyu.n ho

(*fitna*—evil, mischief;
KHaana-viiraanii—laying waste a house)

Is this mischief any less for
turning man's abode to a ruining end—
Why should the skies be inimical
to one you've chosen for a friend

The beloved is often a destroyer for the lover but God is the ultimate preserver. This verse engages with the idea of how devastation is caused to someone by some agency that may be either human or non-human, and sometimes both. In this case, it is the beloved who turns out to be the cause of the lover's devastation. The speaker goes to the extent of proclaiming that she alone is enough to devastate him and lay waste his abode, by which he implies that with her being there, no divine wrath is indeed required to ruin him and his abode.

The speaker who unveils human miseries underlines these aspects quite prominently: (a) it is massively ironical that a friend turns into a foe, and pushes one to a state of dispossession and suffering (b) this friend is, tragically enough, the beloved herself who works on the sly, or acts by design, to devastate her lover (c) devastation is also brought by the divine power, but in this case it is the beloved who acts as the supreme authority of destruction, and (d) the element of irony is marked further and only too well in a human agency acquiring divine power.

Human act is qualified here as *fitna* (mischief), which is associated with the dastardly acts of the infamous Satan. The beloved, addressed here as *tum* (you), is none other than the one who caused devastation to the lover and acquired satanic qualities in this process. As against the embodiment of *fitna*, there is *aadmii* (man), who is the lover himself and is projected as a victim. The dichotomy of *dost* (friend) and *dushman* (foe) is also remarkable here, and is expressed in the most caustic manner— that is, if you become a friend to someone, the sky has no business being his foe. The second line, which reads like a rhetorical question, imparts a wry tone to the verse which adds to its direct appeal. Ghalib's ingenuity makes him approach a subject variously as can be seen here with reference to another verse by him: *nahii.n gar hamdamii aasaa.n na ho ye rashk kyaa kam hai / na dii hotii KHudaayaa aarzuu-e dost dushman ko.*

126

رہیے اب ایسی جگہ چل کر جہاں کوئی نہ ہو
ہم سخن کوئی نہ ہو اور ہمزباں کوئی نہ ہو

रहिये अब ऐसी जगह चल कर जहाँ कोई न हो
हम-सुख़न कोई न हो और हम-ज़बाँ कोई न हो

rahiye ab aisii jagah chal kar jahaa.n koii na ho
ham-suKHan koii na ho aur ham-zabaa.n koii na ho

(*ham-suKHan*—dialogue sharer, interlocutor;
ham-zabaa.n—speaking the same language,
of the same tongue)

Let me go where none lives,
let that be so far-flung
None be there to share my words,
none to share my tongue

Man's quest for the unknown has been a subject of poetical and philosophical discourses. We have the voice of a disillusioned person here who seeks refuge in a world far away from the humming and buzzing one in which we live. His impatience with the bustling human habitat makes us wonder if he is a dejected lover, a disappointed social being, a spiritually inclined human, a philosophically charged human being or the poet himself who speaks through a persona.

The speaker develops a clearly philosophical stance here: (a) he expresses his disappointment with man and his environment without revealing the reason for the same (b) he finds himself all alone, even while living in a congregation of humans, which makes him seek refuge in a location of complete aloofness (c) he considers his own self as his best companion to live and develop a dialogue with, in order to find and actualize himself (d) instead of living a life in meditation, or seeking *nirvana*, he chooses to live by himself to underline a metaphysical truism that man is essentially lonely (e) he also highlights man's capabilities to live in complete isolation with greater satisfaction and fulfilment, even while being a social animal, and (f) in nursing his utopian dream, he desires to live alone with the elements in a state of tranquillity.

This verse bears ample testimony to Ghalib's imaginative vitality which helps him carve out a utopian world for the speaker. Two expressions—*ham-suKHan* (dialogue sharer) and *ham-zabaa.n* (of the same tongue)—are complementary to each other and they create a sense of kinship among men who may communicate with each other. The speaker negates this kinship and expresses his desire to remain alone, which is well qualified by the phrase *koii na ho* (let there be none around). The simple word *ab* (now) underlines his need to be away from everyone at the present moment. This suggests that the experience of living in companionship with others has been neither rewarding nor pleasant. This condition of philosophical detachment takes a comparable turn in this verse by Bedam Shah Varsi: *dasht-e Ghurbat mei.n tire KHaak nashii.n achhe hai.n / chaahiye aur unhei.n be-sar-o saamaa.n honaa.*

127

بے در و دیوار سا اک گھر بنایا چاہیئے
کوئی ہمسایہ نہ ہو اور پاسباں کوئی نہ ہو

बे-दर-ओ-दीवार सा इक घर बनाया चाहिये
कोई हम-साया न हो और पासबाँ कोई न हो

be dar-o-diivaar saa ik ghar banaayaa chaahiye
koii ham-saaya na ho aur paasbaa.n koii na ho

(dar-o diivaar—door and wall;
ham-saaya—neighbour;
paasbaa.n—guard, watchman, sentinel, keeper)

Let a house be made akin
to a door-less, wall-less one
Let there be no neighbour there,
not even a guard, none

This is a contiguous verse to the previous one from the same ghazal. The speaker is a seeker here who extends the idea of his splendid isolation further with a different set of images. He imagines a home with no doors and walls, not even a neighbour and a guard, which amounts to developing a new idea of a dwelling or habitat. This clearly speaks of his disengagement with the material world.

In this highly paradoxical, yet philosophical, verse, Ghalib's speaker unveils the states of his conscious and subconscious mind as follows: (a) he denies all worldly encumbrances that subject human beings to misery, and loss of privacy and independence (b) he speaks to us like a Sufi who denies the burdens of home and hearth (c) he redefines the idea of habitat and reconstructs one that is unworldly and esoteric (d) he also underlines the significance of vacuum, or nothingness, which is filled with greater meaning, and finally, (e) he makes a metaphysical point that human beings cannot apparently perceive everything, because there is so much that may be perceived, or experienced, but only in a state of imaginative ecstasy.

The verse is essentially surrealistic in nature which imparts it a unique strength. The idea of a house without four walls, the dispensability of a gatekeeper, who could keep it guarded and safe, and the denial of a neighbour's presence who could provide company, are aggressively esoteric in nature. This is borne out well by the diction and images executed here. Five visual images of *dar* (door), *diivaar* (wall), *ghar* (house), *ham-saaya* (neighbour) and *paasbaa.n* (guard) join hands to create a sense of worldly possessions, which he denies in entirety with the double use of *na* (no) in the second line. Drawing upon Ghalib in all probability, Nasir Kazmi comes up with his intriguingly individual kind of a composition: *diivaangii-i shauq ko ye dhun hai in dino.n / ghar bhii ho aur be-dar-o diivaar saa bhii ho.*

128

صد جلوہ رو بہ رو ہے جو مژگاں اٹھائیے
طاقت کہاں کہ دید کا احساں اٹھائیے

सद जल्वा रू-ब-रू है जो मिज़गाँ उठाइए
ताक़त कहाँ कि दीद का एहसाँ उठाइए

sad jalva ruu-ba-ruu hai jo mizhgaa.n uThhaaiye
taaqat kahaa.n ke diid ka ehsaa.n uThhaaiye

(*sad*—hundred;
jalva—manifestation, appearance, display, lustre;
ruu-ba-ruu—face-to-face, in front of; in presence of;
mizhgaa.n—eyelash;
diid—sight, seeing, spectacle;
ehsaa.n—kindness, obligation, beneficence)

If one raises one's eyelashes,
there are a hundred sights of being
But do the eyes have the strength
to bear the delights of seeing

God's grandeur is manifest all around for beholders but only if they could see. The speaker is full of gratitude for the divine blessings in this verse. Also, man cannot express his gratitude to the divine in any possible way. Even though divine manifestations are writ large all around, man's capacity is too limited to bear the beneficence of seeing with his mere two eyes that may otherwise survey all, but only superficially.

Ghalib speaks in gratitude for himself, as also for all others and suggests that (a) the world is a splendid gallery of God's grandeur where each manifestation is amazingly different from the other (b) in spite of all his prowess, man is too incapable to enjoy the brilliant spectacle that God has spread out before him (c) there is a mysterious relationship between the object and the seer, and the objects of seeing are of far greater value than the vision man has at his command to see them, and (d) being full of reverence and gratitude for God's innumerable gifts, the poet acknowledges the divine blessings that God has bestowed upon His creation.

Several expressions in the verse hold our attention. *Sad* (hundred) does not necessarily indicate a number but implies the multitudinous manifestations that are presented to man. *Jalva* (display) is another deep word which goes beyond the visual spectacle and stands for God's splendour. The most powerful phrase, *diid kaa ehsaa.n* (the obligation of seeing), comes at the end as a phrase that fastens the sense of veneration for God in the body of the verse. For the reasons of its proximity with Ghalib, a rubaai by Mir Anis is worth referring to here: *gulshan mei.n phiruu.n ke sair-e sahraa dekhuu.n / ya m'aadan-o koh-o dasht-o dariyaa dekhuu.n / har jaa tiri qudrat ke hai.n laakho.n jalve / hairaan huu.n do aankho.n se kyaa kyaa dekhuu.n.*

129

مسجد کے زیرِ سایہ خرابات چاہیے
بھوں پاس آنکھ قبلۂ حاجات چاہیے

मस्जिद के ज़ेर-ए साया ख़राबात चाहिए
भौं पास आँख क़िबला-ए हाजात चाहिए

masjid ke zer-e saaya KHaraabaat chaahiye
bhau.n paas aa.nkh qibla-i haajaat chaahiye

(*KHaraabaat*—tavern, bar, gambling den, ruin;
qibla-i haajaat—one who meets all needs)

A tavern under the shadow of a mosque,
let there be one
Like eyebrows near the eyes, O my giver,
let there be one

The world is not divided between bad and good in absolute terms. Ghalib comes up with an apparently irreverent verse here, the likes of which are sprinkled across his ghazals like salt and pepper. In his typical vein, he thinks of a tavern and a mosque together, and makes them sit alongside to see whether they hold well with each other or deny each other outrightly. He tries to see meaning in their possible integration or separation, as it may be.

There are certain thought-provoking aspects in the seemingly disparate situation this verse creates: (a) the poet draws upon the traditional metaphors of eyes as the wine-house and brows as the prayer-niche of a mosque to build his poetic logic (b) this is well supplemented with the idea of a tavern in the shade of a mosque like eyebrows near the eyes (c) this also suggests that God Himself has made the mosque and the tavern, as well as those who choose to go there (d) while the poet turns irreverent, he actually acknowledges the existence of two institutions and their visitors who deny each other, yet they visit their chosen destinations just as they wish, and (e) that one could understand life fully only if one took cognisance of both, rather than deny any.

Ghalib constructs this verse by putting together the incompatible ideas of the *masjid* (mosque) and *KHaraabaat* (tavern/ruin) in the first line, and the compatible ideas of *bhau.n* (eyebrow) and *aa.nkh* (eye) in the second line. All these finally submit to *qibla-i haajaat* (the provider for needs) for a resolution. It should be rewarding to note that Ghalib uses *KHaraabaat* in both the senses of a tavern and a ruin, and makes the verse doubly complicated. The element of irony may not be missed in the phrase *zer-e saaya* (under the shade) of the mosque, which provides a space to the tavern and suggests, by implication, that life and the world are composed and constituted of opposites and thrive in reconciliation. Mir Taqi Mir's individual apprehension in this context deserves our attention: *masjid mei.n imam aaj huaa aa ke vahaa.n se / kal tak to yahii Mir KHaraabaat nashii.n tha.* It should be befitting in this context to quote Qayam Chandpuri too: *zaahid dar-e masjid pe KHaraabaat kii tuu ne / jii bhii yu.n hii chaahe thaa KHaraabaat kii tuu ne.*

130

مے سے غرض نشاط ہے کس رو سیاہ کو
اک گونہ بے خودی مجھے دن رات چاہیئے

मय से ग़रज़ नशात है किस रू-सियाह को
इक-गूना बे-ख़ुदी मुझे दिन रात चाहिए

mai se Gharaz nishaat hai kis ruu-siyaah ko
ik gunaa be-KHudii mujhe din raat chaahiye

(*mai*—wine, spiritous liquor;
GHaraz—intention, object, purpose;
nishaat—joy, pleasure, ecstasy;
ruu-siyaah—disgraced, dishonoured, damned;
ik guunaa—continuous, incessant;
be-KHudii—rapture, ecstasy, selflessness)

Who cares for wine's ecstasy, who is that damned one
I must remain ecstatic ever, nothing else, none

Wine and its intoxication have been stock subjects of the ghazal. Drawing upon this, Ghalib's speaker makes a plea for a desired state of ecstasy in which he wishes to be and enjoy himself without end. Who intends to drink wine merely for the joys of drinking, he asks rhetorically, and asserts that being in a state of self-intoxication is what he aspires for. He thus assigns a special role to wine as a redeemer and to himself as the redeemed one.

This ostensibly playful verse has its own implications: (a) the speaker seeks pleasure in an unusual way as he does not drink like ordinary men for the sake of temporary intoxication (b) instead, he wishes to be in an exalted state of selflessness and self-absorption day and night, which only the more elevated ones deserve to be in (c) wine, thus, becomes a source of achieving a state of extraordinary rapture which cannot be achieved in the state of consciousness (d) in this state of rapture alone, he may get rid of the mundane matters of life and living (e) this also helps him define his intriguingly individual way of belonging to a physical world, while also being oblivious of it, and (f) being drunk on divine inspiration is yet another aspect of drinking, which characterizes both the mystics and the men of God.

The speaker speaks quite conceitedly in this verse on the strength of five key words—*mai* (wine), *nishaat* (ecstasy), *ik guuna* (continuous) *be-KHudii* (rapture) and *ruu-siyaah* (damned). With the first four words, he reflects his own mood, but with *ruu-siyaah* he segregates a mean drinker, who is literally black-faced and damned, and drinks merely for the sake of simple intoxication, which the speaker abhors. Mir Taqi Mir's famous verse comes naturally to mind in this reference: *be-KHudii le gaii kahaa.n ham ko / der se intizaar hai apnaa.*

131

بے رنگ لالہ و گل و نسریں جدا جدا
ہر رنگ میں بہار کا اثبات چاہیے

है रंग-ए लाला-ओ-गुल-ओ-नसरीं जुदा जुदा
हर रंग में बहार का इसबात चाहिये

hai ra.ng-e laala-o gul-o nasrii.n judaa judaa
har ra.ng mei.n bahaar kaa isbaat chaahiye

(*laala*—tulip, poppy flower;
nasrii.n—white rose;
isbaat—affirmation, recognition, confirmation)

Each blossom—poppy, tulip—is different in its hue
An assertion of spring—must there be in each, anew

Spring is the mirror of beauty, a divine bliss, and is much celebrated in poetry. In this apparently single-layered verse, Ghalib makes a point that is enormously appealing for the multiple messages it embodies with regard to the beauty of nature. He says that all the blossoms in the garden have their own colours, but more importantly each colour affirms the presence of spring in nature. He thus visualizes spring as a permanent condition which every hue of the blossom represents. This brings the verse closer to the poetics of nature poetry which discovers pantheistic shades in it.

In making an assertive statement, Ghalib posits certain subtle suggestions here: (a) it is divine glory reflected through the beauty of nature that primarily holds his attention (b) nature appears to him in many of its resplendent faces, with each one having its own hue (c) he pays his obeisance to this divine glory as a pantheist would do (d) in the way meaning is constructed here, the garden stands for the world, blossoms for the manifestations of the world and colours for the resplendence of divine signs, and (e) metaphorically, Ghalib brings in a mystical dimension to this verse with reference to nature symbolism as found in poetry across languages.

The two blossoms—*laala* (tulip) and *nasrii.n* (white rose)—serve as generic references for the beauty of nature and the existence of spring. The word *ra.ng* (colour) stands here for the colour of nature, as also for the variety of blossoms in the garden. The verse acquires its value in how Ghalib makes the two blossoms paradigmatic of the variety that nature represents, and how they affirm the existence of spring and its resplendence. *Bahaar* (spring) is the key word, representing life in bliss and the permanence of beauty and its resplendence. This reminds, in particular, of 'God's Grandeur' by Gerard Manley Hopkins: 'And all for this, nature is never spent;/There lives the dearest freshness deep down things ...'

132

گھر میں تھا کیا کہ ترا غم اسے غارت کرتا
وہ جو رکھتے تھے ہم اک حسرت تعمیر سو ہے

घर में था क्या कि तिरा ग़म उसे ग़ारत करता
वो जो रखते थे हम इक हसरत-ए तामीर सो है

ghar mei.n kyaa thaa ke tiraa GHam use GHaarat kartaa
vo jo rakhte the ham ik hasrat-e t'aamiir so hai

(*GHaarat*—destroy, vanquish, extinguish;
hasrat—yearning, longing, desire;
t'amiir—construction, building, creation)

What was there left in home that your sorrow
could bring them to nought
The yearning I had once for creation,
with that I'm still caught

Lovers never tire; they ever retain their spirit and express themselves in extraordinary ways. Ghalib's lover addresses his beloved here to make two assertions: (i) on a pensive note, he says ironically that there was nothing more that the beloved could do to vanquish his heart any further, but (ii) on a positive note, he asserts that he still retains his yearning to put things in order once again. The house being referred to here stands for the lover's vanquished heart, but he wishes to keep it thriving, while expecting indirectly that the beloved would keep pace with him in his attempt.

The coats of implicational meaning may be marked in these terms: (a) the house, which is akin to the heart, is broken, but that is not the end of the world for the lover (b) the beloved, as she is, brings misery, but the lover, as he must be, preserves his spirit to rebuild it (b) the lover expresses his grief by stating indirectly that he neither enjoys the beloved's blessings nor the world's favours anymore (c) even in this state of deprivation, he emerges as one without losing his hope and faith (d) this refusal to be vanquished in love only suggests that lovers are not meant to be estranged or separated, but only to stay together, and finally (e) it comes out that grief is inferior to passion and passion cannot be vanquished in any case.

Two expressions—*GHam* (grief) and *GHaarat* (destruction)—that create an onomatopoeic effect, supplement each other with respect to semantic implications and carry the essential burden of the verse. The phrase *hasrat-e t'aamiir* (longing to reconstruct) carries the weight of the lover's optimism and his determination to keep his heart, the home of love, alive and thriving as it was earlier. The lover's tone of yearning adds to the immediacy of appeal of this verse and makes its impact on the reader.

133

غم دنیا سے گر پائی بھی فرصت سر اٹھانے کی
فلک کا دیکھنا تقریب تیرے یاد آنے کی

ग़म-ए-दुनिया से गर पाई भी फ़ुर्सत सर उठाने की
फ़लक का देखना तक़रीब तेरे याद आने की

*Gham-e duniyaa se gar paaii bhii fursat sar uThhaane kii
falak kaa dekhnaa taqriib tere yaad aaane kii*

(*falak*—sky, firmament, heaven;
taqriib—auspicious occasion, ceremony, festival)

From the worries of the world,
if I get a chance of release ever
To look up the skies, evoke your memory,
shall be my endeavour

Suffering and the desire to seek release from suffering keep the balance of living in place. The two lines of this verse, logically related to each other, speak to us in the voice of the lover. The lover plainly states that if at all he gets time to seek release from the worries of the world and raise his head, he would look up to the skies in gratitude, which would also be a ceremonious occasion for him to remember his beloved. This is his frank admission of his predicament to the beloved with which he asserts his steadfastness in love. This verse may be categorized along with those verses that gloss upon the bliss of love and warmth in romantic relationships.

The speaker pays his highest compliments to his beloved as follows: (a) he considers himself to be a victim of the sufferings that this world has brought to him (b) but he asserts that the beloved alone can bring him release from all his sufferings (c) uniquely enough, he equates the act of looking up at the sky with that of remembering the beloved, which is no less than a ceremony (d) in doing so, he asserts his faith as much in the divine power as in his beloved, and (e) this is how he finds her a place there, rather than on the earth, which is so full of sorrows.

The expression *taqriib* (auspicious occasion) holds the key position in this verse. As a potent carrier of meaning, it incorporates multiple connotations of ceremony, festivity and celebration which relate with remembering, or being reminded of the beloved. The act of looking at the sky and the ceremony of remembering the beloved bear out the merits of Ghalib's intensely poetic turn of imagination. The desire for companionship with the beloved remains conditional, however, which is concealed artfully in the smallest unit of the word *gar* (if at all). This is where the element of paroxysm comes out and makes the verse doubly impactful.

134

کیا خوب تم نے غیر کو بوسہ نہیں دیا
بس چپ رہو ہمارے بھی منہ میں زبان ہے

क्या ख़ूब तुम ने ग़ैर को बोसा नहीं दिया
बस चुप रहो हमारे भी मुंह में ज़बान है

kyaa KHuub tum ne Ghair ko bosa nahii.n diyaa
bas chup raho hamaare bhii mu.nh mei.n zabaan hai

(*bosa*—kiss)

That you didn't let the other kiss you,
what a joke—how sleek!
Well, just keep shut;
I too have a tongue in my cheek

A grumpy lover addressing his beloved with certain doubts about her in his mind presents a dramatic sight. Ghalib constructs the image of one such lover here. This lover addresses the beloved sardonically and asks her not to make a false plea for her innocence as he knows well that she had offered a kiss to someone else. He asks her to keep shut and not argue, else he will reveal what he knows and leave her defenceless. The verse is striking for its remarkable merit to amuse the reader. Cautiously enough, the beloved chooses to just listen without getting back to her lover with her words or gestures of any kind.

Even in this characteristically jovial verse, there are interesting aspects of the lover-beloved relationship: (a) the lover is possessive, jealous and complaining, all at the same time (b) as he cannot show proof, he can only cast a doubt on her as lovers are prone to nursing doubts about the fidelity of their beloveds (c) by saying that he too has a tongue in his mouth, he makes two suggestions: (i) he can answer back to vanquish her defence of innocence, and (ii) he may kiss her lips and confirm that she has been kissed by someone else (d) in spite of this, he does not disown or castigate her because he is still devoted to her (e) he complains to her in all honesty, even without expecting a reply from her, and (f) instead of harbouring any malice, he only wants her to be his own and of none else.

The verse has a light tone and a conversational ease to the core. The phrase *Kyaa KHuub* (how smart!) contains light irony and defines the nature of the verse with this very first expression itself. Another phrase—*Ghair* (the other)—is richly ambiguous here, containing multiple implications of a rival, a stranger, an outsider and even a lecherous one. This verse is yet another variation on the theme of the other as rival in Urdu ghazal. Quite interestingly, by telling her *bas chup raho* (just keep shut) he shows his authority over his beloved which she does not challenge.

135

درد سے میرے ہے تجھ کو بے قراری ہائے ہائے
کیا ہوئی ظالم تری غفلت شعاری ہائے ہائے

दर्द से मेरे है तुझ को बे-क़रारी हाए हाए
क्या हुई ज़ालिम तिरी ग़फ़लत-शिआरी हाए हाए

dard se mere hai tujh ko be-qaraarii haai haaii
kyaa huii zaalim tiri Ghaflat-shi'aarii haai haai

(*Ghaflat-shi'aarii*—habit of neglecting, perpetual carelessness)

Now, my pain makes you restive, ah!
Where your neglect, O cruel one, ah!

Even the cruel beloveds turn kind when they see lovers in pain. Here is a special moment of sharing sympathy in love that Ghalib chooses to celebrate. He portrays a lover in pain and a beloved who had been negligent so far, but she is much too concerned now and expresses that through her unmistakable gestures. The lover asks her the cause of her kindness which remains unanswered, but in this very act of her concern for him, lies the proof of her love for him. This is a naturalistic portrayal of a condition in love that is expressed in many ways, sometimes even in as strange a way as this one.

There are certain thought-provoking implications in this verse: (a) the beloved is restless because she can guess that the lover is in pain (b) the lover wonders as to how the beloved, who was negligent so far, has turned sympathetic now (c) he knows quite well that in spite of her indifference, she is as much in love with him as he is with her, and (d) with this, he feels rewarded as a lover as his pain becomes the cause of her restlessness.

A set of two expressions—*dard* (pain) and *be-qaraarii* (restlessness)—join hands as cause-and-effect words. Another set of expressions—*zaalim* (cruel) and *Ghaflat-shi'aarii* (habit of neglecting)—works exactly in the same manner, and they come together to characterize the beloved. Interestingly, after she has shown her concern, she is no longer a cruel and negligent beloved in the eyes of the lover. The refrain of *haai haai* (ah! ah!) provides a sense of curious wonderment and relief, which defines the basic nature of the verse.

136

عمر بھر کا تو نے پیمان وفا باندھا تو کیا
عمر کو بھی تو نہیں ہے پائیداری ہاے ہاے

उम्र भर का तू ने पैमान-ए वफ़ा बाँधा तो क्या
उम्र को भी तो नहीं है पाएदारी हाए हाए

'umr bhar kaa tuu ne paimaan-e vafaa baa.ndhaa a to kyaa
'umr ko bhii to nahii.n hai paaedaarii haai haai

(*paimaan-e vafaa*—promise to love,
bond of love, commitment to love;
paaedaarii—stability, constancy, firmness)

What if you struck a bond of love for life, ah!
But this life does not endure beyond a life, ah!

The idea of life's transitoriness has ever been a subject of literary and philosophical discourses. This verse capitalizes upon this idea in poetic terms. Lovers may form a pact to stay together for life; but life itself is transitory and is subject to reaching a terminal point. Marked by its elegiac tone, the verse makes sense with respect to both—the lover and the beloved—who vowed to keep a bond for life, but, tragically enough, they have no control over retaining life beyond the destined moment of passing away.

As this verse unveils the reality of life and death, it develops both as a dirge and a discourse in the process: (a) none can make a commitment or enter into a bond of love, for all times (b) life is defined by a given times pan which must terminate sooner or later (c) as such, both love and life terminate together when death strikes (d) so, the pledge of togetherness falls flat as it leaves the lovers suffering in separation, and (e) although the verse expresses the lover's sense of obligation and indebtedness to the beloved, they remain destined to part and pine for the lost one.

Two expressions—*paimaan* (bond) and *paaedaarii* (stability)—call for attention as they strengthen the central idea of the verse. A bond is no bond if it is not stable, and since no bond for life can be true, it comes out that life and stability are contradictory ideas. A simple exclamatory-cum-interrogative phrase with a conversational tone—*to kyaa* (so what)—emphatically underlines the feebleness of that bond and makes the verse exceptionally persuasive. The refrain of *haai haai*, as executed in the earlier verse too, adds to the impact of mourning marked presumably by breast-beating.

137

شرم رسوائی سے جا چھپنا نقاب خاک میں
ختم ہے الفت کی تجھ پر پردہ داری ہائے ہائے

शर्म-ए रुस्वाई से जा छुपना नक़ाब-ए ख़ाक में
ख़त्म है उल्फ़त की तुझ पर पर्दा-दारी हाए हाए

sharm-e rusvaaii se jaa chhupnaa niqaab-e KHaak mei.n
KHatm hai ulfat kii tujh per parda-daarii hai hai

(*rusvaaii*—embarrassment, infamy;
niqab-e KHaak—veil of soil;
parda-daarii—veiling)

To go and conceal in the soil's cloak to save infamy, ah!
Ah, the veiling of love comes to end with you alone, ah!

This is yet another verse of the same ghazal we have examined just before this verse. The lover remorsefully meditates upon the passing away of the beloved here, who, in figurative words, has turned her back on life. In leaving this world, she has left behind much to ponder over concerning love as a cause for infamy and love as pretension. This makes the lover muse over his, as well as her, predicament. This verse is remarkable for the unusual suggestions it makes about the passing away of the beloved from this world.

This poignant verse opens up several leaves of meaning: (a) the loved one either fears infamy, or she has already been blamed for indulging in love, which has made her go behind the veil of soil (b) one wonders if she has brought her life to its end on her own or has suffered enough to die a natural death (c) one also wonders if the bond of love is a cause for infamy in this world of false pretensions (d) the departed one has thus put a veil on her love in disappearing from this world (e) she has maintained the secrecy of her love in a manner, which none else would ever do (f) the sense of mourning, writ large on the face of this verse, brings it closer to the tone and tenor of elegiac poetry.

The crucial expressions—*sharm* (shame), *rusvaaii* (infamy), *niqaab-e KHaak* (veil of soil) and *parda-daarii* (veiling)—weave the pathetic plot of this verse together. *Sharm* and *rusvaaii* are broadly synonymous, and carry a tinge of irony, just as *niqaab-e KHaak* and *parda-daarii* are largely identical in import, and spell out the idea of death and disappearance from the face of the earth. This amounts to drawing a veil against the world and all its manifestations, including human beings, who are transitory and are moving towards their demise with every passing moment. These expressions, read in this manner, complete the circle of meaning here.

138

لیتا نہیں مرے دل آوارہ کی خبر
اب تک وہ جانتا ہے کہ میرے ہی پاس ہے

लेता नहीं मिरे दिल-ए आवारा की ख़बर
अब तक वो जानता है कि मेरे ही पास है

**letaa nahii.n mire dil-e-aavaara kii KHabar
ab tak vo jaantaa hai ke mere hii paas hai**

She does not bother to ask after my wild heart
She thinks it's still with me, me alone, my heart

Lovers, being too conscious of themselves, always wonder if they are being cared for by a sulking beloved. This light-hearted verse presents the picture of a young lover who is devoted to one who is yet to be called a beloved in real terms. It is indeed an ironical situation in which the beloved does not really know that there is someone who has already fallen for her. This is both a pathetic and a comic situation for the young man to be in. This lover wishes that she knew about him and asked after him. This is not a matter of feigned pretension of ignorance on the part of the beloved, but of the simple fact that many young ladies do not know how many suitors they might have.

Even in a verse of this kind, Ghalib opens avenues of multiple interpretations as we may see here: (a) the lover's heart has already turned rogue, but he does not confess this to his beloved (b) far from complaining about her, he gets playful about her ignorance that he has already fallen in love with her (c) as he muses over this, he also shares this with a supposed listener who may be amused by his story or sympathize with him (d) he seems to suggest that she is an innocent beloved, and finally (e) the verse makes its mark as a soft soliloquy which reads like an expression of sheer love for the much-aspired one.

Ghalib qualifies the lover's heart as a wandering heart and calls it *dil-e aavaara*. This construction is loaded with a rich meaning because the lover is in a state of wandering and is yet to reach his destination. Even though *aavaara* may have a negative connotation, suggesting that the lover is a frisky figure, it works positively in the context of this verse. The wandering heart is indeed the wandering lover whom the poet presents playfully in a bright light.

139

ہر اک مکان کو ہے بے مکیں سے شرفِ اسدؔ
مجنوں جو مر گیا ہے تو جنگل اداس ہے

हर इक मकान को है मकीं से शरफ़ 'असद'
मजनूँ जो मर गया है तो जंगल उदास है

har ik makaan ko hai makii.n se sharf Asad
majnuu.n jo mar gayaa hai to jungle udaas hai

(*makii.n*—dweller;
sharf—glory, eminence)

Each abode gets its glory, Asad,
with its dweller alone
Now that Majnuu.n is dead and gone,
jungle is sad and forlorn

Here is a verse that poeticizes a truism. Surely, every house gets its glory from its dweller. A house is no house if it does not have a dweller with his or her own distinguishing value. This is just as the jungle got its splendour from Majnuu.n and, with his passing away, it lost that splendour. Ghalib brings in the paradigm of Majnuu.n and the jungle here to enliven his verse with a fascinating implication.

Some thoughtful implications may be marked from what Ghalib intends to suggest here: (a) Majnuu.n is associated with wilderness, not a physical home or an abode, which makes him an enamouring and iconic figure (b) after leaving his home, he found his home in the wilderness, where he wandered all over pining for his beloved, Laila (c) Majnuu.n's presence in the wilderness brought splendour to the wilderness itself and it got associated with his name (d) with the passing away of Majnuu.n, the jungle lost its lover, which makes it mournful (e) essentially, the verse engages with the idea of home and alters its definition, suggesting that even the wilderness can be a home by virtue of someone living in and belonging to that home.

Ghalib often fills his counters of expression with new meaning, as he does here in the case of *makaan* (dwelling) and *makii.n* (dweller). By presenting the jungle as sad, he personifies it and imparts it a human quality, which means that the jungle, too, can mourn Majnun's passing away. Ghalib has drawn upon the stock figure of Majnuu.n in other verses as well, one of which is particularly relevant in the context of his typicality which invokes sympathy: *mai.n ne Majnuu.n pe laRakpan mei.n Asad / sa.ng uThaayaa tha ke sar yaad aayaa*. Ram Narayan Mauzuun has also developed an interesting perspective on this: *Ghazalaa.n tum to vaaqif ho kaho Majnuu.n ke marne kii / divaana mar gayaa aaKHir ko viiraane pe kyaa guzrii*.

140

بستی کے مت فریب میں آ جائیو اسدؔ
عالم تمام حلقۂ دامِ خیال ہے

हस्ती के मत फ़रेब में आ जाइयो 'असद'
आलम तमाम हल्का-ए दाम-ए ख़याल है

hastii ke mat fareb mei.n aa jaaio Asad
'aalam tamaam halqa-i daam-e KHayaal hai

(*hastii*—life, existence, being;
fareb—deception, deceit, illusion;
'aalam—world, condition;
halqa—circle, loop, net;
daam-e Khayaal—net/trap/web/snare of imagination)

Don't be deceived, Asad, by the being's naughty knots
The entire world is only a net, a web of thoughts

Is existence a deception? In addressing this philosophical question, Ghalib appears to us at his philosophical best. He develops a primary discourse about existence in its broadest sense, which incorporates the many shades of life and the world. He unravels the mystery of life and living, being and becoming, illusion and reality, and imagination and ratiocination. By considering the world as a web of imagination, he warns man by imploring him not to be deluded by the tempting and misleading phenomenon called the world.

As Ghalib assumes the posture of a preacher, he suggests that (a) existence is mere deception and the world a trap of illusions (b) one's physical presence in this world cannot be taken as a sign of one's real existence (c) life and creation are nothing but hypotheses and one keeps hovering in a web of illusions (d) this hovering around does not help arrive anywhere, as both the world and existence are merely suppositional (e) human and terrestrial existence bear upon one another, and quite significantly, (f) the problematic of existential angst and the resultant crisis reflect largely upon the illusion of life 'as dreamt' and the reality of life 'as lived' (g) in this respect, Ghalib foreshadows the philosophical discourses of prominent existentialist philosophers like Soren Kierkegaard, Fredrich Nietzsche and Jean-Paul Sartre.

In his characteristic style, Ghalib richly combines two interrelated words—*fareb* (deception) and *daam-e KHayaal* (snare of imagination)—to reflect upon each other and to deepen the meaning of deception. The two together weave a design of the central intent of this verse in relation to the problematic of *hastii* (existence). Similarly, two other corresponding images—*halqa* (circle) and *daam* (trap)—strengthen the primary idea of entrapment. In addition, circle and trap act as metaphors, and they define the nature of life and the world together, and enrich Ghalib's intended meaning. Ghalib's preoccupation with existential crisis is reflected in other verses as well with equal brilliance: *hastii hamaarii apnii fanaa per daliil hai / yaa.n tak mite ke aap ham apnii qasam huve* and *haa.n khaaiyo mat fareb-e hastii / harchand kahei.n ke hai nahii.n hai.*

141

دل ہی تو ہے سیاست درباں سے ڈر گیا
میں اور جاؤں در سے ترے بن صدا کیے

दिल ही तो है सियासत-ए दरबाँ से डर गया
मैं और जाऊँ दर से तिरे बिन सदा किए

dil hii to hai siyaasat-e darbaa.n se Dar gayaa
mai.n aur jaau.n dar se tire bin sadaa kiye

(*siyaasat-e darbaa.n*—guard's politics;
sadaa—call)

After all, it's only my heart; it got scared
of the guard's trick and gall
But well this is me; how could I return
from your door without raising a call

Lovers have rivals not only in the figure of the other; the snooping guard, too, could be a different kind of rival. This is a verse with the lover and the guard facing each other, but supposedly from some distance. The dishevelled lover seeks admittance into the beloved's quarters, but the tough guard, considering his appearance, keeps him away by taking advantage of his position. Scared of the guard's power by virtue of his position, the lover could not even raise a call. The typical lover and the stereotypical guard create a situation that we witness with curiosity only to find that the guard succeeds in his politics in playing the role of a tough deterrent between him and the lady.

Interesting aspects of this drama may be noted as follows: (a) the lover is persistent and unyielding, howsoever difficult it might be for him to assert his position (b) the guard at the beloved's quarter emerges not only as a house guard but also of the lady (c) this guard employs his own tricks of politics to deter the lover and he succeeds in his move (d) the lover is doubly disappointed in that he can neither gain admittance nor raise a call because of the guard's fearful presence (e) the beloved is nowhere in sight but her presence is writ large in the verse along with the guard and the lover, who are the real actors in the drama.

Ghalib employs the conventional symbolism of *darbaa.n* (guard) used in the Urdu ghazal as a figure of deterrence and discouragement. A more fascinating figure, however, is that of the lover here whose desires remain unfulfilled. While the guard is characterized by his *siyaasat* (politics) of keeping visitors at bay, the lover who looks like a disappointed *faqiir* of love, cannot even raise his *sadaa* (call) to the beloved for fear of the deterrent guard and returns crestfallen. In a unique play of his words, Ghalib's constructs the figure of the unfriendly guard in another verse as follows: *phir jii mei.n hai ke dar pe kisii ke paRe rahei.n / sar zer-e baar-e minnat darbaa.n kiye huve and vaa.n gayaa bhii mai.n to un kii gaaliyo.n kaa kyaa javaab / yaad thii.n jitnii duaaei.n sarf-e darbaa.n ho gaei.n.*

142

مقدور ہو تو خاک سے پوچھوں کہ اے لئیم
تو نے وہ گنج ہائے گراں مایہ کیا کیے

मक़दूर हो तो ख़ाक से पूछूँ कि ऐ लईम
तू ने वो गंज-हा-ए गराँ-माया क्या किए

maqduur ho to KHaak se puuchhu.n ke ai laiim
tuu ne vo ganj-haa-e garaa.n-maaya kyaa kiye

(*maqduur*—means, resource;
laiim—ignoble, inglorious, miser;
ganj-haa-e garaa.n-maaya—of precious stock)

If I may have the power to ask,
I'd ask this ignoble earth
What on earth did you do
with those of the precious birth

Many noble faces go to hide in the veil of the soil and merge with the earth. Those left behind are left to mourn, as Ghalib's speaker does here. He addresses the earth and asks where did all those of prodigious worth disappear without leaving any traces behind. The question is left unanswered and makes the readers meditate on this. In this unanswered question lies the possible answer about men of precious stock who disappeared forever and the callous earth failed to preserve them. Perhaps, it establishes the fact yet again that men who rise from the soil go back to the soil, irrespective of their proud stock, or lineage.

The possible implications of this verse may be appreciated with reference to the following: (a) the speaker puts a haunting question to the earth about the whereabouts of those precious souls who adorned the world once and were adorned by the world in return for their merits (b) the one who puts forth this question considers himself of little means, just like the earth, which is of little value and is essentially inglorious (c) in spite of being the mother, the earth is called inglorious because it did not preserve the precious souls (d) the earth cannot answer the moot question regarding the creation and preservation of the noble souls (e) presumably, the soil that composes the earth is destined to blow with the wind and be traceless, like the noble souls who too blew away into nothingness, and ironically enough, (f) the earth is inglorious, but it lives on, while those of the precious stock disappear for good.

The speaker presents himself as one who has little *maqduur* (means). He also presents the earth as *laiim* (inglorious). With this, his question regarding the survival of *ganj-haa-e garaa.n-maaya* (of precious stock) remains unattended. Ghalib's engagement with the idea of those belonging to the precious stock finds its echo in Nietzsche's philosophy of the superman, who is a picture of perfection and evolves his own principles of perfection in a given social order. This brings us to Ghalib's other verse: *vo daad-o diid garaamaayaa.n shart hai hamdam / vagarna muhr-e Suleman-o jaam-e jam kyaa hai.*

143

صحبت میں غیر کی نہ پڑی ہو کہیں یہ خو
دینے لگا ہے بوسہ بغیر التجا کیے

सोहबत में ग़ैर की न पड़ी हो कहीं ये ख़ू
देने लगा है बोसा बग़ैर इल्तिजा किए

sohbat mei.n Ghair kii na padii ho kahii.n ye KHuu
dene lagaa hai bosa baGhair iltijaa kiye

(*sohbat*—company;
KHuu—habit;
iltijaa—entreating)

Was it in the company of the other
she got this habit, I wonder,
How she offers to be kissed
without imploring, without wonder

A very unusual idea about the company one keeps is the subject of this verse. The lover finds it unusual that the beloved should offer a kiss to a stranger even without an asking. He wonders if she developed this habit in the company of the mythical 'other'. This speaks clearly of the lover as one who is possessive and often in doubt about the steadfastness of the beloved. With this doubt in mind, he remains in constant suffering and deprives himself of the pleasures of love.

As this queer idea finds space in the speaker's imagination, exciting aspects of the verse come to the fore: (a) the lover never received a kiss from his beloved without asking but she favoured the other, which casts a dark shadow on her (b) instead of being unhappy or angry, he turns doubtful of the beloved because she has been in the company of others presumably for some time and must have favoured them with a kiss (c) there is an impending sense of jealousy with the other, even as the lover is possessive of her (d) he suffers because he cannot either disengage with her or confront her, and sadly, (e) with his mistrust in her, he puts her in the circle of doubt for no good reason.

With the deft choice of words, Ghalib has turned this experience worthy of literary merit. Even while the word *sohbat* (company) carries a neutral meaning of togetherness, it also has a negative connotation of an illicit relationship. This negative implication of the word haunts the lover and marks his attitude of doubt towards the beloved. The word *Ghair* (other) represents the stock figure of the rival, who is a cause of constant worry to the lover. However, it is the word *kahii.n* (if at all) which gives him some sense of relief. In yet another representation of such a mood, we may look at this verse by Ghalib: *bosa dete nahii.n aur dil pe hai har lehza nigaah / jii mei.n kahte hai.n ke muft aae to maal achhaa hai.*

144

نقش کو اس کے مصور پر بھی کیا کیا ناز ہیں
کھینچتا ہے جس قدر اتنا ہی کھنچتا جائے ہے

नक़्श को उस के मुसव्विर पर भी क्या क्या नाज़ हैं
खींचता है जिस क़दर उतना ही खिंचता जाए है

naqsh ko us ke musavvir per bhii kyaa kyaa naaz hai.n
khe.nchtaa hai jis qadar utnaa hii khi.nchtaa jaae hai

(*naqsh*—painting, image;
musavvir—painter, artist;
naaz—pride)

The portrait is proud of the painter,
proud beyond all praise
The more he draws in, the more it draws out,
beyond all praise

Poetics is all that matters in art and artistic representation. There are three direct subjects of attention here—the painting, the painter and the painted. Indirectly, the speaker who comments on them is the fourth subject himself. All four of them present pictures of excellence individually, but together they represent a condition of far-reaching poetic implications. The painting is a fine work of art, the painter is envious of his painting, the painted is a paragon of beauty and the speaker a worthy admirer of all that he sees.

The implications of the verse are quite rich and they work well in these directions: (a) the painter is well-versed in his art, but this is a special moment when he paints the beloved's image and puts himself to test (b) the painting is proud of the painter's genius but the beloved who is being painted puts him to test (c) in one way, the more he paints, the better her image gets painted with each stroke of his brush (d) in another way, the more he paints, the more her image draws itself away from the painter's reach (e) is the painted one too arrogant, one wonders, that she does not lend herself easily to the artist, just as she does not lend herself to the lover in life, and finally (f) the idea of perfection in art and all kinds of creative works is illusory, yet the artist continues with his engagement to acquire excellence in his art, which brings him close to *saadhnaa* and turns him into a *saadhak*.

The key expression that lends this verse its exceptional beauty is the play on the two words—*khe.nchtaa* (draws) and *khi.nchtaa* (gets drawn). The two expressions brilliantly represent two physical and metaphorical conditions of 'drawing in' and 'drawing out'. This amply reflects the tension of the moment in the act of creation. The poetic excellence lies, in fact, in the poetics of tension that Ghalib, the great craftsman, creates here in this verse.

145

کارگاہ ہستی میں لالہ داغ ساماں ہے
برق خرمن راحت خون گرم دہقاں ہے

कार-गाह-ए हस्ती में लाला दाग़-सामाँ है
बर्क़-ए ख़िर्मन-ए राहत ख़ून-ए गर्म-ए दहक़ाँ है

kaargaah-e hastii mei.n laala daaGh-saamaa.n hai
barq-e KHirman-e raahat KHuun-e garm-e dahqaa.n hai

(*kaargaah-e hastii*—workshop of existence;
laala daaGh-saamaa.n—blot-marked tulips/flowers;
barq-e KHirman-e raahat—lightening of
the rewarding harvest;
KHuun-e garm-e dahqaa.n—peasant's hot blood)

In the workshop of existence, the tulip is marked
with blots of ill breed
The lightening on the rewarding harvest is
the peasants' blood indeed

Certain manifestations of the world evade simple explanations. Ghalib draws upon this idea in one of his more complex verses here. He posits that in this world of multiple manifestations, the tulip is indeed blotted, which robs it of its beauty. He then postulates that the lightning which falls on the harvest is but only the peasant's blood that blots the harvest. Here is a discourse on creation and destruction, and what lies between the two stages of being and nothingness. This may well be considered Ghalib's anticipation of the Marxist socio-political discourse that developed and defined the human predicament from a certain socio-political perspective.

We may infer these possible meanings here: (a) in the world of beautiful manifestations, all manifestations are not so beautiful (b) even the most beautiful of blossoms is not without a blot (c) the peasant puts in his hot blood to produce the blossom, which reflects like blots on the face of the blossom (d) the peasant's hot blood returns like lightning on the harvest, and as such, (e) the entire phenomenon reflects the pains taken by the producer to produce his work, just like the garden where nature takes all the pains to produce the blossoms.

The phrasal construction *laala daaGh-saamaa.n* (blot-marked tulips) is a stroke of Ghalib's creative genius where he qualifies the blot on the blossom in an entirely refreshing manner. In the second line, a parcel of three-pronged phrases—*barq-e KHirman-e raahat* (lightening of the rewarding harvest) and *KHuun-e garm-e dahqaa.n* (peasant's hot blood)—create a solid philosophical foundation for the verse. In addition, the similarity between the red colour of *laala* (tulip) and the red blood of the peasant also deepens the Marxist implication of the verse. A comparative perspective may be explored in another verse by Ghalib: *rag-e Laila ko KHaak-e dasht-e Majnuu.n reshagii baKHshe / agar bove bajaae daana dahqaa.n nok-e nashtar kii.*

146

اگ رہا ہے در و دیوار سے سبزہ غالبؔ
ہم بیاباں میں ہیں اور گھر میں بہار آئی ہے

उग रहा है दर-ओ-दीवार से सब्ज़ा 'ग़ालिब'
हम बयाबाँ में हैं और घर में बहार आई है

ug rahaa hai dar-o diivaar se sabza Ghalib
ham bayaabaa.n mei.n hai.n aur ghar mei.n bahaar aaii hai

(*sabza*—greenery;
bayaabaa.n—desert, wilderness, wasteland, desolate)

The walls are getting covered with green,
Ghalib—all over
I am in the wilderness; at home
it's spring—all over

Wilderness and greenery represent the two conditions of life and nature. Ghalib has a crazy lover here who has chosen to leave home for the desert. He develops a monologue with himself and remembers home, which has changed in its appearance with the passage of time. This condition spells out the unpredictable nature of lovers whose actions cannot be judged with reason. Since it is not stated as to what took this lover to wilderness, his action may be considered idiosyncratic. Further, since wilderness does not offer the protection that a home does, the memories of home come back to him intensely.

The levels of implications are diverse here: (a) first, the lover has gone crazy and has left home for the wilderness, as crazy lovers stereotypically do in their pining for their beloveds (b) second, grass and weeds grow on the doors and walls of his uninhabited home in his absence, which he remembers now with a pang (c) third, spring has already arrived back home, which he misses; this pang is further intensified because he knows that spring will never come to the wilderness (d) fourth, in such a situation, he exudes a sense of sorrow which is subdued but real (e) as such, he underlines the dichotomies of existence by marking the fissure between desire and fulfilment, as much as between the spring and autumn of nature and life.

Looking at the diction, we may easily mark that *ghar* (home) is identified here in metaphoric terms with *dar-o diivaar* (doors and walls) signifying protection from the hubbub of life. This is placed in sharp contrast with *bayaabaa.n* (wilderness), and the two together are alien to *bahaar* (spring). All these dichotomous images, turned into metaphors, represent two conditions of life which is of particular relevance in the context of this verse. The phrase *ug rahaa hai* (it is growing) with reference to *sabza* (greenery) on the walls also shows the arrival of spring at its own natural pace, and it puts the idea of wilderness in complete contrast with the idea of home and adds to the cumulative impact of the verse. A keen representation of *bayabaa.n* which reflects on this verse as well may be marked in another verse by Ghalib: *girya chaahe hai KHaraabii mire kaashaane kii / dar-o diivaar se Tapke hai bayabaa.n honaa.*

147

دیکھنا تقریر کی لذت کہ جو اس نے کہا
میں نے یہ جانا کہ گویا یہ بھی میرے دل میں ہے

देखना तक़रीर की लज़्ज़त कि जो उस ने कहा
मैं ने ये जाना कि गोया ये भी मेरे दिल में है

dekhnaa taqriir kii lazzat ke jo us ne kahaa
mai.n ne ye jaanaa ke goyaa ye bhii mere dil mei.n hai

(*taqriir*—talk, address, speech;
lazzat—relish, delight, flavour)

Look at the relish of eloquence,
look what she said
I found that also lay within my heart,
all that she said

The beauty of communication lies in what one thinks, but is expressed by another. Ghalib glosses over this by bringing us to a lover enamoured by his beloved's words and the magic of her utterances. The lover's fascination with her grows to such an extent that he thinks that whatever she says lies in his heart too. This is as if she is spelling out his own aspirations. So, the lover eulogizes the magical appeal of the beloved's speech, because he thinks she is his own voice and reflects only his aspirations.

This verse foreshadows a theoretical discourse on communication and makes fascinating propositions: (a) Ghalib develops a discourse through his speaker on speech and communication, which prefaces seminal theories of communication in modern times (b) there is a close communion between the delivery and the reception of the message between the two people involved (c) this is exemplified by the speaker, who is the lover, and his listener, who is the beloved (d) this is how they develop intimacy, love each other and understand each other's gestures, (e) this may be considered Ghalib's foreshadowing of what is now known as Discourse Analysis and relates with the process of meaning-making (*m'anii-aafriinii*) as foregrounded in the science of Semantics.

This is one of those compositions of Ghalib's where each unit of expression has a precise and meaningful place in the two lines that we read only naturally and effortlessly. Consider the six verbal blocks of the lover's address and see how admirably they are intertwined to create a structure of intent: *dekhnaa* (look), *taqriir ki lazzat* (relish of speech), *ke jo us ne kahaa* (that which she said), *mai.n ne ye jaanaa* (I thought as if), *ke goyaa ye bhii* (as if this too) and *mere dil mei.n hai* (as if, this too is in my heart). There is not a single word in the two lines that carries lesser weight and has slighter relevance than the other. This indispensability of the exact words and their precise location in a poetical text only validates Mallarme's definition of poetry as the best words in the best order.

148

دیکھو تو دل فریبی انداز نقش پا
موج خرام یار بھی کیا گل کتر گئی

देखो तो दिल-फ़रेबी-ए अंदाज़-ए नक़्श-ए पा
मौज-ए ख़िराम-ए यार भी क्या गुल-कतर गई

dekho to dilfarebii-i andaaz-e naqsh- e paa
mauj-e KHiraam-e-yaar bhii kyaa gul katar gaii

(*dilfarebii-i andaaz-e naqsh-e paa*—attracting ways
of the footprints;
KHiraam-e-yaar—beloved's pace/walk)

Look at the gorgeous élan of her footprints
What waves of wonder did create those footprints!

The beloved's footprints have had a mythical identity in the ghazal tradition. What a gorgeous way Ghalib discovers to describe the beloved's movement and the footprints she leaves behind! It appears as if the beloved's delicate movement on the earth has left wondrous imprints only to be praised with a sense of amazement. Her act of walking resembles the majestic waves of water at a slow pace. It creates, as if, music for the ears and delight for the eyes. The beloved appears, therefore, as a work of art unto herself. Enamoured of her being and her regal movement, the lover invites others to watch this magical phenomenon of sorts.

This verse is decidedly a work of exquisite craftsmanship creating multiple meanings: (a) Ghalib portrays the movement of the beloved's feet as something outstandingly magical (b) as she walked, she created magical images on the soil with her footprints (c) the ground she walked on and the imageries she left behind resemble a garden (d) her swirling movement on the earth has created waves, as if, on the surface of water which is yet another aspect that adds splendour to the image created (e) one wonders if this act of leaving behind magical imprints is an act of creating wonders on the soil or making mischiefs, which is typically associated with the movement of beloveds.

The most vital phrase in the verse is *gul katarna* which holds multiple meanings of cutting flowers, making paper flowers, doing something novel, saying something surprising, acting mischievously, causing turmoil and showing anger. Ghalib's merit lies in making his verse richly ambiguous by leaving his readers with all possible suggestions that this key expression makes. Another important word—*mauj* (wave)— adds yet another dimension to the verse which helps us figure out the beloved's movement, as if on the surface of water, that leaves mesmerizing figures behind. Far from being an example of poetic exaggeration, this verse creates a wonder of words, reflecting the image of the beloved in movement which makes the verse uniquely picturesque.

149

اپنی گلی میں مجھ کو نہ کر دفن بعد قتل
میرے پتے سے خلق کو کیوں تیرا گھر ملے

अपनी गली में मुझ को न कर दफ़्न बाद-ए क़त्ल
मेरे पते से ख़ल्क़ को क्यूँ तेरा घर मिले

*apnii galii mei.n mujh ko na kar dafn b'aad-e qatl
mere pate se KHalq ko kyu.n teraa ghar mile*

(b'aad-e qatl—after assassination/slaying;
KHalq—humanity, creation)

After I'm slain, don't bury me in your lane
for anyone's access
Why should the world ever reach your abode
with my address

Men often wish for the place where they want to be buried, though they hardly ever say where they don't want to be buried. Ghalib engages here with this unusual idea but in the context of a lover's wish. This is a lover speaking to a beloved and asking for relief for himself as well as for her, after he is slain and buried. There are two distinct acts projected here—first, the beloved killing the lover in metaphorical terms and, second, his burial in her lane. These set the stage for the subsequent acts of the people finding the address of the beloved's abode from his address.

Interesting aspects of meaning lie around this verse: (a) the lover knows that the beloved would slay him but he does not want her to be known as his slayer (b) lovers generally want to be buried near the beloved's street but this lover does not want this to happen (c) with the address of the lover's grave, the beloved's address would be identified and she would gain fame because of him (d) he is jealous and does not want anyone to come around to her place and make friends with her (e) his jealousy is also combined with his possessiveness for the beloved even after he is no more (f) he also exudes a sense of superiority by questioning why his spot of burial should be known as the beloved's address, rather than her lane as the address of his grave.

The verse mythicizes the beloved's *galii* (lane) which generally appears in ghazals as a place lovers keep whirling around, day and night. Metaphorically, this is the place where the beloveds indulge in the pleasant act of snaring their lovers with their intermittent appearances and passing looks. The two lines of this verse sound different from each other, but with no sense of break in meaning or continuity of thought. The first line reads like a direction, whereas the second line sounds like a question but put only rhetorically. This defines the mood of the verse for the reader. The expression *qatl* (slaying) must be appreciated here in metaphorical terms, as used in the ghazal tradition, than in literal terms. Ghalib's use of this expression in another verse will bear it out: *'ishrat-e qatl gahe ahl-e tamanna mat puuchh / 'iid-e nazzara hai shamsiir kaa 'uryaa.n honaa*. Another usage of this word in a metaphorical manner may be seen in a verse by Dagh as well: *vo qatl kar ke mujhe har kisii se puuchhte hai.n / ye kaam kis ne kiyaa hai ye kaam kis kaa thaa*.

150

موت کا ایک دن معین ہے
نیند کیوں رات بھر نہیں آتی

मौत का एक दिन मुअय्यन है
नींद क्यूँ रात भर नहीं आती

maut kaa ek din mu'ayyan hai
nii.nd kyu.n raat bhar nahii.n aatii

(*mu'ayyan*—definite, established,
settled, fixed, appointed)

The day of death is appointed, for sure
Why does sleep evade all night, evermore

Death drives a natural fear in human beings. It robs them even of sleep. Knowing fully well that death is inevitable, men are unable to reconcile with the reality of death and remain awfully occupied with the fear of dying. Put against life, which is marked by consciousness and action, death is a state of oblivion and seizure of action. This is a truism that Ghaib configures in poetic terms. The fear of entering this zone of the unknown forms the essential idea of this verse that occupies human consciousness incessantly and fills them with terrible apprehensions.

Even a verse of such one-to-one correspondence with respect to meaning, opens different avenues to enter it: (a) one is destined to die, but not before or after the appointed day (b) man is irrational in denying its reality and fearing it all his life (c) keeping awake all night is a sign of the anxiety of death, which also robs man of sleep and peace of mind (d) the verse is both a dialogue with oneself and the supposed listener, as human beings are prone to sharing their fears and apprehensions (e) here is a vexed psychological state of thanatophobia in which the speaker seeks an answer, but finds none.

Ghalib fills the word *ek din* (one day/someday) with extraordinary weight of meaning. This one day foreshadows all the days and nights of life a man lives. The day is appointed, but its arrival is kept secret which keeps man sick with apprehension and fear. Further, this plain truth of dying one day is made complex with a single word—*kyu.n* (why). This 'why' is a question that has no answer. It is also a psychological curiosity which is unjustifiable at a rational level, but is real at the emotional level.

151

هم وہاں ہیں جہاں سے ہم کو بھی
کچھ ہماری خبر نہیں آتی

हम वहाँ हैं जहाँ से हम को भी
कुछ हमारी ख़बर नहीं आती

*ham vahaa.n hai.n jahaa.n se ham ko bhii
kuchh hamaarii KHabar nahii.n aatii*

I'm there from where—I too do not get
To know where I am—where indeed, yet

In a state of self-absorption, one knows not where one is. Such a condition marks this verse for its deep metaphysical intent. The speaker's inability to understand where he is underlines a unique state of his belonging and unbelonging. This state of his disengagement from the self distinguishes him from ordinary human beings and the ordinariness of life itself. Such a denial of the self and the world around does not turn him into a recluse or a narcissist, but elevates him to the status of a superhuman who is identified on the basis of his noble quality of philosophical detachment.

Ghalib leaves us wondering about the multiple possibilities by which his speaker may be identified: (a) he had been too preoccupied with his self which has led him to negate it now (b) he has reached a state of self-absorption and is completely oblivious of not only himself, but everything around (c) he denies the material world that had captured him so far, because it was too limiting for him and stopped him from rising above and traveling beyond (d) having grown oblivious to everything other than his new-found self, he has reached a world that lies far away and does not look back to the world left behind (e) his new-found self has brought him to a space at par with that of Sufis and saints.

The speaker identifies himself in this verse as *ham* (we/us) instead of *mai.n* (I). He is no longer an individual but a collective presence for men, representing the metaphysically awakened ones. A common word, *KHabar*, generally signifying news or information, is extraordinarily charged here and connotes 'realization' or 'revelation'. With this, he has risen from a plebeian state to a sublime one. This is well borne out by the word *vahaa.n* (there), which signifies the place he has reached now, from *yahaa.n* (here), where he was earlier. It should be pertinent to suggest that 'here' represents the banality of existence and 'there' represents its extraordinariness. These two words suggest the physical distance between two places which this man has traversed and acquired a new identity. The speaker's state in this verse is akin to a state of *be-KHudii* (the state of being beside oneself) which is so well constructed by Mir Taqi Mir: *be-KHudii le gaii kahaa.n ham ko / der se intizaar hai apnaa.*

152

جب کہ تجھ بن نہیں کوئی موجود
پھر یہ ہنگامہ اے خدا کیا ہے

जब कि तुझ बिन नहीं कोई मौजूद
फिर ये हंगामा ऐ ख़ुदा क्या है

jab ke tujh bin nahii.n koii maujuud
phir ye ha.ngaama ai KHudaa kyaa hai

When nothing exists without you, O God!
What is this hubbub then, what for, O God!

The question of God's existence, in spite of all the evidence around, has ever held man's attention. When none else but you alone exist, then what is this hubbub all about, asks Ghalib's speaker in great exasperation. He emerges as a stock questioner about the oneness of God, or his multiple incarnations, including men who consider themselves no less than gods. While he wonders if there is anyone, or anything, else that moves this world, he poses this question to none else but God Himself. This being a rhetorical question, shows his eternal curiosity which defines him for what he himself is. He knows the answer well that there is only one God, yet he puts forth this question in frustration, which only suggests that this question is asked again and again only to underline man's unending inquisitiveness about God's unitary existence.

This interrogative verse opens the following ways of interpretation: (a) there is a firm assertion that God alone exists and nothing other than God (b) this seems to be the voice of a monotheist, who believes in the unity of gods—that is, all gods constitute one God (c) this exemplifies his liberalism and underlines his larger catholicity towards all peoples and their faiths (d) the verse is also a criticism of those who fail to appreciate the real and they quibble only about peripheral matters (e) since there is none else but God alone, there is no room for any argument any further, and finally, (f) Ghalib engages with the idea of God's presence in his individual way, irrespective of Ali's saying in *Nehj-ul BalaaGha* that God is present in everything. This is also what the Bible (1:4, 8:3, 28:16) says, that God does not approximate a physical form, which comes close to the idea of God as *niraakaar* (formless) as it is presented in Hinduism (Yajurved 32:3) and Buddhism.

The idea of an all-pervasive God is carried in the word *maujuud* (present). By implication, this presence stands in contrast with *Ghaaib* (absence), which suggests that God is omnipresent in His absence. The second line, which comes up as a question from the speaker, carries his sense of wonder as well as of inquisitiveness. Remarkably enough, with the very first word of the verse—*jab ke* (when this is so)—he forestalls his answer that there is nothing else that exists. With this, he leaves no space for any argument about God's presence which is only too well established.

153

بستی ہماری اپنی فنا پر دلیل ہے
یاں تک مٹے کہ آپ ہم اپنی قسم ہوئے

हस्ती हमारी अपनी फ़ना पर दलील है
याँ तक मिटे कि आप हम अपनी क़सम हुए

hastii hamaarii apnii fanaa per daliil hai
yaa.n tak mite ke aap ham apnii qasam huve

(*hastii*—existence;
fanaa—mortality, vanishing, perishing;
daliil—evidence, proof, argument, witness)

My existence is proof enough of my mortality itself
I was erased so much; I became a vow unto myself

The idea of existence as a proof of perishing is essentially a metaphysical one. Ghalib's curious speaker comes up with a philosophical exposé on the idea of being and perishing in this verse. He suggests that all that lives has to die and every erasure from the earth is a proof of its being on the surface of the earth. It is also important to appreciate that perishing is the common destiny both for men as well as for the phenomenon, which we know as the physical world. The speaker puts forth his argument to himself and passes them on to us—that this cycle of being and perishing has been repeated so much, and for so many times, that it has become its own argument and its own proof, as well as its own witness and evidence.

The layers of meaning are complicated here and open up these prominent aspects for our attention: (a) man's existence is the ultimate proof of his own perishing (b) existence and perishing go side by side and ascertain each other (c) it applies to human life as much as it does to the myriad manifestations of life and nature (d) man is erased from the script of being so completely that he becomes his own sign of having existed at one point of time and perishing at a subsequent point of time; and in sum, (e) life and death swear by each other.

The verse stands on the internal logic propounded here by two key words of contrastive nature—*hastii* (existence) and *fanaa* (mortality). This opens up the larger discourse regarding being and nothingness, which has engaged man ever since he learnt to develop a discourse. *Yaa.n tak mite* (got erased to such an extent) is a profound phrase that underlines the extent of erasure after which no trace remains. *Qasam* (vow) is the most creative expression here that extends the idea of standing witness to perishing of existence that the verse puts forth. In his persistent engagement with the problematic of *hastii*, Ghalib develops yet another perspective in a different verse on *hastii* as such: *juz naam nahii.n suurat-e 'aalam mujhe manzuur / juz vahm nahii.n hastii-i ashyaa mire aage.*

154

ظلمت کدے میں میرے شب غم کا جوش ہے
اک شمع ہے دلیل سحر سو خموش ہے

ज़ुल्मत-कदे में मेरे शब-ए ग़म का जोश है
इक शम्अ है दलील-ए सहर सो ख़मोश है

zulmat-kade mei.n mere shab-e Gham kaa josh hai
ik sham'a hai daliil-e sahar so KHamosh hai

(*zulmat-kada*—dark house;
shab-e Gham—night of sorrow/grief;
daliil-e sahar—proof of morning)

In my dark dungeon burns bright the night of sorrow
But a lamp sits silent to bear witness to morrow

What do light and darkness signify in real terms? This verse engages with this question, but eludes an easy answer. It seems to suggest, however, that the speaker's dark house is lit up by the radiance of sorrow and the lamp which burnt bright once, sits silent now. From a different perspective, and in philosophical terms, grief can be a redeemer and enlighten human beings to understand the sorrows of life better. In this respect, even a silent lamp in the morning will resume its life the next evening and light up the space. It may thus be surmised in broader terms that in suffering lies the panacea. Similarly, in grief lies the way out of grief, which makes grief an enriching experience.

We may also develop a different perspective on the verse as follows: (a) the first line reads like a simple statement, whereas the second line appears as supportive of the first line with the metaphor of a lamp to strengthen the primary idea (b) the lamp that burnt all night is extinguished in the morning and sits silent all day (c) considering what the speaker says, one is led to wonder whether the lamp burnt at all through the night, or had it been silent since the advent of last evening itself (d) The absence of light through the dark night, even without the dim rays of the lamp in the night, strengthens the idea of gloom (e) this gloom is reflective of the speaker's predicament which he does not complain against, rather takes pride in.

Two opposite expressions—*zulmat* (gloom) and *sham'a* (lamp)—constitute the ideational core of the verse. While gloom is a real experience here, the lamp is presented only as an image that brings no light. The poetic turn in the verse comes with the expression *josh* (spirit), which, ironically enough, stands for the spirit of gloom, as also of light. This is what brings a rich duality of meaning to the verse.

155

آتے ہیں غیب سے یہ مضامیں خیال میں
غالبؔ صریر خامہ نوائے سروش ہے

आते हैं ग़ैब से ये मज़ामीं ख़याल में
ग़ालिब सरीर-ए ख़ामा नवा-ए सरोश है

aate hai.n Ghaib se ye mazaamii.n KHayaal mei.n
Ghalib sariir-e KHaama navaa-i sarosh hai

(*Ghaib*—mysterious/hidden world;
sariir-e KHaama—sound of pen's movement;
navaa-i-sarosh—angelic voice)

These ideas come to me from the spheres unknown, indeed,
Ghalib! The sound of my pen's movement is of angelic breed

Ideas spring from subterranean sources. This is Ghalib's personal admission in the first voice about how he gets his ideas to create his poetry. Then, he proudly announces that his pride lies in the sound created by the movement of his pen, which turns into an angelic voice. By this, he privileges the unseeable over the seeable and the unsayable over the sayable. As poetry comes to the poet in inscrutable ways and acquires its own entity, T.S. Eliot rightly proposed that poetry comes from strange sources like the reading of Spinoza, noise of the typewriter and smell from the kitchen. Once composed, it becomes a music of ideas played by the pen.

Ghalib's statement on his poetics opens up certain other aspects: (a) the ideas coming from the hidden worlds on their own underline the idea of poetry emerging from unidentifiable sources (b) poetry for him is a godsend, and not a deliberate act of composition (c) in such a case, his pen sings its own songs and the act of singing becomes divine (d) this is the height of imaginative ecstasy that a poet enjoys in his state of splendid solitude (e) even though this may be a creative process for all poets, he turns it into an intensely personal experience of creative engagement and enlightenment (f) even while a sense of the poet's arrogance may be seen in the second line, the first line negates it.

In mentioning *Ghaib* (unknown world) as the hinterland of creativity, Ghalib only reinforces an age-old dictum that the domains of poetic imagination lie far beyond the physical space. This space could be mystical, mysterious, indefinable, even mundane at times. Two vital expressions—*sariir-e KHaama* (sound of pen's movement) and *navaa-i sarosh* (angelic voice)—particularize it with respect to Ghalib and impart a unique Ghalibean touch to his verse.

156

گنجینۂ معنی کا طلسم اس کو سمجھیے
جو لفظ کہ غالبؔ مرے اشعار میں آوے

गंजीना-ए मानी का तिलिस्म उस को समझिये
जो लफ़्ज़ कि ग़ालिब मिरे अशआर में आवे

ga.njiin-i m'anii kaa tilism us ko samajhiye
jo lafz ke Ghalib mire ash'aar mei.n aave

(*ga.njiin-i m'anii*—treasury of meaning;
tilism—enchantment, magic)

That's magic from meaning's treasury, consider that for sure
The word that enters my verse, Ghalib, that is a magic pure

A word, or lexis, as nucleus of meaning is a concept of ancient as well as modern poetics. Ghalib draws upon this in his own manner and eulogizes himself for his creative merit. He addresses his readers and asks them to believe that the words which find their place in his poetry are purely magical and create a treasury of meaning. He assigns a lofty position to himself as the high priest of poetics who lays emphasis on thought. He subscribes to the critical dictum that all great poetry must have its foundation in metaphysical thought. It is with these that he creates a rich music of ideas which distinguishes poetry from all other arts.

The verses of *t'allii* where poets praise themselves challenge the readers, even as they open up different ways of understanding the poet. The major layers of meaning in this verse from Ghalib may be marked as follows: (a) words that constitute the poet's diction are carefully weighed and balanced against other counters of expression when used in verse (b) Ghalib is conscious of this and enlivens his words with extra imaginative vitality when executing them (c) these words become the nucleus of meaning and create a complex of connotations in companionship with other words (d) put together in unexpected combinations, they constitute the poet's enchanting world, and create poetry of shocks and surprise, and finally (e) with this, Ghalib invites his reader to unravel this and his other verses known for their complexity.

Ghalib has written a paean to the power of his *lafz* (word) in this verse. Plato considered word (lexis) to be a manner of speaking and divided it into *mimesis* (imitation) and *diegesis* (plain narrative), and made way for perpetual discoursing by poets and critics. Ghalib takes it further and unites it with his own *ga.njiin-i m'anii* (treasury of meaning) and his own *tilism* (magic). He thus charges his words as images, similes, metaphors, symbols and myths from stage to stage. He creates, thus, his own poetics, and his own architectures of word and meaning. He adorns this structure with mirrors to impart the reader with shocks of recognition regarding which this verse makes a seminal statement. In a diametrically opposite stance, Ghalib also makes a garbled complaint in another verse which presents him differently: *na sataaish kii tamanna na sile kii parva / gar nahii.n hai.n mire ash'aar mei.n m'anii na sahii.*

157

اور بازار سے لے آئے اگر ٹوٹ گیا
ساغر جم سے مرا جام سفال اچھا ہے

और बाज़ार से ले आए अगर टूट गया
साग़र-ए जम से मिरा जाम-ए सिफ़ाल अच्छा है

aur baazaar se le aae agar TuuT gayaa
saaGhar-e Jam se miraa jam-e sifaal achhaa hai

(*saaGhar-e Jam*—Jamshed's cup;
jam-e sifaal—clay/earthen cup)

I'll get another one from market if it does break
From Jamshed's cup, my clay cup is better for its make

There are ways to take pride in dearth and deprivation. Ghalib's speaker engages with this idea and comes up with his own way to assuage himself, even though with a fair amount of smugness. He has a clay cup to drink from which may break, but he is proud that he may get another from the market, if it does. He considers Jamshed's cup inferior to his own because the one he drank from is more of a mythical cup. It also comes out through a sly suggestion that cups break in the act of drinking when the drinkers indulge in revelry and it is in these acts that the extra joy of drinking lies. It appears that the speaker has written a eulogy for wine and drinking, and taken pride in doing so.

This verse has these interesting features to take note of and appreciate: (a) Ghalib's drinker takes pride in his ordinariness, rather than in envying the wares of the wealthy ones like Jamshed, the great ruler celebrated in Iranian folklore (b) after all, both the wares are made for drinking and the pleasure of drinking lies in enjoying the drink than in flaunting the cup (c) in positing his clay cup against Jamshed's mythical cup, wherein he could see the world, the speaker presents a stark contrast between the highly powerful and the most ordinary mortal, and on a more serious note, (d) he underlines the difference between the high and low, and privileges the low over the high.

This verse acquires its strength in the way Ghalib highlights a striking contrast between *jam-e sifaal* (earthen cup) and *saaGhar-e Jam*, (Jamshed's cup), also known as *jam-e jahaa.n-numaa* (world's image-bearing cup). Both these images represent the social hierarchy of the high and the low which drinkers defy. In a variation on this theme, Ghalib chose to develop a different perspective on Jamshed and his cup, which is of no less interest: *sultanat dast-ba-dast aaii hai / jaam-e mai KHaatim-e Jamshid nahii.n.*

158

ان کے دیکھے سے جو آ جاتی ہے منہ پر رونق
وہ سمجھتے ہیں کہ بیمار کا حال اچھا ہے

उन के देखे से जो आ जाती है मुँह पर रौनक़
वो समझते हैं कि बीमार का हाल अच्छा है

un ke dekhe se jo aa jaatii hai mu.h per raunaq
vo samajhte hai.n ke biimaar ka haal achhaa hai

(*raunaq*—glow, brightness, splendour, lustre)

A lustre shows up on my face, as I see her face
She thinks this sick one has gotten better apace

If the lover's face gets aglow at the sight of the beloved, the beloved presumes that the sick lover has gotten better now. Ghalib presents here a curious moment in the life of the lover, but in ironic terms. This is, in fact, a travesty of his love because the lover is still in a bad condition, which, ironically enough, she does not realize. This suggests that the lover can never be well as he is destined to remain sick in the beloved's absence. The beloved's sight is a source of rejuvenation for him, but only for a short while, as she has to part with him after a brief meeting. As he is totally given to her, she is the only source of his health and happiness; however, she is hugely unaware of how the lover survives in her absence.

Further responses are noteworthy as well: (a) the lover is presented here as a sick one, but he glows at the sight of the beloved, which leads to the misunderstanding that the beloved has developed about her lover (b) as opposed to this, the beloved is presented here as a naïve one who does not know that the lover is really sick in separation from her (c) a suggestion comes out clearly that this prototypical lover seeks his pleasure in the companionship of the beloved (d) in other words, her presence is pleasure and her absence a pain for the lover, and quite interestingly (e) Ghalib also creates a rich ambiguity as to who really looks aglow—the lover at the sight of the beloved or the beloved at the sight of the lover?

The words *raunaq* (glow) and *biimaar* (sick) that stand against each other, and deny each other in terms of implication, create a paradigm of complex meaning in this verse. One who is sick can have no glow on his face, but Ghalib makes that happen and adds a fascinating dimension to the lover-beloved relationship. The illusive expression *vo samajhte hai.n* (she thinks so) adds an ironic tinge as it suggests that what she thinks is indeed not right. It is essentially the element of irony that enriches the verse. Mir Taqi Mir's verse in this perspective would be of particular interest and relevance: *jin jin ko thaa ye 'ishq kaa aazaar mar gae / aksar hamaare saath ke biimaar mar gae.*

159

دیکھیے پاتے ہیں عشاق بتوں سے کیا فیض
اک برہمن نے کہا ہے کہ یہ سال اچھا ہے

देखिए पाते हैं उश्शाक़ बुतों से क्या फ़ैज़
इक बरहमन ने कहा है कि ये साल अच्छा है

dekhiye paate hai.n 'ushshaaq buto.n se kyaa faiz
ik barahman ne kahaa hai ke ye saal achhaa hai

(*'ushshaaq*—lovers, admirers, suitors;
faiz—bounty, favour, grace)

Let us see what grand favours
the idols offer their lovers
A brahmin has forecast
this is an auspicious year for lovers

Human beings, prone to fancies, are easily pleased by happy forecasts. Let this verse be read as a lively and bright expression of such an experience. The narrator rejoices a Brahmin's prophecy that this year is going to prove good for lovers. So, he looks forward expectantly to the favours that the lovers might receive from their beloveds. There is, however, a trace of doubt here as well, because the narrator in this verse is only watching, rather curiously, to see what the future holds for them.

We may also find the following interesting implications in this verse: (a) the narrator is of a playful disposition who shares his jubilance about what the Brahmin has prophesied (b) he expects good times for all lovers of whom he too is presumably one (c) there is also an element of irony here in what the narrator says: 'let us see what happens even if the Brahmin has said that this would be a good year' (d) yet another interesting layer of meaning lies in the reference to idol and Brahmin, as an idol traditionally stands for lady love in poetry and Brahmin as the keeper of faith (e) interestingly, the Brahmin plays a pleasant role here of happy soothsaying for lovers, which is unlike the usual soothsaying he has been doing traditionally.

Ghalib puts up a scene on the stage with four human figures of *'ushshaaq* (lovers), *but* (idols), a Brahmin (keeper of faith) and a narrator. While the narrator is visible, playing out the drama, the three others are physically absent but referentially present. The Brahmin emerges here as a soothsayer, the lover as an expectant being, the beloved as the centre of all expectations and the narrator as a commentator in the drama. The first word of the first line—*dekhiye* (let us see)—which is essentially gestural, superbly blends the moods of both jubilance and doubt, which imparts a unique appeal to the verse.

160

نہ ستائش کی تمنا نہ صلے کی پروا
گر نہیں ہیں مرے اشعار میں معنی نہ سہی

न सताइश की तमन्ना न सिले की परवा
गर नहीं हैं मिरे अशआर में मअ'नी न सही

na sataaish kii tamanna na sile kii parvaa
gar nahii.n hai.n mire ash'aar mei.n m'anii na sahii

(*sataaish*—accolade, eulogy, praise, appreciation;
sila—reward, recompense, gift)

I've no desire for praise, nor
a care for rewards, or so
If there's no meaning in my verses,
who cares, let it be so

Good poets neither write for a targeted audience nor expect any rewards because the pleasure of writing is in itself the reward for writing. This is the poet, presumably Ghalib himself, speaking directly to his readers with a good reason in mind. He voices his concern about his reception and muses uncaringly that he neither nourishes a longing to be praised nor cares about any rewards. He is also not bothered if some people declare his verses devoid of meaning. However, it brings him joy and satisfaction if the readers appreciate his work.

Some important aspects of this verse may also be marked as follows: (a) Ghalib appears to be unconcerned about his reception by his readers in terms of praise or rewards, but that may not be wholly true (b) he is surely concerned because the idea of praise and proceeds could not have come to his mind otherwise (c) he clearly implies that his verses deserve appreciation, but he does not care if they are considered to be meaningless (d) he is sure that it does not reflect upon the merit of his verse, but upon the readers who are indeed ignorant and he needs no praise from such persons (e) the verse also reflects upon the critical thinking that contemporary readers cannot be fair judges of works of art, as Virginia Woolf suggested in 'How it Strikes a Contemporary', and that (f) good works of art outlive time and make their place in the larger contexts of time, place and readership.

Sataaish (praise) and *sila* (reward) look at each other in unison as both suggest praise and proceeds for the poet. The vital word, however, is m'anii (meaning) which was Ghalib's major concern throughout his career. This is a theme around which the contemporary discourse on the meaning of meaning, meaning behind meaning, and meaning as co-existent and relative has been developed under Foundational and Semantic theories of meaning.

161

رگوں میں دوڑتے پھرنے کے ہم نہیں قائل
جب آنکھ ہی سے نہ ٹپکا تو پھر لہو کیا ہے

रगों में दौड़ते फिरने के हम नहीं क़ाइल
जब आंख से ही न टपका तो फिर लहू क्या है

rago.n mei.n dauRte phirne ke ham nahii.n qaael
jo aa.nkh hii se na Tapkaa to phir lahuu kyaa hai

(*qaael*—agree, convince, consent)

If it flows only through the veins, blood is no blood
What it is, if it does not drip from the eyes' bud

We know blood is something that the heart pumps through the vessels in a mechanical manner. Ghalib imparts a different role to blood and suggests that it embodies the pain of the sufferer and drips from the eyes rather than flow through the vessels. He develops a poet's perspective and suggests that the expression of grief is only a noble and natural act because it sublimates man. This expression of grief takes a natural course through tears, which indeed are drops of blood that swell in the eyes and drip in mourning. They reflect that something tragic has happened inside the sufferer's heart which now flows in the form of blood through his eyes.

We may spell out the verse in these terms thus: (a) tears roll down the eyes when grief exceeds the limits of human forbearance (b) the expression of grief develops into a human discourse here where shedding of tears is akin to shedding of blood (c) running through the veins is a mechanical exercise for the blood and its real dignity lies in dripping from the eyes (d) Ghalib turns an oft-used proverb—*KHuun ke aa.nsuu ronaa* (to shed tears of blood)—into a strong metaphor for the expression of pain (e) this takes us to Aristotle's theory of cathartic expression.

The flow of blood as a mechanical exercise is well carried out in the phrase *dauRte phirne* (running about). While the act of running through the veins is devoid of all passion, the act of dripping from the eyes carried in the phrase *Tapkaa* (drop) conveys deep pathos which imparts certain dignity to the verse. The word *qaael* (convince) carries a strong sense of affirmation. Here, Ghalib uses it to negate the role of tears flowing through veins and affirms its dignity in dripping from the eyes. A close corollary to this verses that capitalizes upon the idea of blood may be seen in another verse by Ghalib that adds an entirely different dimension to the experience of bearing and expressing pain: *rag-e sa.ng se Tapakta vo lahuu ke phir na thamtaa / jise Gham samajh rahe ho vo agar sharaar hotaa.*

162

رات پی زمزم پہ مے اور صبح دم
دھوئے دھبے جامۂ احرام کے

रात पी ज़मज़म पे मय और सुब्ह-दम
धोए धब्बे जामा-ए-एहराम के

raat pii Zamzam pe mai aur sub'ha-dam
dhoe dhabbe jaama-i ehraam ke

(Zamzam—holy water from the harem's well;
mai—wine;
jaama-i ehraam—the white robe worn
during hajj rituals, or entering Mecca)

At night, I drank wine at the Zamzam,
and in the morn
I washed the blots off my *ehraam*,
that I had worn

Irreverence challenges the readers' imagination and engages them intellectually. Ghalib wrote several irreverent verses that place him in a liberal frame, although they inflame his readers' imagination. His speaker in this verse takes pride in drinking wine at the harem's well of the holy water located in Mecca. In another act, as the morning arrived, he washed his white robe that had got blots on it. This is unimaginable for the believers and those visiting the precincts of the holy *ka'aaba*. It appears, however, that the speaker is experimenting here with himself and trying to seek truth on his own.

Ghalib's speaker surprises us by yoking disparate ideas and behaviours together: (a) he suggests that sin and virtue reside side-by-side, although they are hugely different in their nature and impact on human beings (b) symbolically, sin is associated with night's darkness and virtue with day's brightness, which is clearly suggested here (c) sin is visible to him in terms of symbolic blots which appeared on the white robe of the speaker who wore it as he drank his wine (d) the realization of sin moves him to wash it off in the bright light of the day and make an open declaration of his purificatory act, and (e) on washing the robe, he feels easy and announces it with pleasure.

A set of three utterly contrastive expressions—*raat* (night) and *sub'ha* (morning), *Zamzam* (holy water from the Harem's well) and *mai* (wine), and *ehraam* (pilgrim's white robe) and *dhabbe* (blots)—surprise us with the way Ghalib chooses to place them together to construct the complex of his meaning in a very distinct manner. He wants us to appreciate how meaning is constructed in utterly unimaginable ways with finding and locating not only the best words in the best order, but in employing the techniques of surprise to make his statement. Significantly enough, he finds a rakish and naughty speaker to represent this poetic method. In another verse, Ghalib develops an entirely different perspective on this experience which testifies that poetry is the best site to experiment with different modes of expression and experience: *Zamzam hi pe chhoRo mujhe kyaa tauf-e haram se / aaluuda ba-mai jaama-i ehraam bahut hai.*

163

رہا آباد عالم اہلِ ہمت کے نہ ہونے سے
بھرے ہیں جس قدر جام و سبو مے خانہ خالی ہے

रहा आबाद आलम अहल-ए हिम्मत के न होने से
भरे हैं जिस क़दर जाम-ओ-सुबू मय-ख़ाना ख़ाली है

rahaa aabaad 'aalam ahl-e himmat ke na hone se
bhare hai.n jis qadar jaam-o subuu maiKHaana KHaalii hai

(*ahl-e himmat*—courageous ones;
jam-o subuu—cup and jar)

The world prospered with the courageous ones,
not being there
The more the tavern has cups and pitchers,
the more it's bare

The queerness of thought distinguishes this verse and reflects on the angle of vision that man develops to perceive, or see something in a paradoxical manner. The speaker makes an assertive statement that the world can sustain without the courageous ones and leaves us wondering whether that is indeed true. He suggests that howsoever much the metaphorical wine-house, representing the world, is full of its possessions, it does not really have anything of substance, which makes it empty in real terms.

There are different layers of implication in this verse that are essentially philosophical: (a) the worth of this world in terms of the worth of its human beings is only relative (b) all human perceptions, being conditional, are non-definitive (c) the idea of fulness and emptiness is also no different (d) all manifestations are a play of illusion and reality (e) the more the cups are full, the more empty is the winehouse of its stock (f) it may also be surmised further that the world remained in place because it did not have the courageous ones around to ransack it.

The play of illusion and reality is presented here verbally with two antonyms—*aabaad* (populated/fulness) and *KHaalii* (emptiness/vacuum)—put together consecutively in the two lines of the verse. Similarly, both *'aalam* (world) and *maiKHaana* (wine-house) stand as proofs of divine manifestations and they supplement each other. The world is a wine-house and the wine-house a world unto itself. By yet another implication, the world is a wine-house which keeps its inhabitants perennially drunk, as the wine-house is a commune of drinkers who seek their revelry and realization there itself.

164

تو وہ بد خو کہ تحیر کو تماشا جانے
غم وہ افسانہ کہ آشفتہ بیانی مانگے

तू वो बद-ख़ू कि तहय्युर को तमाशा जाने
ग़म वो अफ़्साना कि आशुफ़्ता-बयानी माँगे

*tuu vo bad-KHuu ke tahayyur ko tamaasha jaane
Gham vo afsaana ke aashufta-bayaanii maa.nge*

(*bad-KHuu*—of bad nature/habit;
tahayyur—wonderment;
aashufta-bayaanii—stressed way of saying)

You, such a malicious one, you consider miracle
a mere play
But grief is a tale that needs a sore rhetoric,
to say a say

Wonderment, or miracle, cannot be presented as a mere play, or just as an amazing spectacle. This applies to the experience of pain as well, which needs to be represented, but only painstakingly with a sore rhetoric at hand. Ghalib's contemplative speaker considers pain a constant season that demands a rhetoric of its own kind for its expression. He seems to justify that every shade of experience needs a diction of its own ilk to make it adequately representational.

The points to take note in this discourse are: (a) wonderment, of whatever kind that may be, is a seminal experience of human life (b) it is not merely a piece of an alluring display but something of far greater and deeper significance (c) this experience may thus be portrayed only with the rhetoric of pain that may be worthy of the pain it wishes to portray (d) what the speaker suggests here applies to every representation of pain, from secular to spiritual, as both make human beings undergo tests and trials, and (e) all trying experiences call for their reconstruction in equal terms, which amounts to propounding a theory of creative language and artistic expression.

The addressee is identified here as an inferior being and is addressed in derogatory terms of *tuu* (O, you) and *bad-KHuu* (bad-natured). He is undermined as one who is less enlightened, and less capable to appreciate pain and to represent it. Three nouns, so carefully selected in this context—*tahayyur* (wonderment), *tamaasha* (spectacle) and *afsaana* (tale)—define *Gham* (pain) in three degrees, representing amazement, awe and surprise. All of them richly blended into one essential condition, may be taken as a paean to pain and an enriching experience in love, longing and loss of any kind—physical or metaphysical.

165

دوستی کا پردہ ہے بیگانگی
منہ چھپانا ہم سے چھوڑا چاہیے

दोस्ती का पर्दा है बेगानगी
मुंह छुपाना हम से छोड़ा चाहिये

dostii kaa parda hai begaanagii
mun.h chhupaanaa ham se chhoRaa chaahiye

(*begaanagii*—indifference)

Strangeness is the veil of friendship, a plea
Better to stop hiding your face from me

Friends can also turn into aliens and look for subterfuge. Here is a lover's simple but interesting plea to his beloved in this regard. This keen lover urges his beloved that she should refrain from keeping her face behind a veil and stop acting like a stranger to him. He believes that strangeness is a subterfuge for friendship which she should not indulge in anymore. The lover seems to be forthcoming, but the beloved is still shy and fears those peering eyes that would recognize her face and make up stories. The two together seem to play a game of hide and seek which in itself is a highly romantic and alluring sight for the viewers.

This verse offers multiple ways of interpretation as follows: (a) strangeness is indeed a veil drawn across friendship which the lover wishes to be withdrawn (b) the lover thinks that his beloved's veiling is, in fact, an admission of her love for him which she is trying to hide (c) in spite of this, the lover is possibly suspicious of the beloved which is why he persuades her to stop being shy (d) he also thinks that if she continued veiling her face, people would unnecessarily guess unlikely reasons for her doing so (e) for the veiled beloved, on the other hand, it should also be said that by concealing her face, she actually shows her fascination for her lover, but chooses to feign strangeness for the fear of the peering world around.

The first line of the verse may best be read as an outstanding adage which poetry has the capacity to turn into. The words *dostii* (friendship) and *begaanagii* (strangeness) go against each other and create the basic plot of the verse. The mediating word here is *parda* (veil) which defines their relationship at the present moment, and which the lover wishes to tear off for good. The lover's plea is, however, marked by a tone of persuasion rather than of command. This is well borne out by the phrase *chhoRaa chaahiye* (should stop)— which is spoken in a tone of endearment to the beloved. It should be interesting to mark how Ghalib plays with the idea of the beloved acting strangely in another verse: *vaarastagii bahaana-i begaanagii nahii.n / apne se kar na Ghair se vahshat hii kyu.n na ho* and how his predecessor, Mir Taqi Mir, takes it to another height: *haai re begaanagii kabhuu un ne / na kahaa ye ke aashna hai ye.*

166

ہر قدم دوریٔ منزل ہے نمایاں مجھ سے
میری رفتار سے بھاگے ہے بیاباں مجھ سے

हर क़दम दूरी-ए मंज़िल है नुमायाँ मुझ से
मेरी रफ़्तार से भागे है बयाबाँ मुझ से

har qadam duuri-i-manzil hai numaayaa.n mujh se
merii raftaar se bhaage hai bayaanbaa.n mujh se

(*numaayaa.n*—apparent, conspicuous, visible;
bayaabaa.n—wilderness, arid, desolate, lonely)

Each step tells how distant the goal is from me
My speed makes the wilderness fly away from me

Journey, traveller and destination, being the central concerns of life, appear as strong metaphors in art and literature. Here is a speaker's serious rumination about the pace of his own journey. He accepts that he is too slow in his movement and that even the wilderness has grown impatient with him. He seems to suggest that the wilderness is expansive and limitless, and it makes heavy demands upon him as he does not know if he would arrive anywhere. Howsoever fast he moves, the destination moves farther away from him. He, thus, sends a sad message to himself that he will keep travelling like this forever and his destination will elude him without end.

This verse has several layers of philosophical implications: (a) life is a quest that has kept human beings eternally moving (b) the speaker is a quester who has a supposed destination before him and earnestly walks towards that destination (c) the destination is illusory and the quest itself turns out to be a huge illusion (d) this chasing after illusion despairs man, but he moves with a mixed sense of despair and hope, and finally, (e) the quest is bigger than the quester as the metaphorical expanse of the journey is immeasurable which the human act cannot negotiate with.

The verse clearly works through the larger metaphor of journey. Its structural framework is based on interrelated words in terms of their thematic import, like *qadam* (step), *duuri* (distance), *manzil* (destination), *raftaar* (speed), *bhaage* (keeps away) and *bayabaa.n* (wilderness). Together, they create a picture of a traveller trying to locate himself in the process of his travelling through a challenging space. Most often, Ghalib finds his vocabulary in analogous expressions, as we may mark here, and this helps him create a compact structure of meaning in his verses.

167

چاک کی خواہش اگر وحشت بہ عریانی کرے
صبح کے مانند زخم دل گریبانی کرے

चाक की ख़्वाहिश अगर वहशत ब उरयानी करे
सुबह के मानिंद ज़ख़्म-ए दिल गरेबानी करे

chaak kii KHvaahish agar vahshat ba-'uryaanii kare
sub'ha ke maani.nd zaKHm-e dil garebaanii kare

(*chaak*—tear, rip, split;
vahshat—wildness, savageness;
'uryaanii—nakedness;
maani.nd—like;
garebaan—shirt's collar)

If the wild desires wish to go naked and
tear the collar apart
Like the dawn, the heart's wound may
serve as a collar for the heart

Human desires, like human needs in terms of Malthusian theory, are unlimited. Ghalib richly complicates this thought here. Although man knows that desires are too demanding to be met completely, he does not quite appreciate this and keeps chasing them all his life. In his unreasonableness, he pursues them to such an extent that he reaches a wild stage and tears his collars apart. If that happens, the heart's wound would itself become a guard like the dawn and save it from the disaster caused by the gloom of disappointment.

The implications of this verse are thus: (a) overpowering desires may turn a man wild and drive him towards self-destruction (b) this may happen to the extent of defying reason, which is lost in pursuing destructive passions nakedly (c) such an act robs man of the status of manhood and turns him into a savage (d) in such desperate situations, even the adversities turn into opportunities (e) as such, man's dignity, being greater than everything else, is always restorable.

A group of four corresponding words—*chaak* (rip), *vahshat* (wildness), *'uryaanii* (nakedness) and *zaKHm* (wound)—put together in a consecutive sequence, create a complex paradigm of meaning. All of them reflect the states of ripping, ravaging, stripping and wounding with respect to the plot of savage human desires and their consequences. In another scheme of ideas, we have *sub'ha* (dawn) and *garebaanii* (collaring) that act as agents of the repudiation of suffering. The logical succession of ideas in the two lines, however, is conceived in complex terms.

168

خطر ہے رشتۂ الفت رگ گردن نہ ہو جاوے
غرور دوستی آفت ہے تو دشمن نہ ہو جاوے

ख़तर है रिश्ता-ए उल्फ़त रग-ए गर्दन न हो जावे
गुरूर-ए दोस्ती आफ़त है तू दुश्मन न हो जावे

KHatar hai rishta-i ulfat rag-e gardan na ho jaave
Ghuruur-e dostii aafat hai tuu dushman na ho jaave

(KHatar—danger, apprehension;
rishta-i ulfat—bond of love;
rag-e gardan—neck's vein;
Ghuruur-e dostii—love's pride)

There is an impending danger lest the love-bond
becomes the neck's vein
Love's vanity is but a catastrophe,
may you not be a foe in vain

Apprehension fills man with doubts and despairs. Ghalib appropriates this idea to reflect upon the issue of love here. He has an apprehensive speaker here who wishes to preserve his love, but he is dogged by fears and trepidations as well. He proposes the idea of love as a source of pride, but taking pride in one's love may also turn his beloved into a foe. Taking pride in the beloved's love, and also thinking of her as his foe, is a strange but not an impossible turn of thought.

The uniqueness of this verse may be marked in the fine inferences we may draw from it: (a) love is a boon but an impending danger too, which is caused by none else than the beloved herself (b) inscrutable are the ways of the beloveds for which they are stereotypically known (c) love is never shorn of irony and ironies also make love a subject of discourse (d) vanquishing of the lover is also a vanquishing of the beloved, which this beloved fails to foresee (e) from this perspective, the pride of love may become the cause of love's vanquishing and turn the beloved into an enemy which reiterates the traditional idea of the beloved as a metaphoric killer.

The two compatible words in particular, *rishta-i ulfat* (bond of love) and *GHuruur-e dostii* (love's pride), present love as a positive force. This is vanquished by another expression—*KHatar* (danger)—which defines the impending apprehension of the lover and the predominant mood of this verse. The most vital expression—*rag-e gardan* (neck's vein)—suggesting love's strangulation with the neck's swollen vein turning into a noose, reflects the lover's dark fear. This is the crux of this verse and a comment on the unpredictability of human action, including that of the beloved. This unwelcome idea finds its expression with a variation in another verse of Ghalib once more: *Dare kyu.n meraa qaatil kyaa rahegaa us kii gardan per / vo Khuu.n jo chashm-e tar se 'umr bhar yuu.n dam-ba-dam nikle.*

169

فریاد کی کوئی لے نہیں ہے
نالہ پابندِ نے نہیں ہے

फ़रयाद की कोई लै नहीं है
नाला पाबंद-ए नै नहीं है

faryaad kii koii lai nahii.n hai
naala paaband-e nai nahii.n hai

(*faryaad*—appeal, entreaty, complaint;
naala—wail, lamentation;
nai—reed-flute)

Imploring knows of no tune
Wailing of no reed to tune

Human entreaties need no melodies, tunes or instruments to express themselves. Ghalib glosses over this to make a paradigmatic statement in this verse. He engages with the genuineness of emotion that is best expressed spontaneously which comes close to Wordsworth's observation in his 'Preface' to *Lyrical Ballads* that 'poetry is the spontaneous overflow of powerful feelings...recollected in tranquillity'. Spontaneous expressions, being genuine, are tranquillizing expressions that rise from one heart and reach out to another. Instead of mundane sentiments, these expressions concern sad and sombre emotions which reminds us of Shelley's lines in 'To a Skylark': 'Our sweetest songs are those that of saddest thought'.

Ghalib makes the following suggestions at a metaphysical level: (a) genuine pain has its own magnificence and magnanimity (b) pain is a higher state of being which is more inclusive and empowering than pleasure, which is essentially exclusive and ephemeral (c) this explains why threnodies of pain stay longer with us than the librettos of lighter moments (d) the language of pain has its own rhythm and finds its own appeal in kindred souls (e) this exalted state of being discovers its own language and natural manner to express itself.

In his typical style of setting his words like jewels in his verse, Ghalib chooses three of them—*faryaad* (entreaty), *naala* (wail) and *nai* (reed)—for this verse and uses them in his distinct style. He finds them their individual places and puts them in the close company of other words to construct the essential intent together. Two words in particular—*naala* (wail) and *faryaad* (entreaty)—echo each other semantically and their refusal to accept subservience to any instruments of music is well pronounced in *paaband-e nai* (subservient to reed flute). Finally, the word *koii* (none, in this case) carries a tone of finality and asserts that an entreaty has no fixed tone, except one of its own. The central idea of wailing or lamenting in this verse finds an extraordinary expression in Mir Taqi Mir that complements Ghalib's verse: *naala jab ke.nchntaa hai sar meraa / naala ik aasmaa.n se uThta hai.*

170

ہاں کھائیو مت فریب ہستی
ہر چند کہیں کہ ہے نہیں ہے

हाँ खाइयो मत फ़रेब-ए हस्ती
हर-चंद कहें कि है नहीं है

haa.n khaayio mat fareb-e hastii
harchand kahei.n ke hai nahii.n hai

(*fareb-e hasti*—deception of existence/being)

Don't be deceived by the glosses of being, beware
Howsoever much they say it's there; it isn't there

The phenomenon of existence can be a mere deception. Here is Ghalib speaking as a kind counsel to those who would care to listen to him. He warns human beings against the trickery of existence. He speculates that whatever is being insisted upon here as real is indeed the opposite of that. He considers that the phenomenon known as the world is unreal since it is merely a shadow without substance. It is indeed a place of sorrow and suffering, where beauty is only pretentious and unreal. He suggests that the world holds a false mirror to its manifestations only to reflect unreal images into them.

Ghalib's philosophical speculations may be appreciated in these terms: (a) human life and the physical world are splendid spectacles of deceptions, but they also have a magical quality about themselves (b) he appears to subscribe to the theory of the illusion of reality which says that there is no objective reality as such (c) he also seems to confirm the Neoplatonic philosophy about the hierarchy of existence in which human nature and material life represent the lower level with nothing substantial in real terms (d) he comes quite close to Wordsworth's ode 'Intimations of Immortality', where he considered life as a sleep and a forgetting of a purer state of being in the heavens of which this world is only a reflection, and is merely illusory.

Although the verse reads like a statement, it carries its strength in its simplicity of expression. It begin in an unusual style with an affirmative word—*haa.n* (O, yes)—suggesting as if a part of the story is already told and he is concluding the story with a final piece of advice. The verse is mildly persuasive and appeals through its poetic logic of *hai nahii.n hai* (it's there, it isn't there). This idea is explored in similar terms but much more unassumingly by Mir Taqi Mir: *hastii apnii habaab kii sii hai / ye numaaish saraab kii sii hai.*

171

بہت دنوں میں تغافل نے تیرے پیدا کی
وہ اک نگہ کہ بہ ظاہر نگاہ سے کم ہے

बहुत दिनों में तग़ाफ़ुल ने तेरे पैदा की
वो इक निगह कि ब ज़ाहिर निगाह से कम है

bahut dino.n mei.n taGhaaful ne tere paidaa kii
vo ik nigah ke ba-zaahir nigaah se kam hai

(taGhaaful—negligence;
ba-zaahir—apparently, manifestly)

It took your neglect long to create a gracious look
A look that is visibly far less than a look

The archetypal beloved of the Urdu ghazal is known for acting pricy and being uncaring of her lover, while the lover is known as one ever beseeching her attention. Here is a typical expression of this condition in a lover-beloved relationship. Quite in keeping with their stereotypical roles, the beloved has been neglecting the lover for a long time and the lover has been aspiring for her attention all the while. At last, she cast a sympathetic look at her lover, which makes him acknowledge her favour, yet complain that one look of love from her was indeed far less than a look. This makes him a lover who characteristically needs more favours than one.

In his address to the beloved, the lover in this case makes engrained suggestions: (a) the relationship between the two is of a kind which is yet to be as fulfilling as expected (b) persistence in love pays, but no persistence is as rewarding as anticipated (c) the beloved's sympathetic consideration, even if it is too little, is too precious for the lover (d) by expressing his thanks to her and asking for more, the lover only asserts his commitment to her (e) even while the lover is welcoming, the beloved remains discreetly silent, leaving the lover in the state of constant seeking.

In this lover-beloved relationship of its own kind, two words— *taGhaaful* (negligence) and *nigaah* (look)—spell out the fate of the lover, who has been a subject of negligence and yearns for a sympathetic look from the beloved. Ghalib has ingeniously used the word *nigaah* (look) twice. The first look is a bare look but the subsequent look is qualified by *ba-zaahir* (apparently) which is far less than a look, but it adds punch to the verse and imparts a poetic appeal to it. The experience of beloved's negligence, being a stock theme, has found its expression through all the ages. Ghalib seems to reconfigure this experience of which Amir Khusrau gave one of the finest examples: *ze haal-e miskii.n makun taGhaaful doraae nainaa.n banaae batiyaa.n / ke taab-e hijraa.n na daaram ai jaa.n na kaahe lehuu lagaae chhatiyaa.n.*

172

ہم رشک کو اپنے بھی گوارا نہیں کرتے
مرتے ہیں ولے ان کی تمنا نہیں کرتے

हम रश्क को अपने भी गवारा नहीं करते
मरते हैं वले उन की तमन्ना नहीं करते

ham rashk ko apne bhii gavaara nahii.n karte
marte hai.n vale un kii tamanna nahii.n karte

(*rashk*—envy;
gavaara—tolerate, bear;
vale—but, yet, however)

I do not tolerate even my own envy
I die but don't long for her even in frenzy

Men may sometimes grow eccentric when in love. Here is a lover proud of himself and he cannot compromise with the beloved's negligence. He has, thus, developed an attitude of tough indifference towards her. He goes to the extent of making a frank admission that even though he dies in separation from her, he does not yearn for her. This attitude of indifference towards her, and even of restraining himself in this relationship, indicates that he cannot tolerate his own envy for her.

Here is a verse that portrays an eccentric lover who stands apart in these ways: (a) he negates his own self, which he says is marked by his jealousy for himself as a lover (b) this implies that he cannot tolerate the beloved's indifference towards him (c) he is fiercely individualistic and considers himself no less important than the beloved (d) if the beloved can be proud and reticent, he too can be so (e) he would prefer dying, or dying in desire, rather than desire for her without any fulfilment of his desire, and conversely (f) if she is envious of herself and is possessed by her strong self, he too can be equally strong and choose to remain with himself in pride.

There are two words—*rashk* (envy) and *gavaara* (tolerate)—that represent the belligerent mood of the lover. Two other expressions—*marte hai.n* (I die) and *tamanna nahii.n karte* (don't long for her)—also characterize him further. The verse may be read with greater enjoyment as a character portrayal of a proud and unyielding lover. This sentiment of envy mixed with abhorrence is the subject of another verse by Ghalib which supplements this verse: *nafrat kaa gumaa.n guzre hai mai.n rashk se guzraa / kyu.nkar kahuu.n lo naam na un kaa mire aage.*

173

دیا ہے دل اگر اس کو بشر ہے کیا کہئے
ہوا رقیب تو ہو نامہ بر ہے کیا کہئے

दिया है दिल अगर उस को बशर है क्या कहिये
हुआ रक़ीब तो हो नामा-बर है क्या कहिये

diyaa hai dil agar us ko bashar hai kyaa kahiye
huaa raqiib to ho namaabar hai kyaa kahiye

(*bashar*—human;
raqiib—rival;
naamabar—messenger)

If he has given his heart to her; he is a human,
what can I say
If a rival, let him be, but my messenger too,
what can I say

Condescending lovers offer interesting studies in human nature. Here is one such lover speaking to us about his messenger in a supposedly light mood. Now that his messenger's heart has gone for his beloved, the speaker cannot do much about it because the messenger is a human being after all. And even if he has turned into a rival, he is still his messenger, without whom his messages would remain undelivered and he would ever remain impatient. The messenger, a stock figure of Urdu ghazal, constitutes a part of the ghazal's dramatis personae and adds colour to the plot of romantic love.

Ghalib turns this curious condition into a poetic experience as follows: (a) messengers are known in the ghazal tradition to have turned into lovers of those for whom they carry the lover's message (b) after all, this stereotypical messenger is a human being who has a loving heart, for which he can hardly be blamed (c) the messenger has two roles now, as a lover and a message carrier, which is a curious situation for him to be in (d) the lover, who is the speaker here, is much too yielding and not exactly the messenger's rival, but maybe a confidant (e) those who fall in love know of no constraints, like the speaker here, and they do not act with any caution, as love is uncontrollable, and (f) there is a triangle of three entities in this verse—*bashar* (human), *raqiib* (rival) and *naamabar* (messenger)—and interestingly enough, all three of them are the same person with different faces.

The word *us* (implying she) stands here for the beloved to whom the messenger has given his heart. The lover chooses to remain an onlooker and a commentator himself, who only shows his helplessness with his expression of helpless wondering—*kyaa kahiye* (what shall I say).

174

دیکھ کر در پردہ گرم دامن افشانی مجھے
کر گئی وابستۂ تن میری عریانی مجھے

देख कर दर-पर्दा गर्म-ए दामन-अफ़शानी मुझे
कर गई वाबस्ता-ए तन मेरी उर्यानी मुझे

dekh kar dar-parda garm-e daamam-afshaanii mujhe
kar gaii vaabasta-i tan merii 'uryaanii mujhe

(*dar-parda*—within the veil/curtain;
daama- afshaanii—the act of spreading garment/veil/skirt;
vaabasta—attach, associate;
'uryaanii—nakedness)

My nakedness saw me spreading my skirt secretly
It brought me to my body, but only secretly

The different states of physical being distinguish man in totality. Ghalib engages here with this intense thought regarding the state of man's physical appearance in the two states of dress and undress. His speaker suggests that he was engaged in spreading a garment over the lower part of his body in secrecy, and was, thus, trying to save it from nakedness and shame. When his nakedness saw him doing this, it also helped him restore his body that he was trying to veil from the naked viewing of others.

Multiple meanings may be traced in this intricate verse: (a) the concept of nakedness and veiling is subjective, notional and illusory (b) both nakedness and veiling are not merely the visual states of being, but they are metaphoric conditions of being too (c) the act of spreading the garment is the act of veiling the body, but it is indeed an act of a deceptive veiling (d) this implies that the garment which covers the lower part of the body is only illusory, and nakedness is indeed the veil of flesh within which lie the supportive bones that hold the body together (e) this leads nakedness to do a favour and bring the fleshly body back to veiling, which (f) ultimately unravels the philosophy of nakedness and veiling, and their relationship with the body that was born naked, and finally it comes out that (g) all efforts to veil the body must prove futile.

Although the two lines appear to be logically related, they remain complex in their internal relationship. With the personification of nakedness, Ghalib adds yet another layer of complexity to his verse. The words *parda* (veil) and *'uryaanii* (nakedness) represent two opposite conditions of the body. In corresponding with *daaman- afshaanii* (the act of spreading the veil) and *vaabasta-i tan* (bringing back to body), they complete the circle of the possible meaning.

175

وائے واں بھی شور محشر نے نہ دم لینے دیا
لے گیا تھا گور میں ذوقِ تن آسانی مجھے

वाए वाँ भी शोर-ए महशर ने न दम लेने दिया
ले गया था गोर में ज़ौक़-ए तन-आसानी मुझे

vaae vaa.n bhi shor-e mahshar ne na dam lene diyaa
le gayaa thaa gor mei.n zauq-e tan aasaanii mujhe

(*shor-e mahshar*—din of the doomsday;
gor—grave;
zauq—taste, liking;
tan-aasaanii—ease of body)

Alas, even there the Judgement Day's din
didn't let me breathe easy
Though my love for ease had brought me
to my tomb to make me easy

Exasperation expresses itself in unimaginable ways. Here is a speaker who is in such a state and cannot easily compromise with this annoyance. He asserts despairingly that even on doomsday, he did not get relief from the din around. He adds further that although his liking for quietness and ease had taken him to the grave, he met disappointment when he was raised from the grave to face the din of doomsday. In a massive flight of imagination, Ghalib takes his speaker as well as his readers from one world to another to appreciate his unending dilemma.

The verse implicates the idea of peace and din in these ways: (a) life on this earth is characterized by a kind of din that is inescapable (b) the speaker associates afterlife in the grave with peace and sleep because the body lies there in ease (c) when raised back to life on doomsday, he again faces the commotion he wished to escape while he lived on this earth (d) in sum, life here and hereafter is marked by a ruckus which human beings are destined to suffer.

Two phrases—*shor-e mahshar* (din of the doomsday) and *zauq-e tan-aasaanii* (ease of body)—stand in contrast to each other, one representing the nature of doomsday and the other, the nature of the speaker. The sense of the speaker's frustration is carried out in two vital expressions—*vaae* (alas) and *vaa.n bhii* (even there/there too)—which together spell out his exasperation. This frustration is deepened further in the expression *na dam lene diyaa* (did not allow a breath of peace) for which he aspired in life and did not get even after his death.

176

خدایا جذبۂ دل کی مگر تاثیر الٹی ہے
کہ جتنا کھینچتا ہوں اور کھنچتا جائے ہے مجھ سے

खुदा या जज़बा-ए दिल की मगर तासीर उलटी है
कि जितना खेंचता हूँ और खिंचता जाए है मुझ से

KHudaayaa jazba-i dil kii magar taasiir ultii hai
ke jitnaa khe.nchtaa huu.n aur khi.nchtaa jaai hai mujh se

(*jazba-i dil*—heart's emotion;
taasiir—impact)

God, my heart's passion works,
but only the other way
The more I pull it, the more it gets pulled,
the other way

Even a tug of war can be artfully turned into poetic material. Ghalib represents a fascinating idea as well as a visual condition here, which reflects the speaker's emotional condition. He is in a state of quandary which he cannot negotiate with. He laments unambiguously that what his heart wishes to achieve remains far from his reach. What happens, in reality, is that the effect of his passion is reversed. That is, the more he draws his passion closer to his heart, the more it draws away from him, and leaves him disappointed.

The basic idea of the verse lies incorporated in these aspects: (a) the unhappy speaker is speculative and complains here against his own lot (b) he presents his complain before God, who kindly fulfils the desires of the seekers, but unfortunately, the desire of this speaker is not fulfilled (c) the speaker makes an effort to lessen the distance between his desire and its fulfilment, but it does not happen (d) desire here is the incarnation of his beloved from whom his distance increases, the more he draws closer to her (e) there is thus a sense of irony in the effort of push and pull between desire and fulfilment.

The tone of the verse is set with the very word *KHudaayaa* (God!), which is an address of supplication to God while making a prayer or seeking a favour from the Almighty. Ironically, the phrase *jazba-i dil* (heart's emotion) goes waste and it is expressed with the phrase *magar taasiir ultii hai* (but the impact takes a reverse direction). The poetic merit of this verse lies in the visual picture that Ghalib creates in the tension of pulling back and forth, which is represented in dramatic terms in the second line. The phrases *khii.nchnaa* (to pull towards oneself) and *khii. nchtaa* (get pulled in opposite direction) create a dramatic situation which enlivens the verse and makes it one of his memorable ones. This reminds of another verse by Ghalib where the tension between pulling and getting pulled is dramatically created: *naqsh ko us ke musavvir per bhii kyaa kyaa naaz hai.n / khe.nchtaa hai jis qadar utnaa hii khinchtaa jaae hai.*

177

سنبھلنے دے مجھے اے نا امیدی کیا قیامت ہے
کہ دامان خیال یار چھوٹا جائے ہے مجھ سے

संभलने दे मुझे ऐ ना-उमीदी क्या क़ियामत है
कि दामान-ए ख़याल-ए यार छूटा जाए है मुझ से

sa.nbhalne de mujhe ai naa-umiidii kyaa qayaamat hai
ke daamaan-e KHayaal-e yaar chhuTtaa jaae hai mujh se

(daamaan-e KHayaal-e yaar—the hem/border of
love's thought)

Let me take control, my despair!
what a mess is this
My love's thought is slipping out of my hands!
what a mess is this

No lover would ever let the beloved's thought slip out of his hand. This is what Ghalib presents here by picturizing an anxious lover. The lover is getting disappointed and wants to take control of himself because the beloved's thought is slipping out of his hand. He struggles and implores none else but hopelessness itself to let him take control of his own self. He emerges as one to whom the thought of the beloved is life and any distance from her thought would be a cause of his emotional sinking, leading to his personal doom.

This anxious and worried lover's lot may be appreciated in these possible ways: (a) he personifies hopelessness and makes an appeal to it to let him collect himself (b) his despair makes him think that the world is going topsy-turvy, which reminds him of doomsday, which is now shaking his world of hope and desire (c) the visual representation of the hem of the beloved's thought and its slipping out of his hands underlines the lover's tragic helplessness (d) in this nervous war, the personified hopelessness appears as a winner against hope, which the lover represents himself (e) the lover's address to hopelessness is the address of one nervously losing control over himself.

The visually shattered lover is picturized with the phrase *sa.nbhalne de* (let me take control of myself), which acts like a mirror and presents him in visual terms. The word *qayaamat* (doomsday) holds more than a literal meaning and represents the lover's personal catastrophe. Ghalib's deft use of the phrase *chhuTtaa* creates the nervous condition of the lover that calls for immediate rescuing. The picturesque representation of this condition adds unusual vitality to the verse.

178

بازیچۂ اطفال ہے دنیا مرے آگے
ہوتا ہے شب و روز تماشا مرے آگے

बाज़ीचा-ए अतफ़ाल है दुनिया मिरे आगे
होता है शब-ओ-रोज़ तमाशा मिरे आगे

baaziicha-i atfaal hai duniyaa mire aage
hotaa hao shab-o roz tamaasha mire aage

(*baaziicha*—play, fun, frolic, sport;
atfaal—children, offspring;
shab-o roze—day and night, all the time daily, always)

The world is the children's plaything; I must say
I can see their play go on—night and day

The philosophical reality of the world is that it is a purely mundane spectacle which carries on and on. Ghalib reflects upon this with his own metaphors. His speaker is reflective, but a little less caring, even while sharing such a serious thought with us. He shares his well-concluded conviction that the world is merely a children's plaything, or a toy to him. He can see the play go on night and day without a pause, as if in a mechanical manner. This reminds us of Jaques's words in Shakespeare's *As You Like It*:

> All the world's a stage
> And all the men and women merely players;
> They have their exits and their entrances,
> And one man in his time plays many parts ...

We may consider the following aspects to appreciate the worth of this verse: (a) the world is a plaything for fun or sport, but miseries are staged here too as predestined by God (b) the players on this stage are not only children but adults, too, who are God's own children (c) as such, life represents an astounding variety of human beings (d) we are left wondering if the speaker here is making a judgement, or a comment, or a suggestion, or simply saying so in a mood of 'I hardly care what it is' (e) on a serious note, he is projecting a larger philosophical discourse.

The verse is built on the vocabulary of two closely corresponding kinds of words. The first kind comprises *baaziicha* (playground), *atfaal* (children) and *tamaasha* (sport); and the second kind brings *duniyaa* (world) and *shab-o roz* (day and night) together. Both these sets unravel the drama of life and the world in purely metaphoric terms. The interesting refrain *mire aage* means both 'before me' and 'according to me' and enriches the verse in terms of its implications.

179

عاشق ہوں پہ معشوق فریبی ہے مرا کام
مجنوں کو برا کہتی ہے لیلیٰ مرے آگے

आशिक़ हूँ पे माशूक़-फ़रेबी है मिरा काम
मजनूँ को बुरा कहती है लैला मिरे आगे

'aashiq huu.n pa m'ashuuq-farebii hai miraa kaam
Majnuu.n ko buraa kahtii hai Laila mire aage

(*m'ashuuq-farebii*—deceiving/cheating the beloved)

I'm a lover; my job is to cheat my beloved apace
See, how Laila calls Majnuu.n names to my face

A flippant lover is a prominent dramatis persona of ghazals. Quite vigorously and daringly, he asserts that he is a lover and his job is to deceive the beloved. In saying so, he takes pleasure and feels proud. Further, he seems to assert nonchalantly to himself, as also to us, 'now look and behold, Laila calls Majnuu.n names in my presence'. In saying this with a sense of fun, he creates a typically dramatic situation to seek praise for himself from the listeners rather nonchalantly.

Between the two lines of this verse there is much that is implied: (a) the lover says that deceiving the beloveds is his business, but that is, at best, a glib statement (b) that Laila calls Majnuu.n names is only a prank of a statement because the truth is otherwise (c) the two lines are connected by extended implication insofar as the lover is compared to Majnuu.n, whom his Laila calls names (d) such a statement for Majnuu.n, the archetypal lover, is, at best, a left-handed compliment and, at worst, a travesty of fact (e) in matters of love where Laila and Majnuu.n appear for reference, the present lover brings himself to attention and establishes himself as an ideal lover and his beloved as a playful one who cajoles him, but only playfully to suggest that he is better than Majnuu.n.

The predominant tone of the verse is one of remarkable confidence on the part of the lover. It is frisky at its best and is reflected in the phrase *m'ashuuq-farebii* (deceiving the beloved). This emerges and stays on as a key phrase through the reading of the two lines. It gains in strength with a bolder phrase—*mire aage* (before me/in my presence)—which qualifies this lover as excitable too.

180

رونے سے اور عشق میں بے باک ہو گئے
دھوئے گئے ہم اتنے کہ بس پاک ہو گئے

रोने से और इश्क़ में बे-बाक हो गए
धोए गए हम इतने कि बस पाक हो गए

rone se aur 'ishq mei.n be-baak ho gae
dhoye gae ham itne ke bas paak ho gae

(*be-baak*—fearless;
paak—pure)

So much I cried in love, so much I grew fearless
I was washed so much, I got pure of all the mess

Lovers are as varied as are the conditions of love and the kinds of beloveds. The lover we come across in this verse is quite different from others. He has suffered such grief in love that he has grown fearless, and has emerged innocent and pure. He goes even beyond this to say further that he was predestined to shed tears in love and it was because of this that he achieved a new life altogether. This tone and this idea strike us together for their novelty as well as for the frankness they exude.

While this verse is remarkable for its overriding simplicity, it makes fascinating suggestions: (a) love brings pain and pain brings tears to the lover's eyes (b) the lover might have experienced this because he had been uncouth in love (c) in any case, shedding tears is not necessarily a sign of bearing pain, but of achieving a state of tranquillity after suffering (e) he has not shed his tears once, but so many times that it has turned him serene (f) love, as such, has a cathartic effect which has turned this lover into a truly loving soul rather than a tragic hero.

The rhyming words of *be-baak* (fearless) and *paak* (pure) not only bear the central burden of the verse, they also suggest that those who are fearless must necessarily be pure. The phrase *dhoye gae ham itne* (was washed to such extent) brings in the idea of repetitive washing with a good purpose that qualifies a lover to be a lover. Another word that deserves our attention is *bas* (at last/at best/at the end) which bears out the spirit of pure quietude. Instead of using the personal noun of *mai.n* (I), the lover uses a common noun *ham* (we) for himself which also qualifies all lovers in general who suffered this predicament.

181

جب تک دہانِ زخم نہ پیدا کرے کوئی
مشکل کہ تجھ سے راہِ سخن وا کرے کوئی

जब तक दहान-ए ज़ख़्म न पैदा करे कोई
मुशकिल कि तुझ से राह-ए सुख़न वा करे कोई

jab tak dahaan-e zaKHm na paidaa kare koii
mushkil hai tujh se raah-e suKHan vaa kare koii

(*dahaan-e zaKHm*—wound's mouth;
raah-e suKHan—passage of dialogue)

So long as one does not create
a mouth for the wound
It's hard to make a way with you
to stay well-tuned

Speech, representation and reception are deeper concerns of poetry. Ghalib develops a discourse here that characterizes his own poetics. In literal terms, he says that it is not easy to initiate a dialogue with anyone unless one creates an opening for the wound which is akin to opening a passage for communication. Ghalib intends to suggest that developing a dialogue is tough, especially when it comes to doing so with the beloved.

Ghalib has imparted a metaphoric value to this verse as we may mark here: (a) speaking is as demanding and painful an exercise as that of making a mouth for the wound (b) the wound needs a mouth to bleed through as thoughts need words to speak through (c) as the puncturing of a wound brings relief to the wounded, speaking brings relief to the speaker (d) this implies that as long as the mouth of the wound does not open, the way to speech cannot open (e) the act of speaking becomes all the more difficult when it comes to speaking with the beloved (f) this speaking to the beloved may also mean speaking to the reader for whom the poet writes and with whom he wishes to establish a relationship (g) in developing this idea, Ghalib has, in fact, developed a discourse on the condition of communication between the addresser and the addressee, who could also be the poet and his reader.

Two expressions—*dahaan-e zaKHm* (wound's mouth) and *raah-e suKHan* (passage of communication)—correspond closely with each other in metaphoric terms as well as in terms of two passages or openings. The word *vaa* (open) applies equally well to the opening of a wound as well as of the opening of lips to speak up. The opening of both the mouths mentioned here brings relief to man who had suffered pain. That is, once the opening makes way, when relief comes in; that is, once the poet expresses his pent-up feelings, he achieves a moment of tranquillity.

182

بہت سہی غم گیتی شراب کم کیا ہے
غلام ساقیٔ کوثر ہوں مجھ کو غم کیا ہے

बहुत सही ग़म-ए गीती शराब कम क्या है
ग़ुलाम-ए साक़ी-ए कौसर हूँ मुझ को ग़म क्या है

bahut sahii Gham-e getii sharaab kam kyaa hai
Ghulam-e saaqi-i kauser huu.n mujh ko Gham kyaa hai

(*getii*—life, world, earth;
saaqi-i kauser—one who would offer the heaven's wine,
figuratively Prophet Mohammad)

I bore so much of life's worries, but the wine
was never less to bear those along
I'm a slave of the Kauser's server,
I've my worries, but only for a song

This is once again a verse that draws upon the symbolism of wine and wine-server, but in an entirely new context. The speaker admits that he bore enough suffering in his life, but he sustained them all with his cup of wine with him. He thinks further that in the other world too, he would be well provided for because he is the slave of one who would serve him wine from Kauser, the heavenly fountain, and keep him blessed.

The layers of meaning here are quite exciting: (a) life is full of pain and suffering, and wine is supposedly the panacea (b) the speaker believes that if there are more worries for him in this world, there is more wine available to ward them off and he is not worried about his lot in the world hereafter (c) he is easy and proud that he is a slave of that blissful wine-server of the heaven's fountain, who will provide profusely, unlike the wine-server in this world, who offers drinks in small measures only (e) so, he defiantly considers himself well provided for in both the worlds.

Two contrasting expressions—*bahut* (much), with respect to suffering, and *kam* (less), with respect to wine—embody the essential tension of the first line. Then, in the second line, there is another contrast suggested between *Ghulam* (slave) and *Gham* (worry), which the speaker appropriates to his credit and asserts that a slave cannot be worried as long as the master is around. As usual, Ghalib plays with words and skilfully employs his technique of bringing a register of contrastive dictions together to weave a rich tapestry of meaning. A reference to another verse by Ghalib would also be of interest here: *piyuu.n sharaab agar KHum bhii dekh luu.n do-chaar / ye shiisha-o-qadah-o-kuuza-o-subuu kyaa hai.*

183

مدعا محوِ تماشائے شکستِ دل ہے
آئنہ خانہ میں کوئی لیے جاتا ہے مجھے

मुद्दआ महव-ए तमाशा-ए शिकस्त-ए दिल है
आइना-ख़ाने में कोई लिये जाता है मुझे

mudda'aa mahv-e tamaashaa-i shikast-e dil hai
aaiina KHaane mei.n koii liye jaataa hai mujhe

(*mudda'aa*—intent, purpose, desire;
mahv-e tamaasha—glued to/charmed by spectacle;
shikast-e dil—heart's loss)

My wishes stand charmed by the spectacle
of heart's loss
Someone takes me to a house of mirrors
to see its gloss

The dialectics of desire are poetical and philosophical concerns. Ghalib finds a reflective persona here to gloss over this. He is a victim of desires and is subjected to pain more often than not. He confesses that his desire is only a witness to the loss his heart has suffered in the act of loving and losing in love. He adds that someone is taking him now to a chamber of mirrors where he will watch his loss much more vividly, and realize how much he has suffered in love.

The implications of this well-wrought poetic utterance may be inferred as follows: (a) the lover has suffered in love and his heart has broken into pieces (b) this is just like a mirror breaking into pieces, lying scattered all around (c) the broken pieces make a chamber of mirrors where the lover's desires lie scattered in pieces (d) his desires, broken into pieces, helplessly witness the breaking of the lover's heart (e) to bring the tragic saga to its end, the lover is taken to the chamber of broken mirrors so he may see how he has been devastated in love (f) a deep sense of disappointment added with despair marks the tone of the lover which also characterizes this verse as one typically representing a desolate lover.

The word *dil* (heart) may be read here as a personification of the lover himself who is broken. This is expressed in terms of *shikast-e dil* (breaking of heart) which is akin to the breaking of the lover. *Aaiina KHaana* (chamber of mirrors) may also be read as a metaphor for reflecting the inner desires of the lover, where he is brought only to be inflicted with greater pain in watching his devastation. Ghalib does not say who is taking him to the chamber of mirrors, but one may guess that it is the lover's archetypal lot that brings him to his total annihilation and shows him what he has suffered.

184

ہزاروں خواہشیں ایسی کہ ہر خواہش پہ دم نکلے
بہت نکلے مرے ارمان لیکن پھر بھی کم نکلے

हज़ारों ख़्वाहिशें ऐसी कि हर ख़्वाहिश पे दम निकले
बहुत निकले मिरे अरमान लेकिन फिर भी कम निकले

hazaaro.n KHvaahishei.n aisi ke har KHvaahish pe dam nikle
bahut nikle mire armaan lekin phir bhii kam nikle

(*KHvaahish*—desire, aspiration, wish, will;
armaan—longing, wish, yearning)

Desires in thousands I had, for each I would die
With many I had luck, for many I would sigh

Ghazal, at large, is all about developing the cartographies of desire. In one of his most celebrated verses here, Ghalib defines desire as craving, longing, even dreaming, and the desirer as a helpless subject of desire. In other words, desires are dreams and dreams are often illusive, except that dreams are forgotten, but desires are active and persistent. Pursuing a desire is like pursuing a dream. which brings pleasure, but dreaming up desires is the same as dreaming up illusions, which brings disappointment. The speaker here is an embodiment of desires with a thousand of them crowding his heart. Luckily for him, many of his desires were fulfilled, but his dilemma is that howsoever much they were fulfilled, they were much less fulfilled than he had desired.

Further implications are too varied and worth noting: (a) human psychology testifies that the more the wishes are fulfilled, the more they raise their heads (b) each desire, in the melee of a thousand desires, is stressed here but only modestly (c) each unfulfilled desire leads to suffering and leaves man in despair (d) there were many regrets, but all of them were not expressed (g) every longing is paid for in terms of dying, which implies that many a desire mean many a death (h) life is a web of desires and desires appear in many forms as yearning, wishing, craving and suffering.

Even while Ghalib uses two broad synonyms—*KHvaahish* (desire) and *armaan* (longing)—he posits many more shades of implications into them. The word *hazaar* (thousand) used here in plural does not stand for numbers, but it appears only as a proverb for many. The phrase *dam nikle* (lose breath) does not imply dying, or dying of suffocation, but extreme yearning. We cannot miss the tension of meaning Ghalib creates here with *bahut* (many) and *kam* (less). Ironically enough, many stands here for less and adds beauty to this poetic expression. Ghalib seems to draw upon Mir Taqi Mir's verse here: *saraapa aarzuu hone ne banda kar diyaa ham ko / vagarna ham KHudaa hote gar dil-e be-mudda'aa hote.*

185

محبت میں نہیں ہے فرق جینے اور مرنے کا
اسی کو دیکھ کر جیتے ہیں جس کافر پہ دم نکلے

मुहब्बत में नहीं है फ़र्क़ जीने और मरने का
उसी को देख कर जीते हैं जिस काफ़िर पे दम निकले

mohabbat mei.n nahii.n kuchh farq jiine aur marne kaa
usii ko dekh kar jiite hai.n jis kaafir pe dam nikle

(*kaafir*—idolator, infidel, metaphorically
the tormenting beloved)

There is no difference in love between
living and dying
I live by looking at her, the one for whom
I keep sighing

There is no love that is either all pain or all pleasure. Lovers are both tormenters and redeemers, which makes the relationship between the lover and the beloved very special. Ghalib brings a lover here who enacts this in precise terms. He strikes a difference when he makes his speaker share an individual experience that is universal too. Living and dying are the same for this speaker, because love has brought more pains to him than pleasures. After making this general statement, he comes up with a more sublimating, yet ironical, statement that he lives by looking at the same one for whom he keeps dying as well.

Playing upon words, Ghalib makes fascinating points worth noting with respect to loving and dying: (a) in saying that there is no distinction between living and dying in love, the speaker makes an axiomatic statement in the first line (b) he personalizes this further by asserting that the one who is the cause for his living is also the one for whom he keeps dying day and night (c) dying does not imply death, but it underlines his irremediable suffering which is as good as dying (d) he thus underscores his dichotomous relationship with the beloved as tormenter and tormenter as beloved, which is typical of the beloved in the ghazal tradition.

From the artistic point of view, one can mark that while the first line reads like a maxim, the second line comes up as a unique paradox. This paradox is built on the interplay of living as dying and dying as living. This is well brought out by juxtaposing *jiine* (living) and *marne* (dying) in the first line and *jiite hai.n* (I live) and *dam nikle* (I die) in the second line. The expression *dam nikle,* however, is a painful and prolonged way of dying than dying naturally and instantaneously. This is a typical Ghalibean way of putting the opposites together to bear upon one another and to find the meaning midway. One may not also miss that he identifies the beloved as *kaafir*, like all other ghazal poets, not in the sense of an infidel but as an entity who brings pain, pining, grieving and suffering to the lover.

186

کہاں مے خانہ کا دروازہ غالبؔ اور کہاں واعظ
پر اتنا جانتے ہیں کل وہ جاتا تھا کہ ہم نکلے

कहाँ मै-ख़ाने का दरवाज़ा ग़ालिब और कहाँ वायज़
पर इतना जानते हैं कल वो जाता था कि हम निकले

kahaa.n maiKHaane ka darvaaza Ghalib aur kahaa.n vaa'iz
per itnaa jaante hai.n kal vo jaataa thaa ke ham nikle

(*maiKHana*—tavern;
vaa'iz—preacher)

Tavern's door and preacher's steps—both are
worlds apart, no doubt
I only know this much Ghalib—he walked in,
as I walked out

What is concealed is sometimes revealed in the strangest of ways. Ghalib capitalizes upon a scene to write a typically tongue-in-cheek verse. He asserts that the tavern's threshold and the preacher's steps are never supposed to meet each other. However, the speaker saw the preacher entering the tavern when he was coming out of it yesterday. By bringing these two persons in the scene, Ghalib leaves much to our imagination.

Some interesting aspects of this dichotomous situation come up quite prominently here: (a) Ghalib puts two uncompromising institutions face-to-face here which leaves us bemused (b) he seems to suggest that appearance and pretension do not go together, but when they do they bring out the essential nature of the pretenders (c) the poet's comment on the preacher being there is gently sardonic, but not markedly scornful (d) the preacher's presence there, irrespective of the fact whether he was just passing by the tavern or was around to mark as to who was emerging from there, are less important (e) contrarily, it is far more important that he was noticeably there, betraying the institution he represented (f) no indication is given whether he drank there but it comes out by implication that wine is indeed irresistible, even for those who preach against it, and that is how he fell prey to drinking.

The distance between the tavern and preacher's steps is expressed here with the simplest word *kahaa.n* (how come), not in terms of physical distance but in terms of surprise as the ways leading to the two institutions cut across each other. Ghalib makes his expression quite forceful by putting together the acts of going in and coming out as represented in *jaata thaa ke ham nikle*. However, the pithier expression is *per itnaa jaante hai.n* (only this much I know) which surpasses even the subtlest of the mocking comments.

187

خموشیوں میں تماشا ادا نکلتی ہے
نگاہ دل سے ترے سرمہ سا نکلتی ہے

ख़मोशियों में तमाशा अदा निकलती है
निगाह दिल से तिरे सुर्मा सा निकलती है

KHamoshiyo.n mei.n tamasha-adaa nikaltii hai
nigaah dil se tiri surma-saa nikaltii hai

(*surma-saa*—bearing the quality of collyrium
that is a kind of dark eyeshadow)

In silence, the spectacles wear
a wondrous look
The looks from your heart appear
as the collyrium-eyes look

This is one of the more complicated verses of Ghalib where he refers to collyrium, an antique term, used for medicated eyewash, known in different cultural traditions since the fourteenth century. This is also mentioned in Islamic traditions and Prophet Mohammad, too, is known to have referred to this and mentioned antimony as the best kind of collyrium for eyes. Ghalib uses the idea of collyrium and suggests that the beloved has consumed collyrium, instead of applying it to the eyes, and is thus rendered speechless. So, her gaze is her speech which is so very fascinating unto itself.

Several layers of meaning can be marked here: (a) tongue and eyes are the two sources of human communication, but here the beloved cannot speak, as she has consumed collyrium and has, as a result, lost her voice (b) thus, she can only see and her seeing has a wondrous quality, as it bears the quality of dark collyrium (*surma*) (c) since the putting on of collyrium adds to her coquetry, her seeing which is more of a gazing, has become much more charming (d) her gaze is deep and profound also because it emerges from her heart (e) interestingly, her silence is more expressive and intense compared with her tongue (f) it would not be too far to seek a mystical implication here as the gaze could also be the gaze of a mystic falling sharply on the devotees around.

Two expressions—*tamaasha-adaa* (bearing the quality of a spectacle) and *surma-saa* (bearing the quality of collyrium)—carry the entire burden of meaning and magic of this verse. By adding *adaa* in the first line and *saa* in the second, Ghalib turns the two nouns into adjectives. With this, he turns the entire experience of looking into the beloved's eyes into a magical one. In addition, the linguistic gesture that Ghalib adopts here to portray a situation affirms his spectacular artistry.

188

دل مدعی و دیدہ بنا مدعا علیہ
نظارہ کا مقدمہ پھر رو بکار ہے

दिल मुद्द'ई-ओ-दीदा बना मुद्दआ अलैह
नज़्ज़ारे का मुक़द्दमा फिर रू-बकार है

dil mudda'ii o diida banaa mudda'aa alaih
nazzara ka muqaddama phir ruu-ba-kaar hai

(*mudda'ii*—plaintiff;
diida—eye;
mudda'aa alaih—defendant;
ruu-ba-kaar—in front, appear, face-to-face)

The heart became a plaintiff,
defendant became the eyes
Spectacles' matter is up again
for a ruling, or advice

Courts, arguments and judgements are not sacrosanct to the judiciary alone. Ghalib's genius appropriates these in love's context as well. As always, the heart has become a plaintiff here and the looks of the beloved the defendant. Together, they make a case regarding the act of seeing, which is certainly a suitable matter under hearing in the court of love. The judgement is awaited and the charm of the verse lies in the waiting for how the matter between the two is settled. As poetry does not offer answers or judgments, it only makes suggestions pregnant with deeper meaning(s); this verse leaves much unsaid but gains only with implied intents.

The constituents of this verse make it worthy of our critical attention: (a) we have a plaintiff and a defendant standing against each other, but there is no counsel or judge around (b) the case is that the heart is a plaintiff and the eyes of the beloved the defendant, and they stand as opponents (c) the plaintiff cannot keep his eyes away from the defendant and the defendant cannot always accept those peering looks of the plaintiff (d) so, a case stands out against the plaintiff (e) the two have to act as counsel-cum-judges to defend their individual cases in which there can be no loser or winner (f) this is because in love there are tiffs and the two lovers, acting as plaintiff and defendant against each other, rest their cases with no judgement delivered or received since no judgement can ever be made in their matters.

Three words—*mudda'ii* (plaintiff), *mudda'aa alaih* (defendant) and *muqaddama* (lawsuit)—drawn from the domain of the judiciary, are well applied in the romantic context of this verse. With this technique, Ghalib imparts a unique character to this verse and makes it a pleasurable reading experience for us. Ghalib extends this idea in another verse as: *dil-o mizhgaa.n kaa jo muqaddama thaa / aaj phir us kii ruu-ba-kaarii hai.*

189

دل مت گنوا خبر نہ سہی سیر ہی سہی
اے بے دماغ آئینہ تمثال دار ہے

दिल मत गंवा ख़बर न सही सैर ही सही
ऐ बे-दिमाग़ आइना तिमसाल-दार है

dil mat gavaa.n KHabar na sahii sair hii sahii
ai be-dimaaGh aaiina timsaaldaar hai

(*timsaaldaar*—keeping resemblance)

Don't lose heart, let that not be a news,
but a jest altogether
You brainless one, the mirror only
bears the two together

Love needs counselling and redeeming at times. Ghalib brings a speaker who counsels the forlorn lover here. There is no reason to grieve and ruin the heart, he persuades, because human hearts can also bear pain sometimes. He convinces by saying that this heart is, after all, a repository of both dear and dreary conditions in love, and all of them have to be valued.

We need to keep the following aspects further in mind to appreciate this verse: (a) the heart should not be ruined as it is a mirror that reflects human aspirations as well as disappointments (b) it should not be destroyed even if it is not enlightened with the mysteries of the divine (c) ruining the heart's mirror can itself be a sad reflection on human limitations (d) one should seek pleasure in the manifestations available to man in this world, rather than mourn for what is lost or not achieved (e) the addressee here could be an irascible beloved, who is being persuaded not to reject the gift of the heart, which is indeed a mirror and where images find their reflection.

The most striking phrases here are *aaiina* (*mirror*) and *timsaaldaar* (bearing resemblance). While *timsaal* is a noun meaning an image or picture, it becomes an adjective with the suffix of *aar* and qualifies it as a keeper or reflector of images. Ghalib thus attributes far greater richness to it than the mirror and posits the central argument of this verse in this single word. This implies that a mirror is not only a reflector of an image but something that brings out resemblances too; in this case, between ordinary and extraordinary pleasures. The space for this is created in the first line by distinguishing *KHabar* (news) and *sair* (sport/pastime) against each other). While *KHabar* is an ordinary happening, *sair* is a surprising phenomenon with which Ghalib chooses to express his intent and enrich the verse. We may refer to another verse by Ghalib to appreciate the suitable conformity of thought between the two verses: *sach kahte ho KHud-biin-oKHud-aaraa huu.n na kyu.n huu.n / baiThaa hai but-e aaiina-siimaa mire aage.*

190

آئینہ کیوں نہ دوں کہ تماشا کہیں جسے
ایسا کہاں سے لاؤں کہ تجھ سا کہیں جسے

आईना क्यूँ न दूँ कि तमाशा कहें जिसे
ऐसा कहाँ से लाऊँ कि तुझ सा कहें जिसे

aaiina kyu.n na duu.n ke tamaasha kahei.n jise
aisaa kahaa.n se laau.n ke tujh saa kahei.n jise

(*tamaasha*—show, play, display, splendour)

Why shouldn't I bring a mirror that may bear
a splendid scene
Where do I get one like you, there's none of
that very sheen

Beauty can be praised without end. Here is one of Ghalib's many extraordinary ways of praising the beauty of the beloved. His speaker reflects his own enamoured state and he knows not where he would possibly get someone who would be as grand as her. While he reflects every lover's emotion here, he also registers his own appreciation for her. So, he offers a solution: May she be given a mirror so that she may look into it herself to see what the lover really means. Ghalib puts this idea in a converse sequence of the two lines to put his intent across.

The speaker makes some fascinating suggestions overall: (a) is there anyone available anywhere to stand in comparison with the beloved (b) is there someone somewhere by looking at whom one would say that she is as beautiful as her (c) to resolve this, a mirror may thus be brought to the beloved herself who would present a spectacle to the onlookers by looking into it (d) that is, by looking into the mirror, the beloved will be amazed at herself (e) the very view of her amazement would be a spectacle for the onlookers, and (f) the beloved is incomparable indeed and stands as the ultimate measure of beauty.

There is a richly curious relationship between *tamaasha* (spectacle) and *tujh saa* (like you) here. Both bear upon one another as the spectacle is as miraculous as is the spectacled one herself. The word *tamaasha* is not used here in the negative sense of an ordinary display of objects or a bizarre show by the roadside; it represents just the opposite and drives home the idea of splendour and glory that the beloved is incarnated into. Another striking image is that of the *aaiina* (mirror) with which the verse begins and projects the inverse sequence of the speaker's logic, which finds its corollary in the second line. It is thus well suggested that this mirror is not a silent spectator, but it becomes the image of beauty itself in reflecting the beauteous one. It would be pertinent to bring in Siraj Aurangabadi here, whose verse would help appreciate the authentic portrayal of this sentiment: *chiraagh-e meh sii.n raushan tar hai husn-e be-misaal us kaa / ke chauthe charKH per KHurshiid hai aks-e jamaal us kaa.*

191

تمثال میں تیری ہے وہ شوخی کہ بہ صد ذوق
آئینہ بہ انداز گل آغوش کشا ہے

तिमसाल में तेरी है वो शोख़ी कि ब सद ज़ौक़
आईना ब अंदाज़-ए गुल आग़ोश-कुशा है

timsaal mei.n terii hai vo shoKHii ke ba-sad zauq
aaiina ba-andaaz-e gul aaGhosh-kushaa hai

(*timsaal*—bearing resemblance;
ba-sad zauq—with all sweet attention;
ba-andaaz-e gul—like/in the manner of flower;
aaGhosh-kushaa—with open arms to embrace)

Your image is so naughty that
with all love and grace
The mirror opens up
like a blossom to embrace

Innumerable are the ways and manners of lovers and beloveds, and countless, too, are the methods to praise the magnificence of the beloved. This is yet another novel way of Ghalib praising the beloved. He helps his speaker come up with an entirely novel style of doing this. The mirror has opened its arms like the petals of a blossom to reflect her splendid image. The lover believes that this is so because the mirror itself is like the blossom with its arms open to welcome the beloved.

This verse makes the following suggestions: (a) the playful reflection of the beloved captivates the lover (b) it also captivates the mirror and makes it impatient, just like the lover (c) for holding her reflection close to its bosom, the mirror unfolds its embrace just as a blossom opens up its petals before the viewers (d) the playfulness of the beloved's reflection implies the impatience and playfulness of the beloved herself.

There is a well-wrought poetic argument in the comparison made between *aaiina* (mirror) and *gul* (blossom), as both open up in two different ways. The verse acquires its true appeal in the expressions from the same poetical register, like *shoKHii* (playfulness) characterizing the beloved, *ba-sad zauq* (with all sweet attention) underlining the willingness of the mirror, *ba-andaaz-e gul* (like the blossom) projecting the appearance of the blossom and *aaGhosh-kushaa* (with open arms to embrace) representing the mirror's willingness to embrace. These expressions depict the nature and mood of Ghalib's configuration of the beloved which is typically romantic. In comparison with Ghalib, a verse by Abdul Hameed Adam would be relevant to quote here: *im-shab gurez-o ram kaa nahii.n hai koii mahal / aagosh mei.n dar aa ke tabiiyat udaas hai.*

192

گو واں نہیں پہ واں کے نکالے ہوئے تو ہیں
کعبے سے ان بتوں کو بھی نسبت ہے دور کی

गो वाँ नहीं पे वाँ के निकाले हुए तो हैं
काबे से उन बुतों को भी निसबत है दूर की

go vaa.n nahii.n pa vaa.n ke nikaale hue to hai.n
k'abe se in buto.n ko bhii nisbat hai duur kii

(*nisbat*—bond, relationship)

No longer there although; they are those turned
back and beyond
But with the k'aba, those idols have had
a distant bond

In order to create a context for the intended subject of this verse, Ghalib takes us back to the crucial episode of Islamic history when as many as three hundred sixty idols were expelled from the inner chambers of the k'aba to establish the Islamic faith in one God. It is suggested that they are no longer in the k'aba but they have had an old association with it as they had been there in the pre-Islamic days with Hubal as their head. With this allusion, Ghalib's speaker seems to develop a different narrative of human love, where the beloveds, also known as idols in poetry, are deprived of their lovers sometimes.

The inferences we may draw from this verse include: (a) the idols being referred to here were none else but the beloveds themselves who were worshipped by the pagans—that is, those who did not believe in one God (b) the idols are no longer in the inner chamber of the k'aba from where they had been expelled—that is, they are no longer in the inner chambers of their lovers' hearts (c) in spite of this, the relationship these idols had with the k'aba, can neither be undone nor forgotten (d) the beloveds still take an unusual pride in being once in the inner chamber of the k'aba—that is, the inner chambers of the lover's heart (e) this also explains the relevance of the expression *k'aba-i dil* (the holy precinct of heart)—where beloveds reside with pride (f) in this respect, the speaker looks at the lover-beloved relationship in a new perspective and ponders that the idols who were expelled still live in the memories of their lovers-cum-worshippers.

The verse makes its mark with its tonal and gestural richness. Two words in particular—*nikaale hue* (expelled) and *nisbat* (association)—bear out the nostalgic gloom of the idols. They also bear out how the beloveds, driven out of the lovers' hearts, still recall their association with them. This feeling is strengthened further with the word *duur kii* (of distance) which suggests, by implication, that the relationship that had been so close once has turned so remote now.

193

کیا فرض ہے کہ سب کو ملے ایک سا جواب
آؤ نہ ہم بھی سیر کریں کوہ طور کی

क्या फ़र्ज़ है कि सब को मिले एक-सा जवाब
आओ न हम भी सैर करें कोह-ए तूर की

kyaa farz hai ke sab ko mile ek saa javaab
aao na ham bhii sair kare.in koh-e Tuur kii

(*farz*—compulsory, obligatory, essential;
koh-e Tuur—Mount Sinai)

It's not for sure that everyone gets
the same reply, well-nigh
Come on now, why don't we too,
take a stroll at Mount Sinai

We need to keep the religious allusion according to the Torah, the Bible and the Qur'an in mind to appreciate this verse. The followers of Moses insisted that they would not join the faith he proclaimed unless they saw the Lord for themselves. This brought Moses to the mount of Sinai (*Jabal-e Musa / Tuur Siniin*, The Qur'an 25:2) and address the Lord to show His radiant beauty. Instantly, Moses got a reply that he cannot see the Lord. This was followed by three things—a lightning strike which burnt the date palm at Mount Sinai, an earthquake and Moses falling unconscious. The implication here is that it is not essential that everyone gets the same reply necessarily as Moses got. The speaker thus persuades the addressee to take a stroll at Mount Sinai to seek an answer.

In the light of this, the implications of the verse are: (a) everyone is not Moses whose call would not be heeded to, as the first line suggests (b) in the effort to achieve a goal lies the possibility of reaching a goal and be in the presence of the beloved (c) the speaker wishes to try and take a stroll to Mount Sinai for himself as well as for the benefit of others (d) this underlines the human desire to discover what lies undiscovered for lack of human courage.

The tone of the speaker here is clearly persuasive. This is borne out by the phrase *aao na* (oh, why not come along). This persuasion is strengthened by the logic that everyone may not necessarily get the same reply Moses got, but a different answer of acceptance may also come along. The logic for this persuasion is foregrounded in the first three words of the first line—*kyaa farz hai* (is it compulsory?)—which carries a question but more prominently a sense of incredulity because the consequence of the visit may leave the stroller wonder struck. A verse by Mohammad Iqbal serves as a gloss on Ghalib's verse: *khi.nche KHud-ba-KHud jaanib-e Tuur Musaa / kashish terii ai shauq-e diidaar kyaa thii.*

194

نے تیر کماں میں ہے نہ صیاد کمیں میں
گوشے میں قفس کے مجھے آرام بہت ہے

ने तीर कमाँ में है न सय्याद कमीं में
गोशे में क़फ़स के मुझे आराम बहुत है

ne tiir kamaa.n mei.n hai na sayyad kamii.n mei.n
goshe mei.n qafas ke mujhe aaraam bahut hai

(*sayyad*—hunter;
kamii.n—ambush;
gosha—corner;
qafas—cage)

No arrow in arch; no hunter in ambush to gauge
I am so much at ease in a corner of my cage

A moment of blissful ease in life and living is much yearned for but seldom achieved. Ghalib expresses this idea in a metaphorical framework of hunting. This context is equally applicable to human beings among whom there are the hunters and the hunted, and where the abodes of the hunted are always at risk. This may be appreciated with reference these points: (a) the fear of arrows and hunters keeps the birds ever threatened, and their absence brings a sense of relief to birds, as it does to human beings (b) even the cage, which keeps the birds trapped, becomes a safe retreat for them to rest, just as it happens in the case of human beings (c) for both the birds and the human beings, this could be a place of retreat and safety (d) the attackers attack from behind in ambush as they work through deceit, which is also true of attacks on human beings, and quite significantly, (e) this context may help us further appreciate the predicament of lovers and beloveds who face these dangers too and can't celebrate life only in safety and ease

A verse thickly populated with as many as six contiguous images in three sets—*tiir* (arrow) and *kamaa.n* (bow), *sayyad* (hunter) and *kamii.n* (ambush), and *gosha* (corner) and *qafas* (cage)—weaves a plot of living and surviving. These pairs of images complement each other, but there is a deeper sense of irony in a hunter spreading out an ambush and a corner turning into cage. The plot spills over from the apparent context of a bird and a hunter to reflect upon the human lot of precarious living and safe surviving. In this context, a reference to a verse by Haider Ali Atish would of interest: *sayyad-e gul-'azaar dikhaataa hai sair-e baaGh / bulbul qafas mei.n yaad kare aashiyaana kyaa.*

195

خوں ہو کے جگر آنکھ سے ٹپکا نہیں اے مرگ
رہنے دے مجھے یاں کہ ابھی کام بہت ہے

ख़ूँ हो के जिगर आंख से टपका नहीं ऐ मार्ग
रहने दे मुझे याँ कि अभी काम बहुत है

KHuu.n ho ke jigar aa.nkh se Tapkaa nahii.n ai marg
rahne de mujhe yaa.n ke abhii kaam bahot hai

(*marg*—death)

My heart hasn't turned into blood;
it hasn't dropped from my eyes yet
O death, let me live here longer;
I've so much to do yet

W ho can address death, but the poets alone? This verse is a bold address and a soft request to death. Ghalib's speaker asserts that what lies between life and death is suffering, which is an eternal human condition. He impels death to allow him more time because he has so much to achieve and to suffer still to realize the meaning of his existence. This is his philosophical way of looking at suffering as an empowering agency.

The implied shades of meaning in this entreaty to death may be apprehended as follows: (a) the speaker emerges here as a protagonist in the theatre of life who has retained his resilience and faced all adversities (b) he appears before death as a plaintiff for a longer life and death emerges as an award giver before him (c) he asserts that he has endured much and has enough potential still to endure further (d) he suggests that the world is a place where life's business never comes to end, but life comes to an end itself at the fixed hour which does not allow man to accomplish all that he yearned for (e) the speaker could be the lover himself for whom there is much more suffering in store than he has faced so far, and he has to suffer them all before leaving the world; that is why the plea for a longer life.

The cause-effect relationship between the two lines of this verse works in the form of imploring in the first line and its substantiation in the second line. The idea of the heart turning into blood and dropping from the eyes (*KHuu.n ho ke jigar aa.nk se Tapkaa*) is a proverb of common usage which implies that suffering finds its way through tears. The speaker appropriates it to his purpose with gain. That the world is a place of endless preoccupations is brought out in *abhii kaam bahut hai* (I have enough to accomplish yet). This brings to mind a characteristic verse by Mohammad Iqbal to develop a comparative perspective: *qanaa'at na kar 'aalam-e rang-o buu per / abhii 'ishq ke imtihaa.n aur bhii hai.n.*

196

کرتا ہوں جمع پھر جگر لخت لخت کو
عرصہ ہوا ہے دعوت مژگاں کیے ہوئے

करता हूँ जमा फिर जिगर-ए लख़्त-लख़्त को
अरसा हुआ है दावत-ए मिज़गाँ किये हुए

kartaa huu.n jam'a phir jigar-e laKHt laKHt ko
'arsa huaa hai daavat-e mizhgaa.n kiye hue

(laKHt laKHt—piece by piece, in pieces;
daavat-e mizhga.an—a fare of eyelashes)

Once again, I put together my heart's pieces—
piece by piece
It has been long putting up a fare of
eyelashes—apiece

Lovers have extraordinary appetite, skill and power to negotiate with pain. Ghalib brings us here before an enduring lover who is used to bearing pain, and still has the extraordinary appetite to bear more. He tells his addressees that it has been long since he put his scattered heart-pieces together. So, he would like to do so now once again and offer those heart-pieces to the eyelashes of the beloved for a feast of her eyes. He thus emerges as a typical lover who suffers and wishes to suffer more to show his devotion to his beloved.

Further layers of meaning behind his act may be marked as follows: (a) the lover's heart is already broken to pieces which he wants to collect once again (b) once again, he wishes to put those pieces together and present them as his heart to the beloved's eyelashes in the form of a feast (c) he does this for one who has been the cause of his heart's tearing into pieces (d) the image of the eyelashes as a tent of eyes brings home the idea of eyes as precious possessions that preserve images and are kept protected by eyelashes.

This verse does not work with words alone; it presents a graphic scenario through words invoking a vision. The picking of the pieces of the heart adds a picturesque quality to the verse. This is followed by yet another visual image of *mizhgaa.n* (eyelashes). With the heart-pieces and eyelashes brought together, the speaker creates a plot and invites us to come along and watch how the eyelashes feast upon the heart. Ghalib engages with this idea in another verse as well: *jalva az-bas-ke taqaazaa-i nigah kartaa hai / jauhar-e aaiina bhii chahe hai mizhgaa.n honaa.*

197

غالبؔ ہمیں نہ چھیڑ کہ پھر جوشِ اشک سے
بیٹھے ہیں ہم تہیۂ طوفاں کیے ہوئے

ग़ालिब हमें न छेड़ कि फिर जोश-ए अश्क से
बैठे हैं हम तहय्या-ए तूफ़ाँ किये हुए

Ghalib hamei.n na chheR ke phir josh-e ashk se
baiThhe hain ham tahayya-i tuufaa.n kiye hue

(*josh-e ashk*—turmoil of tears;
tahayya—resolve, determination)

Don't ever tease me Ghalib; I have my restive tears ready
I sit with a resolve; I'll bring a deluge of frenzied eddy

A lover, already devastated, does not want to be devastated any further, but yearns only to resume his spirit of loving. Ghalib presents here the picture of a lover in his own voice. If teased, he would take revenge as if against his own self by raising a turmoil of tears. This presents the beloved in a cruel image, who has caused such misery to the lover.

Some layers of meaning may be explored along these lines: (a) one of the ways to ease oneself is to shed tears which have a calming effect on the sufferer (b) suffering and love keep company, and it appears to be so in his case too (c) the lover does not want to be teased because he is already teased enough and cannot bear anymore (d) in case he is teased, his grief will find its expression through a devastating swirl of tears to drown everything (e) in spite of his suffering, he stays steadfast to his beloved, which testifies his utmost sincerity to her.

Two expressions—*josh-e ashk* (turmoil of tears) and *tahayya-i tuufaa.n* (resolve to raise a turmoil)—hold the key to the predominant temper of the verse. Together, they take us back to the operative verb *chheR* (tease) in the first line which could cause the turmoil of tears. The subsequent phrase—*baiThe hai.n* (I sit prepared)—shows the speaker's determination to react if he is teased for no reason. This gesture is not one of self-pity but of assertion on the part of the beloved. Consider here a verse by Ghalib to mark how he seeks another way of expressing this idea: *rone se aur 'ishq mei.n be-baak ho gae / dhoe gae ham itne ke bas paak ho gae.*

198

گدا سمجھ کے وہ چپ تھا مری جو شامت آئی
اٹھا اور اٹھ کے قدم میں نے پاسباں کے لیے

गदा समझ के वो चुप था मिरी जो शामत आयी
उठा और उठ के क़दम मैं ने पास-बाँ के लिये

gadaa samajh ke vo chup thaa miri jo shaamat aaii
uThaa aur uTh ke qadam mai.n ne paasbaa.n ke liye

(*gadaa*—beggar;
shaamat—misfortune, bad luck;
paasbaa.n—guard, gatekeeper)

He thought I was a beggar;
he kept silent till I set the stage
I stood up and reached out to the guard
only to cause his rage

Lovers may look like beggars, or may become one in love. Here is a scene where the interaction between two people presents a drama of sorts. The person who has arrived at the abode of the beloved resembles a beggar and he considers the gatekeeper to be a kind person. So, he chooses to approach him but only to be rebuffed. This dramatic situation may be appreciated in these terms: (a) there are two persons face-to-face here—the visitor, who looks rumpled like a beggar, and the gatekeeper, who appears tenacious and unyielding (b) the way they are, they represent powerlessness and power respectively (c) when his misfortune struck, the supposed beggar took a step closer to the gatekeeper (d) with this, the gatekeeper could make out his purpose that he wished admittance to the inner quarters of the beloved (e) this implies that he was not a beggar, but a lover who had reached this miserable state in separation from the beloved (f) the gatekeeper could not recognize him because he looked quite messy and could not be allowed to visit the inner quarters (g) since the gatekeeper did not turn him away considering him a beggar, the lover took him to be a gracious person and approached him expectantly (h) we may not, however, entirely reject another possibility that he was mistreated by the gatekeeper when he approached him and touched his feet.

The last bit of reading above is dictated by two words in particular—*shaamat* (misfortune) and *qadam* (step)—which Ghalib keeps ambiguous to impart richness to his verse. The expressions, *uThaa* used in the sense of 'I moved forward' and '*uTh ke qadam mai.n ne paasbaa.n ke liye* suggest 'I approached the gatekeeper' as well as 'I touched the gatekeeper's feet'. Another verse by Ghalib comes to mind in this context: *de vo jis qadar zillat ham ha.nsii mei.n taale.nge / baare aashnaa niklaa un kaa paasbaa.n apnaa.*

199

بہ قدر شوق نہیں ظرف تنگنائے غزل
کچھ اور چاہیے وسعت مرے بیاں کے لیے

ब क़दर-ए शौक़ नहीं ज़रफ़-ए तंगना-ए ग़ज़ल
कुछ और चाहिये वुसअत मिरे बयाँ के लिये

*ba-qadr-e shauq nahii.n zarf-e ta.ngnaa-i Ghazal
kuchh aur chaahiye vus'at mire bayaa.n ke liye*

(*ba-qadr-e shauq*—according to taste;
zarf—tolerance, capacity;
ta.ngnaa-i ghazal—ghazal's difficult task/demand;
vus'at—breadth, extensiveness)

The Ghazal's narrow straits, not to my taste at all
I need a greater expanse for me to take a call

Ta'alli, or self-praise, is not uncommon among poets. Ghalib always considered his potential in superlative terms. While speaking to himself here, he speaks to his listeners who may be both his admirers as well as his detractors. He says that the form of the ghazal does not really give him enough space to express himself fully. So, he aspires for greater space to be able to exercise his imagination. This is one of those verses where Ghalib asserts his worth without any reservation or uncalled for humility.

This is possibly how we may approach this verse further: (a) poets are well known for their heightened confidence in their talent, which Ghalib represents here in clear terms (b) his aspiration for space could mean imaginative space that he surveys and rules over, as well as the larger space that poetical forms like *qasiida, mathnavii* and *marsiya* offer (c) the ghazal, composed in two lines, offers him lesser space to say his say (d) his opinion on the form of the ghazal, in which he excelled undoubtedly, may be read as an expression of his humility, and (e) saying that the ghazal cannot hold all that he has to offer and yet he does express himself with such distinction, only underlines his special love for the form.

The rudimentary phrase *zarf* (capacity) qualifies Ghalib's personal potential which he considers to be intense and immeasurable. This speaks of his personal stance as much as it expresses the potential every poet must have to be able to write and reach a point of supposed, or aspired, excellence. Ghalib's reference to the narrow straits of the ghazal may not be entirely accurate as ghazal is a series of climaxes with one verse after another, and each verse carrying a hidden space between the two lines that challenge as well as tickle the readers' imagination. The other word—*vus'at* (breadth)—characterises Ghalib's desire to operate at broader levels.

200

ادائے خاص سے غالبؔ ہوا ہے نکتہ سرا
صلائے عام ہے یاران نکتہ داں کے لیے

अदा-ए ख़ास से ग़ालिब हुआ है नुकता-सरा
सला-ए आम है यारान-ए नुकता-दाँ के लिये

adaa-i KHaas se Ghalib huaa hai nukta-saraa
salaa-i 'aam hai yaaraan-e nukta-daa.n ke liye

(*nukta-saraa*—appreciator, connoisseur;
salaa-i 'aam—open call;
nukta-daa.n—the discerning ones, nitpickers)

Ghalib has opened his lips, as a connoisseur,
with a unique elan
Here is an open call for discerning friends to join,
if they can

In spite of all their pride in their work, artists also put their work to people's scrutiny. It is rather instructive that Ghalib, so full of self-pride, chooses to do so in one of the verses at the far end of his *diivaan*. He says, without any reservations, qualms or misgivings, that he has expressed himself in his distinct style. He gives an open call to all his readers, both ordinary and extraordinary, to judge his work which has had its critics. This call reaches out beyond his time and applies to all his readers including even the contemporary readers.

This verse exudes a rare sense of confidence and can be appreciated further in these ways: (a) it seems that he wants to objectively hear what his readers and critics have to say about his accomplishments (b) before he gives his open call, he slyly certifies his extraordinary style for himself in the first line (c) while the first line is a personal certification, the second line is an open call for scrutiny of his work (d) it may be inferred that with the first line he has already conditioned his readers and closed the door for disagreement, and yet (e) in the second line he gives an open call to the readers of taste to evaluate his work.

There are three central words—*adaa-i KHaas* (special style), *nukta-saraa* (connoisseur) and *nukta-daa.n* (the discerning ones or even the nitpickers)—that contain the intent of the verse. In using the word *nukta-saraa* (connoisseur), Ghalib defines the nature of his poetry which opens up avenues of mundane as well as metaphysical apprehensions of the poetic kind. The expression *nukta-daa.n* refers to all kinds of readers. This makes space for his *salaa-i 'aam* (open call) to his readers. Interestingly, both the implications appear equally relevant in the context of this verse. This verse, in particular, speaks of his inimitable style which he openly proclaims to have. This oft-quoted verse by Ghalib supplements another verse by him and reaffirms his faith in his extraordinary ability as a poet: *ganjiin-i m'anii kaa tilism us ko samajhiye / Jo lafz ke Ghalib mire ash'aar mei.n aave.*

TRANSLITERATION KEY

Scan this QR code to access the detailed Transliteration Key.

ACKNOWLEDGEMENTS

Frances W. Pritchett's website on the Urdu ghazals of Ghalib, A Desertful of Roses: http://www.columbia.edu/itc/mealac/pritchett/ooghalib/index.html

Rekhta Foundation's website for works by and on Ghalib: https://www.rekhta.org/

Vinay Dharwadker for writing the Foreword. Frances W. Pritchett, Satyanarayana Hegde, Daisy Rockwell, Mehr Afshan Farooqi, Tabish Khair, A. Sean Peu, Anjum Hasan for their generous endorsements.

Tabassum, Yasser, Munazzah and Rabee at home for making my engagement with Ghalib a pleasurable one. Maria and Tabrez for offering me a cosy Ghalib corner in their home in the USA, where I stayed for two long spells of time to complete this work.

Udayan Mitra, Amrita Mukerji, Kadambari Kumari and Shreya Mukherjee at HarperCollins for making the book what it is.

Devangana Dash for a brilliant cover design.

ABOUT THE AUTHOR

Anisur Rahman is a literary critic, translator and bilingual poet in English and Urdu. Formerly a professor of English at Jamia Millia Islamia, a central university in New Delhi, and a senior advisor at Rekhta Foundation (www.rekhta.org), he has worked and published in the areas of comparative, translation, postcolonial and Urdu studies. His recent publications include *Earthenware: Sixty Poems* (Rubric Publishing, 2018), *In Translation: Positions and Paradigms* (Orient Blackswan, 2019), *Socioliterary Cultures in South Asia* (Niyogi Books, 2019), *Hazaaron Khwahishein Aisi: The Wonderful World of Urdu Ghazals* (HarperCollins, 2019) and *Hazaar Rang Shaairi: The Wonderful World of the Urdu Nazm* (HarperCollins, 2022).

Rahman has been a Shastri Fellow at the University of Alberta, Canada (2001–2002) and a visiting scholar at Purdue University, USA (2007).

HarperCollins *Publishers* India

At HarperCollins India, we believe in telling the best stories and finding the widest readership for our books in every format possible. We started publishing in 1992; a great deal has changed since then, but what has remained constant is the passion with which our authors write their books, the love with which readers receive them, and the sheer joy and excitement that we as publishers feel in being a part of the publishing process.

Over the years, we've had the pleasure of publishing some of the finest writing from the subcontinent and around the world, including several award-winning titles and some of the biggest bestsellers in India's publishing history. But nothing has meant more to us than the fact that millions of people have read the books we published, and that somewhere, a book of ours might have made a difference.

As we look to the future, we go back to that one word— a word which has been a driving force for us all these years.

Read.